THE
HERITAGE
OF ISLAM

For Irv, Ari, and Kennedy

THE
HERITAGE
OF ISLAM

WOMEN, RELIGION, AND POLITICS IN WEST AFRICA

•

BARBARA CALLAWAY
LUCY CREEVEY

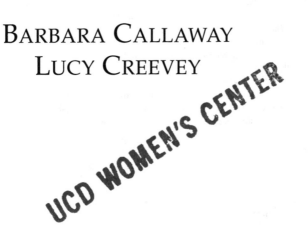

LYNNE RIENNER PUBLISHERS • BOULDER & LONDON

Published in the United States of America in 1994 by
Lynne Rienner Publishers, Inc.
1800 30th Street, Boulder, Colorado 80301

and in the United Kingdom by
Lynne Rienner Publishers, Inc.
3 Henrietta Street, Covent Garden, London WC2E 8LU

Callaway, Barbara.
    The heritage of Islam : women, religion, and politics in West
Africa / Barbara Callaway, Lucy Creevey.
        p.   cm.
    Includes bibliographical references and index.
    ISBN 1-55587-253-0 (alk. paper)
    ISBN 1-55587-414-2 (alk. paper : pbk.)
    1. Women—Africa, West—Social conditions. 2. Women—Legal
status, laws, etc. (Islamic law)—Africa, West. 3. Muslim women—
Nigeria. 4. Muslim women—Senegal. 5. Islam—Social aspects—
Africa, West. I. Creevey, Lucy E. II. Title
HQ1810.C35   1994
305.42'0966—dc20   93-35396
                                                     CIP

British Cataloguing in Publication Data
A Cataloguing in Publication record for this book
is available from the British Library.

Printed and bound in the United States of America

The paper used in this publication meets the requirements
of the American National Standard for Permanence of
Paper for Printed Library Materials Z39.48-1984.

CONTENTS

TABLES

PREFACE

Africa has been the center of our academic lives for all the years since our first visit in 1960. In the course of preparing this book we drew on the resources of many people from whom we have acquired advice, information, and encouragement. We apologize to those we cannot directly acknowledge here, but we do express our gratitude directly to the following people.

• • •

C. S. Whitaker and Richard L. Sklar, two pioneering scholars of Nigerian politics, have long provided inspiration, guidance, and assistance to me [Barbara Callaway]; their studies endure as seminal contributions to understanding the early dynamics of political forces in that country. As a committed scholar of the Nigerian state, Jean Herskovits has no peer; she has been unfailingly helpful and encouraging over the years as working in Nigeria has become more difficult, and she has been a thoughtful critic of my work. For his intense commitment, his enormous energy while in the field, his prodigious work in writing and editing manuscripts and organizing conferences both in the United States and Nigeria, and his unfailing and wholehearted support for the work of others, Larry Diamond deserves special thanks and acknowledgment. John Paden and Mary Smith wrote enormously sensitive and pathbreaking books in 1960, books that have stood the test of time and still provide the models for scholarship and field work in northern Nigeria.

Enid Schildkrout and Priscilla Starratt, who were in Kano during the 1980s, have made particularly important contributions to my own research. Enid Schildkrout's books on women and children have provided the foundation for all my work, and Priscilla Starratt's conscientious study of women scholars in Islam has greatly informed my understanding. I also owe a deep intellectual debt to a remarkable group of women who have focused their considerable talent on the study of the changing status of women in Hausa society: Jean Boyd, Catherine Coles, Nicole Echard, Polly Hill, Beverly Mack, Margaret Knipp, Renee Pitten, and Jean Trevor have been particularly important in this regard.

In recent years an emerging body of scholarship has been of crucial significance to those of us who seek to understand the world of Hausa women. Ayesha Imam, Zainab Kabir, and Bilkisu Yusuf deserve a special salute for putting forth a courageous critique of their own society and offering consistent and sensitive insights into the world of Islam and Hausa women. In providing context and comprehension, Jerome Barkow, M. K. Bashir, Anthony Kirk-Greene, Mervyn Hiskett, Murray Last, and M. G. Smith are particularly noted.

My students in the early 1980s at Bayero University in Kano helped develop and administer surveys and contributed enormously to their collation and interpretation. Bikisu Mohammad, Sani Mohammed Kura, Indo Aisha Yuyuda, Bikisu Ismail, and Mohammed Jabo are owed special thanks in this regard. My teaching assistants, Omar Farouk Ibrahim, Salisu Yusef, and Ibrahim Muazzum, were enormously supportive and hard working. (Omar Farouk later came to Rutgers University as a Ph.D. student and was helpful in every way, and members of his family were extraordinarily generous hosts when I returned to Kano in 1985.) The chair of the Department of Political Science at Bayero University in Kano, Yolamu Barongo, secured the necessary university clearances and helped me find the resources necessary to run the SPSS program on the university computers. Dennis and Cynthia Sunal patiently helped develop the computer program and coached me through many technical problems that arose.

In opening their homes and providing friendship and hospitality through the years, Betty dan Bappa, Rabi and Ahmed Es Hak, Husseini and Magajiya Adamu, Isa Hashim, Barbara Gaba, Kiki Munshi, Charles and Mercia Okafor, and Uma and Njansi Eleazu have become enduring and cherished friends. Nigerian hospitality is legendary; there are many, many debts I can never repay. To the many Nigerians in university and government offices, in the Kano City women's centers, in the offices of newspapers and radio and television stations, in homes and offices, and in the city and in the villages where I worked, I owe much, and I will never forget your many kindnesses and crucial help.

—*Barbara Callaway*

• • •

I [Lucy Creevey] have been studying Muslim Brotherhoods and Islam in Senegal for more than thirty years. However, I began to study the impact of Islam on women in West Africa as a direct result of Barbara's first study of Hausa Muslim women in 1987. I collected information on Islam and women in Senegal from 1988 to 1991, and in 1991 I got the opportunity to do more extensive, in-depth field research on the subject.

I would like to acknowledge the Research Foundation at the University of Connecticut, which provided the grant supporting the survey I conducted, in collaboration with the faculty at the Ecole Nationale d'Economie Appliquée (ENEA), in Senegal in July and August of 1991. Equally necessary for this work to have been done at all was the invitation from Dean Richard Vengroff to join the linkage program between the University of Connecticut and ENEA. This program, funded by USAID, paid for my trip and living in Senegal and allowed collaboration with the ENEA faculty.

I also have a great obligation to the faculty at ENEA. Many people there helped; only a few, who bore the greatest burden, can be named here. Dr. Samba Dione, Director of ENEA, facilitated all the arrangements with his faculty. Bara Gueye, head of the research division at ENEA, arranged all the necessary contacts and organized help among the faculty. He patiently answered myriad questions and helped solve the innumerable problems usual in any research project. Abdourahman Thiam bore the burden of being the field supervisor of the project. He found people to administer the survey, helped choose and train them, and helped refine the survey. He also went to the field to check on their progress—despite numerous difficulties, such as a car breakdown, when he had to push the vehicle for miles. Thiam tolerated considerable pressure caused by the short timing of the study, but he always responded with kindness and efficiency. Mor Gaye acted as driver for the project. Despite being handicapped by continuous breakdowns and multiple conflicting assignments, he was always cheerful and willing. Amadou Diouf and Khassan Diallo, both members of the statistics faculty, coded the bulk of the returned questionnaires, working day and night for the last several days of my stay, and remaining calm and organized throughout. Finally, I wish to thank the women who administered the survey: Katy Diop, Marieme Gueye, Daguene Fall, Aminata Bousso, Aissatou Thiam, Madeleine Ndiaye Fall, Marieme N'Diaye, Deguena Ka, Mame Ndiaye Kane, and Aicha Diop. They faced countless problems—including, for one team, being robbed—but their work was nonetheless thorough and professionally competent.

Many others in Senegal also helped this study. I am most deeply indebted to Lilian Baer. She invited me to her home and offered limitless hospitality. She and her friends, especially Sonia and Yasine, made me feel that I had people to support me whatever happened in my work; they also put me in contact with numerous others who helped in a thousand ways. If there is one person who made it possible for me to complete the task it was Lilian. I am also also grateful to Maryese Fall at the USAID Women in Development Office. She shared documents on women in Senegal that were very helpful and introduced me to several people who gave me very useful information. Finally, there were many Senegalese scholars who shared their research and ideas. The two who helped the most, whose superior expertise in the area of women and Islam in Senegal I wish to acknowledge, are Penda M'Bow and Fatou Sow. I am indebted to them both. A number of government officials took time from busy schedules to answer questions and help otherwise. One of these, Awa Thongane, director of the Statistical Office, went far out of her way to help obtain government statistics and answer questions. I am very grateful to her for her help.

The last debt I have is the greatest. Momar N'Diaye of the faculty of ENEA (currently obtaining his doctorate in political science at the University of Connecticut) has been a mainstay of this work. He helped with all the research plans and made arrangements at ENEA and with other friends of his in Senegal. When I returned to Storrs, Momar spent countless hours helping tackle the statistical analysis of the data. There is no way to repay his kindness. In the most direct sense I could not have written my portion of this book without him.

—*Lucy Creevey*

1

INTRODUCTION: DOES RELIGION SHAPE OR REFLECT SOCIETY?

West Africa is a vast land area containing many states, each of which contains within its boundaries a number of different ethnic groups. Increasingly, its population is becoming Muslim. Table 1.1 indicates the percentage of West Africans who belonged to the Islamic faith in 1966 and in 1983. These figures underrepresent the current number of Muslims, as the religion continues to grow dramatically. Brought from North Africa and the Middle East beginning in the seventh century, Islam expanded rapidly at certain historical points and has continued to spread since independence. Only in two countries—Nigeria and Ghana—did it appear to lose ground between 1966 and 1983. And only the coastal countries to the south have remained primarily non-Islamic.

There are several reasons that Islam has been so successful. Some of these have to do with the way it was spread, the compatibility between the cultures of the proselytizers and the proselytized, and the flexibility of the faith itself in its absorption of existing customs and traditions. Other explanations may have a more political base: For example, Islam has acted as a buffer against Western Christian invaders and has reinforced nationalist movements. Whatever the reasons, the conversion to Islam has a long and deep impact on all members of West African society. In this book we focus on the impact of Islam on the lives of West African women.

In each major region of each country, the impact of Islam is different. Its impact on the population is affected by (among many other things) the percentage of the members of various ethnic groups who convert; whether or not those who control political power are conservative or radical Muslims; the amount and intensity of contacts with the West, the Middle East, and North Africa; the level of economic and social development of the population in general and of Muslims in particular; and the culture and society that existed prior to the arrival of Islam. Across West Africa these factors vary greatly. No study can reasonably blanket the region with one set of generalizations about how Islam interacts with society and shapes

1

Table 1.1   West Africa: Muslim Population and Basic Indicators

Country	Population (millions) 1990	GNP per capita (dollars) 1990	Percentage Muslim 1966	Percentage Muslim 1983
Benin	4.4	113	15	16
Burkina Faso	8.5	274	22	44
Cameron	11.2	475	15	22
Chad	5.4	160	50	51
Côte d'Ivoire	11.2	322	23	25
Gambia	>1	—	80	87
Ghana	14	400	19	15.1
Guinea	5.4	430	65	69.3
Liberia	2.1	—	15	21
Mali	8	230	—	68
Mauritania	1.9	480	96	99
Niger	7.3	300	85	87.4
Nigeria	110.1	290	50	45*
(northern Nigeria)	60	—	—	90
Senegal	7	650	82	91*
Sierra Leone	3.8	—	39	39.5
Togo	3.4	370	8	16

Sources: For population and GNP per capita (except for Gambia and Sierra Leone): World Bank, 1990, p. 178. Sources for percentage Muslim 1966: Mitchell, Morrison, and Paden, 1989, p. 47. Sources for percentage Muslim 1983 and population figures for Gambia and Sierra Leone: Weekes, 1984, pp. 882–911.

Notes: Estimates for the different years are made on slightly different bases by Weekes and Morrison, so the trend comparison is not exact.

a. National figures are much higher.

the lives of women, and we will not attempt that here. Instead, we examine two cases—Nigeria and Senegal—illustrating quite different situations for Muslim women. These two countries, for reasons that we discuss, illustrate the very different ways in which Islam may affect the lives of West African women.

In any country, religion provides a value and belief system; Islam is something more: Again and again in West Africa, the refrain "Islam is a total way of life" is heard. In Islamic societies, religion governs everything from law and banking to dress and appropriate behavior when eating or even bathing. There is no division between the public and the private nor between the secular and the religious. And increasingly, Islam provides an ideology for anti-Western nationalism. In the non-Western world, the materialism, corruption, and lawlessness of Western societies are emphasized, and the Islamic alternative is praised.

The patriarchal nature of most Islamic societies reinforces the pervasive belief that Muslim women are more subject to the control of men than are women in most other societies. This control is dramatic in the case of Muslim Hausa women in northern Nigeria. They are literally secluded immediately upon marriage; that is, they are removed from contact with men (other than relatives) and rarely allowed to move about in public. Islam is quite clear that "marriage is the only road to virtue and that in marriage wives must be submissive and obey their husbands (Minaie, 1981, p. 18). Girls generally marry between the ages of ten and twelve.

In Senegal, the submission of women is less dramatically exhibited; women are not veiled or secluded. The discrimination against them, however, is still obvious in law codes that allow polygamy and unequal inheritance laws (Sow, 1991; Creevey, 1993).

Feminist scholars have argued that analyses based on the examination of public and private domains (Rosaldo, 1974) are not applicable to non-Western societies where power is exercised within kin groups rather than in public forums (C. Nelson, 1974; Nicholson, 1986; Sudarkasa, 1986; Yanagisako and Collier, 1987; Comaroff, 1987). Hence, even in societies where they are secluded, women may exercise power from within their households. These scholars have argued that the definition of power should be broadened to include the invisible control of events by women, which gives them a certain status and position (Whyte, 1978; Ortner and Whitehead, 1981; Mukhopadhyay and Higgins, 1988). In societies such as those examined here, kinship and lines of descent are important, and consequently women's power is most visible as they mature and develop the ability to influence the lives of others in their immediate kin and descent groups (Coles and Mack, 1991, p. 13; Mack, 1988). In these societies, high-status aristocratic women in particular have power in their ability to influence the actions of their sons, husbands and other male relatives. Among the Hausa and the Wolof (the largest ethnic group in Senegal), royal wives and mothers have influenced the outcome of contentious succession disputes; played a role in starting and ending wars; and taken part in the dealings of their husbands with colonial and state officials. Today they are effective in pressing their concerns with emirs, marabouts, and other important public officials (Mack, 1988).

In this work, we will argue that influence and power are not identical or necessarily coterminous. When power is defined as the ability to make people do things they would not otherwise do, the use of force to compel such action if necessary is implied. In few, if any, societies today are women able to wield this kind of power, at least at the national level. However, they are not unable to *influence* their world or the events that concern them; they simply do not command the power to *compel* decisions or behavior, to *determine* what choices are made. How Muslim women in West African society use their influence to acquire power is one focus of this study. (See a related discussion on North Africa in Moghadem, 1992.)

Senegal and the northern states of Nigeria present good case studies from the West African experience through which to examine the interaction between religion, culture, and state policy and to study perceptions about the nature of power and the changing status of women. Islam was firmly established in northern Nigeria by the fifteenth century and in Senegal during the eighteenth and nineteenth centuries, although large numbers of people had converted in earlier periods. Both countries were subjected to European colonialism for the first half of the twentieth century. The French established a protectorate over most of Senegal in 1881 and had full control of the colony by 1901. The British had subjugated the Hausa states of Nigeria by 1903. Other important structures in both Senegal and Nigeria are the *sufi* brotherhoods, to which most Muslims belong. In the northern areas of Nigeria, the brotherhoods have close ties to Saudi Arabia. The Qadiriyya brotherhood is dominant. In Senegal, most Muslims belong to brotherhoods originating in North Africa, and the Tidjaniyya and Muridiyya (a specifically Senegalese order) brotherhoods are the most important. Northern Nigeria experienced a reformist Islamic holy war, or *jihad,* at the beginning of the nineteenth century, which purified Islamic practices. Senegal was subjected to *jihads* by Muslim leaders bent on purification and elimination of corruption in the middle and end of the nineteenth century. These *jihads* did lead to a measure of reform in Islamic practices, but for the majority of the population Islam remained more permissive, allowing much greater emphasis on magic, mysticism, and personal attachment to a leader.

Yet the most important leader of the Senegalese *jihads,* al-Hadji Umar Tal, spent his formative years in Sokoto, the religious capital established in northern Nigeria by the leader of the Islamic *jihad* there, Usman dan Fodio. Thus, there is an interesting religious connection between the two countries, one further expanded in modern times by the proselytization in

Nigeria of a twentieth-century marabout (Muslim leader) from Senegal, al-Hadji Ibrahima Niass. He converted many thousands to his Tidjaniyya brotherhood, including the Emir of Kano at one point. But overall, the form and practice of Islam remains very different in the two case studies. Thus, they allow the formulation of hypotheses concerning the importance of the development of Islam in a specific setting and the different factors that help explain the forms it takes in different places.

A syncretic blend of Islam and local cultural prescriptions shapes women's lives in both Nigeria and Senegal. In both societies, the local culture is clearly patriarchal, making it difficult to distinguish what part of current culture comes from Islam and what pre-Islamic influences remain. The pre-Islamic record in both northern Nigeria and Senegal suggests important public and political roles for royal women. It is clear from historical accounts and pre-Islamic legends of the Hausa and Wolof peoples that the incorporation of Islam into the society profoundly changed the cultural, political, and social conditions under which women live and work (Hiskett, 1973, 1984; Mary Smith, 1981; Boyd and Last, 1985; Sow, 1991; Creevey, 1993). Prior to the coming of Islam, women of aristocratic origin seem to have participated in public affairs, to have held offices designated for them, and on occasion assumed positions of control over the state apparatus. Non-royal women also had political and economic roles at the local level but had less power than their male counterparts. Men controlled the only asset, land. However, there was a relatively small gap between the sexes: Each suffered equally the poverty and dangers of their society. Both were subject to capture and enslavement without any protections whatsoever. By comparing the situation of today with the pre-Islamic society, then, there is a basis for assessing the impact of Islam on both royal and common women in the Hausa states of northern Nigeria and in most parts of Senegal as well.

In several other ways, the impact of Islam on women is demonstrably different in northern Nigeria than in Senegal, particularly in the areas of women's work and wife seclusion. Contemporary Islamic Hausa women in Nigeria do not generally work on farms, and most live their adult lives in strict seclusion. Women of most ethnic groups in Senegal have always farmed and, other than the wives of some Muslim leaders and a handful of strictly orthodox women, are not subjected to Islamic rules of dress restriction or physical seclusion. In recent years Muslim women in Nigeria have become much more vocal and even radical in asserting their rights from within Islam. In Senegal, by contrast, the feminist movement is more secular in orientation, although most of its leaders are Muslim, and many of its battles are with radical Muslim reformers, or fundamentalists, who see women's rights as a corrupting Western influence (see M. Marty, 1992, pp. 15–23; Caplan, 1987, pp. 1–22).

The 50 million Muslims of northern Nigeria constitute the largest Muslim population in Africa. The Hausa/Fulani people here are the largest ethnic subgroup in Nigeria, Africa's largest nation, and together with their brethren in southern Niger form the largest ethnic group in all of Africa. In addition, they have historically been traders, and therefore the Hausa have had a cultural impact on much of West Africa. Because of their precolonial Islamic culture and impressive state structure, the Hausa regions of northern Nigeria and southern Niger have been intensively studied by colonial officials, linguists, historians, anthropologists, and Islamic scholars. At least as much has been written on this society as on any other in West Africa (Palmer, 1914, 1950; M. G. Smith, 1960, 1978; Mary Smith, 1966; Hogben and Kirk-Greene, 1966; Dunbar, 1970; Last, 1967; Hiskett, 1973, 1984; Whitaker, 1970; Greenberg, 1946; Hailey, 1944; Hill, 1971, 1972, 1974, 1986; Nicolas, 1981). Also, large parts of a precolonial record written in Arabic survive and thus provide a foundation upon which hypotheses can be built about the structure and nature of the precolonial Hausa state system (*The Kano Chronicle,* translated in Palmer, 1928, Vol. 3). Hausaland's blend of Islamic prescriptions and local cultural mores present a special challenge to anyone attempting to analyze the determining effect of either.

Senegal has a much smaller population (6.7 million) than Nigeria; its largest ethnic group, the Wolof, numbers only about 3 million people. But Senegal was the capital of the colonial French West African Federation and the location of the earliest foothold of French influence in Africa. Much has been written about Senegal because of its long colonial contacts, its relative accessibility, its unique position in the colonial federation, and the interesting system of French/Muslim cooperation established there (Sy, 1969; Sow, 1989; Diop, 1985; Cruise O'Brien, 1971; Creevey Behrman, 1970; Marty, 1917; Coulon, 1990; Gellar, 1982; Brigaud, 1962; Robinson, 1975; Fatton, 1987). There never was a very large French settler population here, so the policies of the French had to be implemented through indigenous rural leaders. By the early twentieth century these were the marabouts, heads of Muslim brotherhoods.

The French needed the marabouts to be legitimate rulers and to control the rural population. The marabouts needed the French, who provided them with various privileges and interfered when their authority was challenged by an outsider, even another Muslim leader. This interdependence limited the authority of each side and acted to balance and restrict their degree of influence on the lives of the subject population.

By contrast, under the British colonial policy of "Indirect Rule," the Hausa state apparatus was left largely intact to rule the large population of Northern Nigeria. The traditional authority of the emir and lesser officials remained virtually unchanged by the colonial presence. Rules and customs came from the traditions of preceding generations. We contend here that because the French totally undermined the authority of preexisting kingdoms, all subsequent power devolved from the top (the French administration), resulting in a more "modern" power structure. The marabouts, who filled the rural vacuum and took on the power of the former aristocrats (and married into their families) were, if not a creation of the French, at least a result of the French presence.

Senegal, furthermore, had much more intensive interactions with France and the West than Northern Nigeria had with Great Britain and Europe. The geography of the two countries provides an explanation. Landlocked and remote, Northern Nigeria had few resident Europeans, and no one traveled through just because they needed to reach somewhere else. Most of its precolonial trade contacts, established over centuries with the Middle East and North Africa, remained open and active. Conversely, Senegal has always had extensive contact with the West. Dakar, the capital of Senegal, was the major port of entry into West Africa for Westerners until recently and the point of embarkation on the way to other African countries. Railroads into the interior had begun be built by the end of the nineteenth century, and a new cash crop, peanuts, introduced and encouraged by the French, had begun to transform the local economy and society long before World War II. Senegal was reoriented to its coast and trade with the West. Old trade routes through the Sahara to the north rapidly decreased in importance, and soon even the areas northeast on the Senegal River, which had most directly participated in the precolonial trade, were now principally exporting men to new job opportunities in Dakar (and soon in metropolitan France as well). Thus, the influence of the West was considerably more widespread and of deeper impact in Senegal than in northern Nigeria.

One result of this different set of relations with the West is a divergence in governmental structures. In Senegal, a secular government, modeled on the French government, rules the country, although its positions are filled by a body of men who are overwhelmingly Muslim. Government institutions from the national level down to the communal assemblies for rural towns and urban centers, are also modeled on the French pattern. The law is French, except for a section of the Family Code (applying only to those who declare themselves Muslim), which is a modified version of Malekite Islamic law. Politics in northern Nigeria have a stronger religious tinge. Muslim rulers stress adherence to Islamic law, and Islamic personal law is protected by the Nigerian constitution. However, the constitution of Nigeria as a nation is secular because a large part of the population, mostly in the south, is not Muslim. There is a continuing tension between the persistence of Muslim laws and traditions, which have been applied for centuries in the north, and the body of law and governmental institutions the national government has promulgated. The Western/modern institutions and laws are being extended into the north and gradually will affect it more and more deeply. But for the present, the contrast between Senegal and northern Nigeria in regard to the saliency of Islamic law is very striking.

Muslim women in Senegal and northern Nigeria, like women all over West Africa—indeed all over the world—have much less access to the cash economy and wage labor than do males. Muslim women in particular experience limits to inheritance imposed by Islamic law, which hinders their control of wealth and denies them whatever power and influence direct access to wealth brings. Yet they are not altogether unsuccessful in developing strategies to counter the control of assets by men. They manipulate their marriages to their advantage, and they retain control over their own resources and income. From within their polygamous marriages they form bonds of female solidarity completely separate from the world of men. It may well be that the restrictions imposed by Islamic law are reinforced and magnified by state structures that institutionalize both Western and indigenous elements of patriarchy. All come together to disadvantage women vis-à-vis men. But it is also true that such disadvantages exist in all societies. The degree and type of disadvantage differs from culture to culture, but the fact of disadvantage is universal and certainly not unique to Islamic societies. The forms that discrimination may take in Islamic West Africa are illustrated in our two cases, Senegal being representative of a secular Muslim society, Hausaland of a more theocratic Muslim society within a secular state.

In this book we discuss the roots of the present situation of women in Senegal and northern Nigeria by looking at the history of the coming of Islam and its initial impact on pre-Islamic traditional society, specifically on the roles of women in each society. After examining the historical setting, we explore the current situation, first considering how Muslim women are socialized in the two countries and what expectations they develop about themselves and their place in society. Next we look at two common indexes of modernization that promote change in society—specifically, formal Western education and economic growth with resulting "modernization"—and ask what role women play in these processes and with what results. Finally, we look at the political activities of women, including both their roles in influencing decisions and their access to direct political power. We focus on what women are doing to change their situation and how circumstances are changing to increase or decrease their power and authority at all levels of society. We demonstrate the ways in which Islam influences the lives of women in West Africa, at the same time acknowledging how that impact is itself shaped by other forces in society throughout the region.

2

THE ISLAMIC ENCOUNTER

The expansion of Islam beyond Arabia to Egypt was the result of a war of conquest begun in 640 A.D., only eight years after the death of the Prophet Muhammad. During the next ten years the Islamic holy war, or *jihad,* spread to Tripoli and south to the Sudan. By the end of the century the Islamic armies had reached Tunisia (Tunis and Carthage), and within twenty years the entire northern rim of North Africa was subjugated (Fage, 1978, pp. 143–157). Islam was being spread not only as a religion but, indeed, as a civilization. The language (Arabic) and the social and political organization of the conquerors were imposed. Many features of pre-Islamic customs would survive, but throughout the territory there were major changes in peoples' lives and expectations.

Islam itself would change markedly as it spread across Africa, reflecting the political struggles of those who sought to claim authority as the heirs of Muhammad and the effort to reach ever more, and more varied, groups of people. As the religion moved inward in Africa, brotherhoods, or *turuuq* (singular: *tarika),* grew in importance as a means of making Islam more intelligible to the uneducated masses. Brotherhoods were mystical orders tightly organized into hierarchies, each headed by a *shaikh.* The *shaikh* often experienced some mystical revelation from Muhammad or Allah, which gave him the ability to interpret the holy writ and intercede for his followers. The teachings of the *shaikh* would be transmitted to his subordinates. These included the *khalif,* who directed the brotherhood in a given territory; the *muqaddam,* who was also a territorial leader; and various levels of brothers whose positions depended on their study and practice of the order's doctrines. The base of the pyramid was the mass of followers, or *talibes* (students). The followers' basic role was to be obedient to their *shaikh* and his appointed leader, the *khalif* (Massignon, 1929).

The *turuuq* spread throughout the Muslim world beginning in the twelfth century. They were orthodox, or Sunni, organizations—that is, they followed the main line of Islamic descent and accepted Ma'awiya and

9

his descendants as *khalifs*. They also adhered to one of the four main schools of Muslim law—in West Africa principally Malekite law. But the leaders of the *turuuq* were certainly influenced by the Shi'ite minority, which did not accept Ma'awiya. Instead, the Shi'ites talked of a "hidden" Muslim ruler who would be revealed as the rightful ruler and, as *mahdi*, would prepare for the second coming of Muhammad.

The original *jihad* in the seventh century was a vast military conquest that moved from Arabia in the west to the eastern edge of North Africa. Despite—or perhaps because of—its success, the region did not remain unified. The Muslim world was rent by warring would-be leaders whose armies fought each other, as well as the infidels, in the name of Islam. Their religious justification was often based on claims of legitimate descent from the Prophet or his closest companions or, in later years, on the need to revitalize and purify Islam. These claims would be echoed again in the western Sudan, when local prophets and *mahdis* would lead their own *jihads* throughout the area.

THE HAUSA

Early in the advance of Islam, before the brotherhoods had expanded through the Muslim areas, proselytizers were already reaching West Africa. The elaborate trade networks of the Mande and the Hausa brought the word of Islam peacefully. So did the Arab traders moving through the area—and the scholars whose writings form the basis of much of what we know about the ancient kingdoms of the Sudan. But Islam also came into the region through holy wars and conquest. In 1076 the puritan Muslim Almoravids swept south and defeated the rulers of the empire of Ghana in central West Africa, which resulted in the conversion to Islam of the ruling and noble classes, although the mass of the population did not become Muslim at this time.

Prior to the first arrival of Muslim traders and missionaries in the twelfth century into what is today northern Nigeria, the Hausa peoples had developed a highly bureaucratized state structure. The pre-Islamic Hausa state system was characterized by an essentially patriarchal and hierarchical class system, in which occupations were determined by birth and a woman's status was determined by marriage. When Muslim traders and teachers began arriving in the twelfth century, they were incorporated into an already highly stratified, specialized society. Over the centuries, the Hausa have demonstrated again and again that they are both flexible and cohesive, and they assimilated easily to Islam, incorporating those aspects of it that enhanced the traditional culture and making accommodations with those that did not. The accommodations made in the early twentieth century, between the British colonizers and the Hausa rulers serve as a case study of the adaptability of this culture. The intersection of patriarchal Islam, British colonial rule, and Hausa cultural values was not traumatic.

Legends concerning the origins and early development of the Hausa city-states in the area of present-day northern Nigeria and southern Niger are revealing. The Bayajidda legend of Daura, for example, recounts the mythical establishment of the seven dominant and six subordinate Hausa states. The people of Daura (an emirate in the northernmost part of northern Nigeria) link their ancestors to people who migrated from Canaan and Palestine to Baghdad and Tripoli. According to the oral traditions of the area, in the middle of the tenth century A.D. a son of the king of Tripoli, Abdul Dar, fled the city upon his failure to inherit his father's throne. He crossed the Sahara to an oasis at Kusugu, in what is today the city of Daura. He produced only daughters, who ruled the emerging city-state after his death. The city is named after his ninth daughter, Daura, who later became queen. Daura subsequently married a prince named Bayajidda, and their seven sons were the founders of the seven Hausa states. (Six prior sons of Bayajidda's concubine became the founders of the six lesser, or "bastard," Hausa states). This legend of origin appears to establish two things: that there were ancient historical ties between this area of Nigeria and Islamic regions to the north, and that before that time daughters of kings could become rulers.

Many historical commentators hypothesize that the Bayajidda legend records the transition of Hausaland from matrilineal to patrilineal descent and succession patterns (M. G. Smith, 1978; Palmer, 1936; Last, 1967; Hogben and Kirk-Greene, 1966; Pitten, 1979). Most concur that between the tenth and thirteenth centuries, a pattern of matrilineal descent was replaced by a patrilineal one, but deference to the mother, sister, and wife of the ruler was maintained. In several Hausa states, titles given to individual women of outstanding character in the royal families continued to represent a remnant of female authority and sometimes considerable responsibility up until the Islamic *jihad* in 1804. From the thirteenth century on, however, the influence of Islam became ever more pervasive, and women's public roles, titles, and offices gradually disappeared or were transferred to or assumed by men (Pitten, 1979).

By the twelfth century, the largest and most powerful Hausa state was Kano, a large trading city-state in the center of present-day northern Nigeria. According to the *Kano Chronicle,* the first Muslims came to Kano about 1150 A.D. from the area of present day Timbuktu in Mali. Two centuries later, the fifth Hausa king, Yusa, received forty Muslim missionaries (c. 1380), built a mosque, and ordered all the people to pray five times a day (Hogben and Kirk-Greene, 1966, p. 188). During the reign of Muhammad Rumfa (1463–1499), missionaries came to Kano directly from the Islamic holy city of Medina (in present-day Saudi Arabia). These Muslim missionaries found the soil of Kano to be "the same" as that of Medina, thus establishing a special mystical and religious relationship between it and Kano. By the end of the reign of Rumfa, women of high social status were secluded, and a very orthodox form of Islam had been firmly established (Hogben and Kirk-Greene, 1966; Palmer, 1928).

The advent of Islam led to substantial changes in women's status. As late as the fifteenth or sixteenth century, instances of women in important public roles, including at least two queens who led wars of conquest, were recorded in the history of the Hausa states surrounding Kano, but there are no records of such women in Kano itself (Hogben and Kirk-Greene, 1966; Palmer, 1928). After this time, however, ruling-class Hausa women in all the Hausa states experienced a steady diminution of their influence and were systematically deprived of their authority and autonomy in every area of life (Pitten, 1979). Even traditional titles and offices relating to authority over women and redress of their grievances have now become nominal or have been discarded altogether.

By the sixteenth century, the erosion of the standing, influence, and authority of women titleholders coincided with the growing influence of Islam. First dominant in Kano, Islam became an established presence in all the Hausa states by the end of the fifteenth century. Until this time, women in royal families, in addition to fulfilling their public roles, were closely identified with a pre-Islamic religion characterized by spirit possession: Bori. Bori was, in effect, a state religion led by women of the ruling class. The continued success of the state was dependent in large measure on the efficacy of the Bori rites performed (Greenberg, 1966). Although ruling lineages and their followers increasingly identified with Islam, they continued to participate in the rites of Bori (Palmer, 1914). Until the nineteenth century, Islam coexisted with Bori, and individuals participated in both without perceived conflict (Greenberg, 1966).

Under the influence of North African Arab traders and teachers, a few of whom settled permanently in Kano, a small number of Kano men became literate in Arabic and scholars of the Quran. They were usually attached to the emir's palace, where they served as religious teachers, scribes, advisors, and even physicians. These men studied books on Islam brought from North Africa and began to write on religious subjects, producing a small body of learned Islamic literature, c. 1700–1750, that is still preserved in Kano (Hiskett, 1973). Neither the Arabs nor the local Hausa Muslim scholars at this time objected to local custom or the coexistence of Bori and Islam. By the end of the eighteenth century, however, Muslim teachers, or *mallams*, began to voice their disapproval of that part of the surrounding Hausa culture that was not purely Islamic, particularly the practice of Bori, the "nakedness of women," and the mixing of the sexes in public in defiance of Islamic law (Bivar and Hiskett, 1962).

One explanation for the existence of a more orthodox Islam in Nigeria than in Senegal is the nature of the *jihad* experienced by the Hausa states at the beginning of the nineteenth century. As devout Muslims here became increasingly dissatisfied with the contrast between daily Hausa life and the Islamic ideal, the stage was set for the Fulani Islamic reformer, Shehu Usman dan Fodio. Between 1789 and 1804, dan Fodio experienced visions in which the "Sword of Truth" instructed him to launch a holy war in order to purify the area of the Hausa states for Islam (Hiskett, 1973). In his *Kitab al Farq,* the Shehu listed various sins against Islamic religious teachings on the part of the Hausa (*Kitab al Farq* has been translated by Hiskett, 1960). He saw the authority royal women held over other women as one of the fundamental manifestations of the un-Islamic nature of Hausa society (Hiskett, 1960, p. 67). Dan Fodio denounced the inappropriate roles of royal women, both in Bori and in Hausa custom (which let these women resolve their own grievances), and deplored the nearly universal ignorance of common women concerning their rights in Islam. He decreed that all women should live according to the teachings of Islam and advocated that they be taught Islamic religious doctrine and basic literacy in Arabic so they could read the Quran. As an example, he taught his own daughter, Asma, to read the entire Quran in Arabic (dan Shehu, 1971).

The *jihad* reinforced adherence to orthodox Islam and proved a special boon to that part of the Hausa population subject to constant slave raiding by the emirs. Most people not of royal lineage were subject to enslavement during the constant raiding of one state by another. Women in particular were taken away from their homes and forced into harems as concubines for the emirs and their sons. Common women had virtually no rights in the Hausa states. The Shehu objected, warning that women should be protected as specified in the Quran. Thus, whereas royal women dramatically lost status and titles after the establishment of Islam, common women gained protections previously unknown to them before the *jihad.*

Dan Fodio's *jihad* was fought between 1804 and 1812, during which time Fulani rule was superimposed over the Hausa and Hausa titles were transferred to the holders of new, Fulani-sanctioned offices. Over time the Fulani were absorbed into Hausa culture, and we speak today of the Hausa/Fulani as one culture, Hausa.

Rather than being regarded as a conqueror, the Shehu was increasingly viewed in Hausaland as a religious leader and teacher of great knowledge. He traveled constantly, teaching and preaching as he went. A corps of scholarly followers accompanied him, revealing to the common people many of the rights and protections of Islam of which they were ignorant. In so doing, he touched a foundation of both discontent and Islamic acculturation that had been developing for seven centuries (Hiskett, 1973, pp. 76–77).

The political system that evolved during the next century was essentially the original Hausa system with a strong Fulani and Islamic overlay (M. G. Smith, 1960; Whitaker, 1970). Based on a system of patronage and fiefholding, the authority of the emirs (the former Hausa *sarki,* or kings) was maintained through the institutionalization and extension of Islamic courts, a complex system of taxation, and an elaborate administrative machinery.

For royal women, the most important consequence of the *jihad* was the loss of their ritual authority in Bori and thus the primary foundation of their influence in political matters. The ascendance of Islam forced Bori underground; it lost its legitimacy, and its adepts lost their influence. This venue of power for ruling-class Hausa women continued to decline and when the British arrived at the turn of the century, northern Nigerian women were already political minors, a fact made apparent by the dearth of reference to them in official documents, except for the inevitable mention of marriage and divorce patterns. (Presumably, the absence of women in public places and the systematic exclusion of women from political authority and influence in Hausaland did not offend British sensitivities. In the years between their conquest of the area and Nigeria's independence in 1960, the British showed no concern over the absence of women in the public sphere. The subordination of women to men was not unique to Hausa or Islamic culture.)

As the area came under the domination of the British in the early twentieth century, a sharp change in the development of the Hausa states occurred. By declaration they became a part of the Protectorate of Northern Nigeria in 1903. The leader of the British conquest and the first governor of the protectorate was Sir Frederick Lugard, the principal architect of overall British colonial policy known as "Indirect Rule." The core of this philosophy was that whenever possible, the metropolitan power should seek to recognize and rule through traditional authorities in accordance with their indigenous social and political institutions and mores (Lugard, 1970). As part of the overall policy of Indirect Rule, virtually no Christian missionaries were allowed into the Muslim areas of Northern Nigeria, thus assuring that Islam there was protected from the liberalizing impact of Christian converters and the schools established by them in southern Nigeria (Coleman, 1960). Islam became ever more deeply entrenched, and Usman dan Fodio's legacy of ideas remains part of the ethos of the area to the present time.

Thus, the colonial state provided the stable conditions necessary for Islamic culture to grow and deepen. Under Hausa/Fulani rule and British protection, the Islamic (*Sharia*) courts were at the heart of the culture. An elite conservative and orthodox class of *mallams* flourished with considerable influence under the security provided by Indirect Rule. To this day, when there is a conflict between Islamic orthodoxy and modern ideas, the *mallams* hold sway. Hence, any effort to enhance the rights of women here must be done within the bounds of Islamic sanction and must meet the requirements of Islamic law.

British rule in northern Nigeria was relatively short, particularly in comparison to the development, over the centuries, of an Islamic culture. By the 1940s nationalist political parties in southern Nigeria were calling for independence from the British. In 1951 the northern political elite established the Northern People's Congress under the leadership of the Sardauna of Sokoto, Sir Ahmadu Bello. Ahmadu Bello was the great-great-grandson of Shehu Usman dan Fodio. Songs of praise from that era link the Sardauna through the Shehu directly to the founder of the Qadiriyya brotherhood of Islam and to the Prophet himself (Paden, 1973). Thus, religious and political authority has continued to be connected in the Hausa areas of Nigeria from the time of the *jihad* to the present.

Islam's primacy in Hausaland had significant consequences for women. In the first two decades after independence in 1960, Islamic women in northern Nigeria were severely disadvantaged in both education and politics compared to their non-Islamic sisters in southern Nigeria. In southern Nigeria, Christian missionaries established roughly twice as many schools for boys as for girls. No such schools were established in northern Nigeria for either boys or girls, although the colonial government did establish a few schools for the sons of the ruling class. At the time of independence in 1960, literacy for women in the Igbo areas of southeastern Nigeria was about 20 percent, whereas the literacy rate (in English) for Hausa women in the north was .02 percent (Coleman, 1960). Whereas women in the predominantly Christian states of southern Nigeria were given the right to vote in 1952, women in the Islamic states of the north did not receive this right until a 1976 military decree gave it to them. The Nigerian constitutions of 1960 and 1979 relegated to the states matters covered by "Islamic personal law." Hence, matters of vital concern to women (marriage, divorce, child custody, property rights) are regulated by Islamic law in the northern states (Callaway and Schildkrout, 1985). Southern Nigerian women are widely admired for their trading skills and control of markets, but women are absent from the markets of the Islamic north. Indeed, wife seclusion is widely practiced there today, and although this is an Islamic tradition, in Hausa Nigeria it takes the extreme form of actual physical seclusion rather than the more modified form of veiling, as practiced in some Muslim societies, or simply modest behavior and decorum, as emphasized in Senegal.

For centuries the Hausa states have reflected the religion and culture of North Africa. Since 1952, when political parties were permitted to form in Nigeria, parties in the northern part of the country have been identified with radical and populist Islamic movements. Today, Islamic women's organizations have formed to bring about dramatic changes in the position and status of women based on Islamic precepts and within the confines of Islamic culture and traditions. The call for a fundamental reconsideration of the position of women has occasioned great public controversy. The juxtaposition of opposing currents in this debate will be explored later in this study.

SENEGAL

The territory of present-day Senegal overlaps with the boundaries of several precolonial kingdoms. Each was ruled primarily by leaders of one of the distinct ethnic groups located in the region. Over time, however, power came to be shared by a mixture of peoples, as other ethnic groups conquered or merely settled in the various polities. The peoples of central Senegal, including the Wolof, the Lebou, and the Serer, spoke languages more closely related to each other than to those spoken by ethnic groups to the east of them. They are considered to belong to a language subfamily, the West Atlantic, which is a branch of the Niger-Congo family of languages and quite distinct from the family comprising the Mandingo and related groups. The people that spoke these languages were agriculturalists who raised cattle. They had a sophisticated farming system and craft industry, and they used metal for their tools and equipment. They did not have as extensively developed a trading system as did their neighbors to the east, perhaps because the Mande (as well as the Fulani, or Peuhl, people, who also spoke a West Atlantic language) formed a barrier that blocked them from the stimulus of trans-Saharan contacts (Fage, 1978).

It is not clear when the Wolof or Serer migrated into the vicinity. Oral tradition and archaeological investigation suggest that prior to the arrival of either, as early as the tenth century A.D., two groups—first the "Soose" and later the "Manding"—may have had highly organized civilizations in this geographical zone (Diop, 1981). By the eleventh century there were already Serer in Senegal, and by the end of that century Wolof were appearing among them. Some sources say that the fall of the empire of Ghana (to the east) led to this Wolof migration (Gastellu, 1981). In any case, the Wolof confined the Serer into smaller and smaller spaces and gradually took political control of most of the region. Certainly remnants of the previous population remained and intermarried with the Wolof, perhaps shaping the current dual-lineage pattern. But many Serer also remained in their own more or less unmixed ethnic communities within the Wolof polities. The kingdoms controlled by the Serer were pushed to the south, so when the first Portuguese explorers came to the coast of Senegal in the fifteenth century, they found Wolof kingdoms in the central area (Diop, 1981).

According to tradition, the Wolof empire was founded by N'Diadiane Ndiaye (descendant of the Almoravid conqueror of the empire of Ghana) in the fifteenth century, at which time the ethnic group supposedly took its name from the words "Wa," meaning people, and "Lof," meaning territory. The dates of this founding are unclear, estimates ranging from the eleventh to the thirteenth century, and the belief that the name "Wolof" corresponds to this founding is not universally accepted. In any case, in this period the state became organized and took command of the region. Later, in about 1550, this empire broke into its component states, so that by the end of the eighteenth century there were four Wolof kingdoms: Walo, north at the Senegal River; Cayor, to the south on the coast; Baol, south of Cayor; and Djolof (the largest state), east of the other three. The Serer, meanwhile, had the kingdoms of Sine and Saloum to the south of the Wolof territories. The Lebou, directly related to the Wolof, had their own state on the end of the Cape Verde peninsula (Brigaud, 1962).

The Tukulor, also of a related language group, had a different history. They were Fulani people (called Peuhl by the French) whose name originated from their settling in the Tekrour, northeast on the Senegal River. The Fulani apparently were first pastoralists in the area that later became the center of the Ghana empire. As that agricultural society developed the Fulani were pushed out and ended up settling in the area east and west of the upper Senegal River. Whatever the Fulani's original language may have been, their proximity in the Tekrour to the Wolof and Serer seems to have influenced their present language, which is closer to the latter two than to other, more easterly groups (Fage, 1978). One part of the Fulani remained in the Tekrour when the kingdom took shape in the ninth century, but the rest migrated through West Africa, a large group settling in the Fouta Djallon of what is now Guinea and an even larger contingent ending up in present-day northern Nigeria. Arabic explorers noted the kingdom of the Tekrour in the eleventh century, although it was in existence previously. The first dynasty is said to have ruled from 850 to 1000 A.D. and the last from 1776 to 1881, when its territory became a French protectorate (Brigaud, 1962).

The political structures of the societies established by the different ethnic groups in Senegal vary, but among the largest central and northern groups there is one important common feature: These were hierarchical caste societies. The middle caste—the free farmers—was the largest. The low caste groups were smaller and included blacksmiths, *griots* (musicians and storytellers), and other artisans. Slaves and tributaries would form a separate low caste group in any of these given societies. The small noble and warrior castes would have the highest status and would normally possess political control.

The Tukulor were apparently the most rigidly organized; social distinctions were stricter than in other groups. As a result, the Tekrour area is said to have a different sociocultural base than the rest of Senegal. It is characterized as Saharan, as opposed to the central zones of Senegal, which are characterized as Sahelian. Saharan culture appears to have a much more strongly hierarchical social structure than does Sahelian culture, with a stronger patriarchal authority system, although the caste structures of the two are very similar. The Tukulor social system was marked by a preeminent Islamic patriarchal structure without the strong surfacing of pre-Islamic cultural practices observed among the Wolof. The Tukulor also were patrilineal, tracing their important family lines through the father's family (as opposed to the dual lineage of the Wolof and Serer). Saharan class structure reflected much greater and more rigid social distinctions than exist among either the Serer or Wolof. Tukulor elites descended from dominant warrior and maraboutic groups who invaded the Senegal River valley at various points beginning in the early sixteenth century. These included several noble subcastes. The larger freeman group was distinctly marked off from the privileges of the nobles, as were the slaves, the tributaries (those who owed allegiance and tribute by virtue of originally being a foreign group), and the nomadic pastoralists (Sow, 1991).

Although the Wolof castes were less sharply divided than the Tukulor, the Serer are said to have been the most democratic, with less significant gaps between social groups, less authoritarian leadership, and more collective work patterns (Gastellu, 1981). Both the Wolof and Serer have inheritance and family relationships partially determined by matrilineal patterns, although the Wolof have fewer traces. The lack of written material predating the first contacts between the Wolof and Muslim missionaries makes it difficult to tell whether the two groups originally were more similar and both matrilineal, as some scholars have claimed (see Diop, 1960).

Despite these differences, all three societies had noble/warrior families as rulers, and most of the more powerful political positions were filled by people from the uppermost noble families closely related to the king. The king was not all-powerful, and there were not great gaps of wealth or distinct differences in living styles between the upper castes and the free farmers (as there were in medieval Europe). Politics revolved around the control of land and the armies. The king was the leader of the armed forces and the most influential noble. He was the chief patron, whose followers expected his services in the form of rights to use the land and protection from enemies. In return, he could expect a tribute from them (in the form of crops) and their service in his army when necessary.

One important difference among the Tukulor was the absence of a leadership role for women. By contrast, in the Wolof states there were two distinct and important political positions held by women. The first of these was the *lingueer,* usually the mother or maternal sister of the king, or *brak* (called the *bourba* or *damel* in some states), and appointed by him. The second was the *awa,* the first wife of the *brak.* These women had significant political power. They controlled some of the king's land and administered it through captives, provided food and maintenance for the entourage, and gave important gifts to various nobles to assure their loyalty.

They were an integral part of the clan system, patrons in their own right, whose good opinion had to be wooed by any aspiring politician (Barry, 1985). The same titles were given to royal women in the Serer kingdoms of Sine and Saloum. The *lingueer* was the most powerful. She had a particular religious role, being guardian of the fetishes, and she had numerous girls from noble families as her followers and many captives as well. She controlled several villages, the contributions from which she could use as she saw fit. These villagers also cultivated a field of grain for her. The *awa,* the first wife of the *bourba,* had as much influence as her Wolof counterpart (Brigaud, 1962).

At times the *lingueer* apparently played an extremely important role in the politics of the warring Wolof and Serer kingdoms. Fatou Sow cites the history of Djembet, who married the king of Trarza (in Mauritania) in 1833. At the death of *bourba* Fara Penda Adam Sal in 1841, it was she who selected the king to succeed him. She made her own marriage, against considerable opposition within Walo, to stop the expansion of French control in the region. Her sister, N'Daate Yaala, also took decisive political action in refusing to ally herself with the French in opposition to her sister, whom she succeeded in 1846. She did not permit her son to contest the accession of Djembet's son so as not to break up the power of the unified kingdom (Sow, 1973; Barry, 1985).

In the Tukulor kingdom, however, there are no recorded ruling female roles prior to the colonial invasion. In this regard, it seems that the influence of Islam, reinforcing (or perhaps creating) the strongly patriarchal nature of the regime, eliminated whatever public leadership positions for women might have existed (see M'Bow, 1989). This interpretation is supported by the fact that the Tukulor, like the Hausa, were introduced much earlier to Islam than were the Serer or Wolof. The first dynasty had Muslim rulers among its members, and Islam was introduced to the majority of the Tukulor in the eleventh century (Brigaud, 1962). In contrast, the Wolof did not become Muslim until the end of the nineteenth century, and the Serer only began to convert in large numbers in the twentieth century. Although Islam in fact improved the position of women in Arabia when it was spread (see Coulson and Hinchcliffe, 1978), it did not have this effect in the largely agrarian, bilinear societies of the Wolof and Serer, where women already had a measure of status. Whether or not these Senegalese ethnic groups had been totally matrilineal societies at some point is moot: Elements of matrilineal transmission of values, characteristics, and kinship endured alongside patrilineal descent patterns even after the spread of Islam.

Patrilineal values may have existed among the Wolof and Serer prior to the introduction of Islam, as the development of castes and classes apparently predated it (Sacks, 1974; Leacock, 1986). In any case, even after these cultures became Muslim, their women continued to have greater freedom and power than was common in the Middle East or in the Hausa states. Women never controlled the state apparatus among the Wolof or Serer peoples, but they did have greater "centrality" (James, 1978). Islam affected this value structure, but among the two ethnic groups in central Senegal the new religion remained largely intermingled with preexisting values and customs. Pre-Islamic customs certainly play an important role in the lives of the Tukulor as well, but the "centrality" of Tukulor women was reduced by comparison with Wolof or Serer women.

Muslim Tukulor women were never veiled or forced to live in seclusion in the precolonial kingdoms, whereas Muslim women in the Hausa states were. The explanation for this difference may be related to the date of conversion of the Tukulor, the nature of the conversion process, and the impact of the French colonial invasion. The major anticolonial *jihads* in Senegal were led by the Islamic leader al-Hadji Umar Tal. By the time of his birth in 1795, the Tukulor were already Muslim and had been subjected to many raids and conquests by Muslim warriors in decades past.

Umar Tal, a member of a warrior caste, spent twenty years away from his country, passing much of this time in what is now Sokoto, Nigeria. He also traveled to the Middle East and made the pilgrimage to Mecca, where he joined the Tidjaniyya brotherhood. This was a newer order than the Qadiriyya order, which had been founded in the eleventh century and originally spread through the western Sudan by Muhammad Abd al-Karim al-Maghrib in the fifteenth century. It was, however, one of al-Maghrib's disciples, al-Mukhtar ibn Ahmad (1729–1811), who had founded the Qadiriyya motherhouse north of Timbuktu, which became the center for the order in West Africa. The Tidjaniyya brotherhood, in contrast, was founded by Ahmad ibn Muhammad al-Tidjani (1735–1815) in Ain Mahdi (Morocco) in approximately 1781, following a revelation from the Prophet. Because of this revelation, al-Tidjani was able to dispense with the chain used by most shaikhs to link their teachings with those of Muhammad through a series of spiritual masters. He also forbade his followers to swear allegiance to other brotherhoods (multiple allegiance had been previously permitted). Eventually his brotherhood would be known, in contrast to the Qadiriyya, for its relatively uncomplicated prayers, litanies, and exercises, the simplicity of which facilitated the understanding of its teachings and practices by uneducated followers (Andre, 1922; Rinn, 1884; Depont and Coppolani, 1897; Gouilly, 1952; Trimingham, 1959).

The first spread of the Tidjaniyya brotherhood to the western Sudan was led by Muhammad al-Hafiz ibn al-Mukhtar ibn Habib al-Baddi, a missionary from the Ida Ou Ali ethnic group in Mauritania. He successfully converted his people and began proselytization of a large area of territory nearby, including portions of northeastern Senegal (Trimingham, 1959). But it was al-Hadji Umar Tal who would have the greatest success in spreading Tidjani adherence through the region. Influenced by the Islamic revivalist movement in Arabia, the Wahhabi movement, and the reforming fervor of the Tidjani, he returned to the Futa Toro in 1838. He soon broke with the aristocrats in his home region and left to set up his own religious retreat. Umar Tal recruited many younger aristocrats and many others, and he skillfully played on the animosities and histories of the people, drawing those who were enemies of the Bambara and Mandinka rulers to his armies. It would be a holy war against the "pagans," although, of course, Islam had long been present in the targeted societies. But the religion practiced was seen by Tal as lax and impure. Interestingly, Tal had obtained weapons from both the British and the French, yet one of the major aims of his campaigns certainly was to try to stop the French from taking control of more territory in eastern Senegal and the Sudan (See Robinson, 1985; Fage, 1978).

Al-Hadji Umar Tal led his first major war of conquest in the Senegal area out of the Fouta Djallon (in present-day Guinea), entering the region near the upper Senegal River and defeating the Bambara kingdom of Kaarta in 1854. He turned south thereafter and for two years, 1857–1859, he fought the French. The battles were bitter and long, and the economy of the region was devastated. In 1859 the French negotiated a settlement with Tal, after which he turned his attention to the east. By 1861 he had conquered the Bambara kingdom of Segu, but in that year he was killed, thus ending his expansion drive. Tal's *jihad* had a profound effect on the whole western Sudan, leading to the full conversion of the majority of the societies to Islam and making the Tidjaniyya brotherhood the dominant order in the region. Tal's wars of conquest were based on the purification of Islam, the establishment of the "real" faith and expulsion of the perversions he saw in the "so-called" Islamic states he was attacking. In this respect his *jihad* bears a strong resemblance to that of Usman dan Fodio, by whose teachings he was certainly influenced. He never established a regime based on his reformist principles that endured for any period of time because he died; within twenty years of his death, the French had effective control of the entire region of Senegal.

The Wolof, in the central region of Senegal, were strongly affected by al-Hadji Umar Tal's battles, although he did not fight directly in their central zone. By the nineteenth century many of them had already converted to Islam, despite the rejection of Islam by the Wolof ruling classes in the sixteenth century. The earliest European travelers found Muslim nobles ruling a pagan population, but apparently the more or less superficial conversion of the rulers disappeared after the late fifteenth century. Gradually, however, Islam spread through Wolof society, and by the end of the nineteenth century only the nobles and kings had not converted. In this period the power of the ruling classes was being directly undermined by the French invaders, and conversion to Islam was at least in part a reaction to this loss of status and authority. Umar Tal and his followers were major agents in the process, and conversion became wholesale, sometimes by force and sometimes by persuasion.

The most important marabout in the process of the Islamization of the Wolof was Ahmadu Bamba, born Muhammmad ibn Muhammad ibn Habib-Allah, in M'Backe, Senegal, in approximately 1850 (Creevey, 1979; Cruise O'Brien, 1971). Ahmadu Bamba was born into a Wolofized Tukulor aristocratic family whose father was a marabout and had instructed the children in the ways of the warrior marabout, Maba Diakhu. Following the death of his father, Ahmadu Bamba joined the Qadiriyya *tarika* and even traveled to Mauritania to be initiated by the famous Qadiri leader, Cheikh Sidia. He founded his own order, the Muridiyya, in 1886, when he had a revelation telling him that Touba (Senegal) was to be the site of the motherhouse. The French viewed him with trepidation. He seemed to attract numerous followers who were identified with anti-French resistance. But Ahmadu Bamba did not in fact lead a holy war against the French. He was exiled and suffered other persecutions at their hands; by the end of his life, he was accepted by the colonial authorities as essentially peaceful. His order has never been the largest in Senegal (the Tidjaniyya brotherhood has more members), but it began to play a central role in Senegalese politics and has done so ever since the period of French occupation.

The basis of the political power of the Muridiyya, like that of the brotherhoods in North Africa in the nineteenth century, was the total allegiance of the followers to their *khalif*. The Muridiyya brotherhood went further in emphasizing discipline and work as the path to salvation. The specific circumstances of the economy and polity in Senegal in the late nineteenth and early twentieth centuries made this formula take on a new and special meaning. The prescribed rituals and prayers of the Muridiyya were quite similar to those of its mother order, the Qadiriyya, but the Mouride disciples quickly became distinguishable from other disciples for their blind obedience and hard labor, especially in producing the new crop strongly encouraged by the French in this period: peanuts. Peanut production was changing the rural economy, and it was the Mourides who most strongly capitalized on this. The French, now confident of their control of the region, saw the potential of the Mourides as intermediaries in the various campaigns they envisioned for their new colony. Other brotherhoods in Senegal would also organize their followers to grow peanuts, and other *khalifs* would regularly use their position to influence political decisions the way the Mouride leaders, following Ahmadu Bamba, were increasingly able to do. But no other *tarika* rivaled the Muridiyya in its degree of political control or its emphasis on economic production.

Conversely, the power of the brotherhoods in North Africa rapidly declined in the twentieth century. There, the French did not collaborate with them as they did in Senegal, and orthodox Muslim clerics opposed them strongly for their impure Islamic practices. By the time of the independence of Algeria and Morocco, the North African politicians had established power bases even in rural areas, where in most cases they were quite distinct from the brotherhood structures. In Senegal, by contrast, the Mouride and to a lesser extent the Tidjani marabouts remained central to both the economy and the politics of the country. The French and then Senegalese politicians used them to reach and organize the rural peasants in the countryside, and their authority remains largely intact even at present. Thus, the brotherhoods succeeded in their final conversion efforts because people sought a social and political identification to replace their traditional political allegiances, which were undermined by the power of the French. In fact, a primary brotherhood identification was often perceived as a way of resisting the French. Nonetheless, the French were able to limit the power of these organizations and eventually turn that power to their own use (Creevey Behrman, 1971).

In North Africa, the French fought and defeated Muslim leaders, never establishing a policy of cooperation and support with them. But in Senegal, the French actually ended up becoming dependent on rural Muslim leaders for the administration of the country. This development is particularly interesting because the colonial authorities, aware that they had helped to spread Islam, initially intended not to support or increase the power of Muslim leaders. Their strategy was threefold. First, the various religious groups were to be kept small and separate. Islam, which the French saw as divided into small warring sects, would be kept divided. They would maintain divisions within ethnic and religious groups by ceasing to appoint indigenous chiefs to govern large territories. Instead, each small ethnic area would have a local ruler who would report directly to the French administrators, without the intermediary of African provincial chiefs. Second, French culture and ideas were to be encouraged in all possible ways. Thus, the colonists attempted to shut the Muslim courts, restrict and reform the Quranic schools, and spread Western education through French language formal schools as rapidly as possible. Finally, marabouts were to be cut off from their source of power—i.e., the contributions of their followers. A 1911 law sought to arrest for "vagabondage" any marabout found living off the alms of his followers (Creevey Behrman, 1970).

In practice, though, the French needed to have effective channels to the rural people. Because their numbers were few and their language and customs so different, the French could not communicate directly with the mass of the Senegalese to maintain control and get their own needs met (such as collecting taxes) or to embark on any new plan (such as spreading the growth of peanuts throughout the country). Strong rural leaders were very useful. By World War II, the pattern was very clearly established. The brotherhoods were far more than little splintered groups; they unified much larger areas of the country. Their leaders were national leaders, and the French found it expedient not only to let this be so but to promote it. They interfered in brotherhood politics when they felt it necessary, but generally they left the marabouts to do as they pleased (including living off the alms of their followers) as long as they did not challenge French authority. They used the marabouts and were used by them, and the recipical relationship worked out well for both. Ironically, the strategies making up their original policy did not work, either. They were forced to re-open the Islamic family courts. Their efforts to control the Quranic schools bore little fruit, and their own schools never reached more than a handful of children in the urban areas. Meanwhile, Islam continued to spread. In 1912 it was estimated that 66 percent of the population was Muslim. In 1960, the year of independence, Muslims made up 90 percent of the population, and in 1992 the figure was 94 to 95 percent (Creevey Behrman, 1970).

What the French had successfully done, however, was to limit the authority of the brotherhoods. Political power on the national level emanated from the top down, from the French ruler to the people via the intermediary of the brotherhoods. After the beginning of the twentieth century there were no Muslim leaders (other than Ahmadu Bamba, who did not ever lead a military resistance) who had the political strength to threaten French control in any but a small, regional context. The laws, institutions, and structures of government through which the French exerted their power were, from the outset, modern secular administrative and political institutions modeled on those of the French. At first these structures had little significance outside the larger towns, but by the 1950s, when the French permitted the Senegalese to vote for delegates to the French National Assembly, national political parties were organized around Western-educated elites. Like the French before them, these elites went to the leaders of the brotherhoods to get out the vote, but they devised political platforms and programs based on French concepts of modern administration and development. The marabouts had been sequestered. Unlike the British, the French did not turn government over to the Muslim rulers but imposed their own form and bribed and pressured the marabouts to accept it. Convinced of France's military might and desirous of the privileges it offered, the marabouts accepted their limited role. The French were careful not to attack Islam and thereby push the Muslim leaders to a final conflict. In these circumstances the Senegalese Muslim leaders retained significant political power—the allegiance of the rural majority—but they did not have political control of the institutions of government or the weapons of enforcement (Creevey Behrman, 1970).

Islam continued to spread and reach ever larger numbers of people; just by virtue of being there longer, the religion deepened its hold among its converts, who came to have a more thorough understanding of the religion and its teachings. However, this process did not occur in a vacuum in which other versions of social order were absent. Rather, it took place in a setting where modern economic programs, including the spread of cash crops and the introduction of formal Western education and other training programs, were being introduced. Thus, the model of medieval Middle Eastern Islamic society that may have accompanied the Islamic conversion of the Hausa had much less significance in Senegal. The relatively open pre-Islamic society continued to exist with an Islamic overlay that changed it but did not destroy its basic characteristics. Strict, orthodox Islam did not predominate; the French had not given it a chance to take hold. The brotherhoods were more tolerant and certainly less orthodox than in Nigeria. In Senegal, women were not veiled, even among the Tukulor; they continued to work in the fields, and, although there was a distinct time lag, girls began to get education and move into the wage sector, following their male peers.

Ironically, while the French may have been the reason that Islam did not place more dramatic restrictions on women than removal from public office, they were also the major reason that in the modernization of agriculture and the economy, men had a considerable advantage over women. The French had their own customs, attitudes, and beliefs about women, which would seriously affect the situation in Senegal. Their original, principal goal for the territory they conquered was to make it profitable. Slaves were the first major export commodity, but as this trade decreased, the French turned to encouraging the cultivation of cash crops. Other trade items, such as gum (used in the textile industry), gold, ivory, and hides, were profitable, but not enough as far as French merchants were concerned. Peanuts became the crop of choice. Particularly in the central zones of the country, Senegalese farmers began to grow them, with encouragement from their marabouts, who recognized the possible profit for both themselves and their followers. Eventually this shift in cultivation would have a serious impact on the provision of food for the country, but even in the beginning years the introduction of this cash crop distorted the family farming system, in particular downgrading the status of women in production.

The French presumed that the production of peanuts would be a specifically male responsibility. A wife might work on her husband's farm, but her husband would receive the incentives—the selected seeds or fertilizer or credit, for example. He was also the one to be trained in new production techniques, the use of new tools, and so forth. Women would benefit in some ways—for example, more of their labor might be needed on the larger fields cleared by the new animal-drawn plow, or their husbands might use the plow to clear their fields after the main family field was done—but they were removed from direct control or authority over the new tools of production. The French systematically excluded them from participating in the new cash crop system of production except as dependent laborers. Eventually they would grow peanuts in their own plots, and they would certainly work in the peanut fields of the family, but their relative economic position had been seriously altered. Not only was their status lowered, their relative ability to produce was undermined because they were not to be taught improved production methods. Thus, their relative capacity to generate revenue was also reduced (see Creevey, 1993).

The same attitude was embodied in the recruitment and staffing of the new industries and commercial establishments set up by the French in St Louis and in and around Dakar, the capital city. Men were trained first and hired, and women were only to be drawn into the new wage labor market in a second phase. Left in the rural areas when men migrated to Dakar to find employment, women were now responsible not only for their traditional tasks but also for the obligations men used to meet and for their work in the family field. Thus, the second legacy of the French-inspired economic revolution in Senegal was increased work and responsibility for women, whereas men gained the option of joining the new economic hierarchy, whose rewards were salaries, benefits, and status.

Rural Senegal did not face the same distortion from migration that countries in southern Africa did, because the industrial/mining job opportunities were much fewer and agriculture was correspondingly more important. Even at present the male/female ratio in rural areas is not heavily unbalanced overall. Women make up 52 percent of the population in both rural and urban areas of Senegal. Approximately 350,000 people, or only 5 percent of the population, are reported to be living away from their zone of residence, and 60.3 percent of these are men (Recensement Générale de la Population et des Habitats [RGPH] 1988, Table 1.1). Some areas of the country, however, do show strong evidence of this problem. The Senegal River region, in particular, has faced a serious drain of male workers both to Dakar and to France, resulting in 30 percent of today's households now being headed by women (RGPH, 1988, Table 2.01). The effect of this development on the position of women has been wide-ranging and severe.

The social and cultural impact of the French was no less severe for women. The number of French remained small, but they established towns that acted as nuclei for the spread of French ideas and culture, affecting the cultures already existing in the countryside. Many of the townspeople in fact became Catholic, and Catholicism would provide the moral rhetoric of the French civilizing mission. (The French were careful not to threaten their collaboration with the marabouts, however, and did not even train African missionaries to spread the Catholic faith—see Hargreaves, 1977.) But the Catholic message was clearly also that women had a secondary role to play in life. Catholicism condemned polygamy (and in this attacked Islam), but otherwise the two faiths had a similar message. As Penda M'Bow writes:

For the Church, the essential mission of woman is motherhood and the foundation of a home. . . . the personal dignity of the woman is shown by the exchange of matrimonial vows in full liberty and equality by both spouses but the equality between the spouses is limited by their natural gifts, by the hierarchy necessary for family society. (M'Bow, 1989, p. 45)

The Islamic and French invasions of Senegal, then, combined to undermine the status of women. By independence in 1960, women were seriously disadvantaged relative to men in their access to the benefits of society, including political office, inherited wealth, the status of paid jobs, the advantages of education, the ability to get credit or inputs for agricultural production, and ownership of the major resource of an agricultural society: land. Women were not, however, powerless or silent. Neither Islam nor the colonial era had removed women's freedom of movement, their ability to participate in the market, their right to control what they earned, and their readiness to speak out for what they wanted. Senegalese society has remained more open than Hausa society, a mixture of elements drawn from all sources—the precolonial traditional states, Islam, and the West.

It remains to be seen which of these influences will attain dominance and how this will change under the impact of economic growth and continuing exterior forces, including the wave of anti-Western fundamentalist nationalism now sweeping the Islamic world.

3

SOCIALIZATION AND THE
SUBORDINATION OF WOMEN

*Were our state a pure democracy, there would still be excluded
from our deliberations women who, to prevent deprivation of
morals and ambiguity of issues, should not mix promiscuously in
gatherings of men.*   —Thomas Jefferson

*The Bible provides all the valid excuses men need to assign lowly
places to women. . . . Subordinating women to the will and rule
of men was an immediate divine punishment imposed in the heat
of anger . . . when Eve took the serpent's advice and ate the
forbidden fruit. . . . Adam made a good job of perpetuating it. And
all men like it.*   —Dan Agbese in the *Nigerian Outlook*

*Let your women keep silent in the churches, for they are not
permitted to speak but they are to be submissive as the law also
says. And if they want to learn something, let them ask their own
husbands at home for it is shameful for women to speak in church.*
                                            —First Corinthians 11:34

*How is it that this world always belonged to the men and things
have begun to change only recently? Is this change a good thing?
Will it bring about an equal sharing of the world between men
and women?*   —Simone de Beauvoir 1974

In recent years the scholarship on women has firmly established the uni-
versality of a constraining view of women that informs nearly every culture and major religion. Islam differs from other major religions, however,
both in the emphasis it places on the proper behavior of women and the
protections it provides for them. Approximately one-third of the *akham*, or
legal injunctions, in the Quran relate to women and the family (Khurshid,

29

1974). The Quran is taken literally as the word of God; it gives both men and women complete instructions for living, and it prescribes the proper society. The Quran and the laws that flow from it (the *Sharia*) cannot be altered, although new interpretations may be made. The interpretations of the words of the Prophet Muhammad by his disciples have led to four schools of Islamic law. Their emphases are slightly different, but all four schools of Islamic law provide instructions for every aspect of public and private life. Women are meant to be wives and mothers. Marriage and childbearing are religious duties. The roles of husbands and wives are viewed as complementary rather than unequal, and although both men and women are equal before God, men stand a step above women in society (Quran 2:229). Thus, the family is hierarchical and patriarchal in structure.

The Quran treats a woman's identity from the point of view of a jealous husband. She cannot appear attractive outside the home, she cannot have friends beyond the family circle, and she cannot have a life free from the supervision of her husband. She is to blame if a man is attracted to her, for sin originates in her, not in her male counterpart (Sabbah, 1984). Within the family, a wife has both rights and duties, and men have obligations to support their wives. Wives who disobey their husbands may be beaten and lose their right to receive support.

The Quran states that a man may marry as many as four wives if he can support and treat them equally (Quran 4:4), but a woman may marry only one man at a time (she may remarry after a divorce or the death of a husband). A man may divorce his wife at will by declaring his intention three times in front of three witnesses but is enjoined to do so only for serious cause. Should a woman seek a divorce, she must do so in Islamic court. In court the testimony of two women is equal to that of one man (Quran 3:283). However, it is clear that women are not compelled by the religion to tolerate mistreatment or nonsupport. In spite of their disadvantages in court, women in most Islamic societies have developed strategies for manipulating seclusion and divorce procedures to their own advantage (Pitten, 1979b). Divorce rates are quite high in Islamic regions of Nigeria, the divorce rate being almost equal to the marriage rate. In Senegal, where women are neither veiled nor secluded, divorce is also common, especially in urban areas, but it is not as widespread as in Nigeria. Thus, the degree of constraint of women called for in Islamic culture does not necessarily predict the degree of independence women will have in their personal lives. Context to some extent modifies content.

The separation of marital property as required by Islamic law may have advantages, as early marriage and frequent divorce are the norm. Women have a right to the money they themselves earn, and the rules of inheritance are among the most highly developed and distinctive characteristics of Islamic law. Strict mathematical for division of inheritable assets in every conceivable situation. Briefly, daughters inherit one-half the share of a son, and a wife inherits one-eighth of her husband's estate if there are children and one-fourth if there are no children. If a man has more than one wife, the wife's share is divided among them (Quran 4:12). Thus, although the laws of inheritance are unequal, women have rights and advantages they did not have in pre-Islamic society. As one example, under Islam widows theoretically have the means to live should they choose not to remarry.

Unlike most other religions, then, Islam does concern itself with the rights of women, even if those rights are not equal. Although it views women as sexual temptresses and for that reason dictates how they should dress, circumscribes their behavior, and reinforces their subordination to men in marriage, Islam also admonishes husbands to be responsible and obligates them to support their wives and children (J. Smith, 1987):

> Men are those who support women, since God has given some persons advantages over others, and because they expend their wealth on them. Men have authority over women because Allah has made the one superior to the other and because they spend their wealth to maintain them. (Quran 4:35)

The traditional ethos of male domination and the Islamic emphasis on female submission to men combine to limit opportunities for Muslim women in Nigeria and Senegal. It is clear, however, that Hausa culture has combined with Islam to limit women's choices and life horizons to a much greater extent than has been the case in Senegal. As Islam became more deeply entrenched in Hausa society, women lost any independent rights they may previously have had to engage in public trade, to work, travel, or remain unmarried. Whereas a hundred years ago only the wives of religious leaders, emirs, royalty, and wealthy individuals were secluded, seclusion is now the norm in both rural and urban areas in northern Nigeria. It may be that in the countryside, women actually preferred seclusion to hard work in the fields. In any event, in northern Nigeria, Muslim women of childbearing age do not generally work in the fields, trade in the markets, or go out into the streets during daytime hours. At night they go out only to visit homes sanctioned by their husbands and must be accompanied at all times. In Senegal, by contrast, daily routines of women, such as working in the fields, appearing freely in the markets, or moving openly about in public places, were not altered by the conversion to Islam.

PRE-ISLAMIC CULTURES

Islamic teachings are not imposed uniformly in all West African cultures. Thus, the written law of Islam interacted with each specific set of pre-existing customs and traditions to create distinctive Islamic societies that differ, sometimes strongly, from each other. Thus, in Nigeria and Senegal, women's lives today are shaped by a syncretic blend of local cultural prescriptions and the teachings of Islam. As the precolonial cultures were certainly patriarchal, it is difficult to determine which parts of current culture come from Islam and which from predisposing elements in pre-Islamic society.

In Nigeria, there is a small subgroup of Hausa people in the southernmost part of Hausaland, the Maguzawa, who were outside the Hausa state structure and did not convert to Islam. Christian missionaries were welcomed here, and today the Maguzawa are predominantly Christian rather than Muslim. A number of scholars contend that the Maguzawa represent an earlier Hausa social order. Women here are not secluded, work in the fields, have a significantly higher literacy rate than Muslim women, and are not disadvantaged in law compared to men. It is difficult, however, to generalize from this case, because the Maguzawa live in a few very small villages in a remote part of Hausaland. They received Christian missionaries and schools, which greatly altered their traditional culture. It would be as difficult to disentangle what is indigenous and what is syncretic here as in any other society. For the purposes of this study, Hausa culture applies to the 99.9 percent of Hausa people who are Islamic and live in northern Nigeria.

In Senegal, pre-Islamic societies contained a mixture of matrilineal and patrilineal traditions. Among the Wolof, for example, women were believed to transmit character and intelligence to their children, as well as less desirable qualities such as susceptibility to certain illnesses and the gift of sorcery or witchcraft. Among nobles and aristocrats, women passed on the family status, and certain items (such as land and slaves) would be inherited through the female line (Diop, 1985, pp. 19–22). Men were believed to transmit courage and other social values, including honor, power, and authority. Significantly, for the commoners and lower castes, the male line determined property ownership (it was transmitted through them to their male heirs). Caste, furthermore, was determined by the male and his inherited profession (Diop, 1985, pp. 22–23). As mentioned in Chapter 2, political posts of importance were held by women in the Wolof kingdoms before the arrival of Islam. But even then, women held a secondary political position to men and were economically disadvantaged. Men controlled the only major resource (land), and only they could inherit it. Whether this custom was the result of the development of patriarchy concomitant with the development of castes and classes is not known. The point is that it was not the result of the spread of Islam.

When Islam was spread throughout the Tukulor, Wolof, and Serer kingdoms, it reinforced the patriarchal values of these traditional societies, justifying in the law and the Quran the subordination of women to men.

One consequence here, as in Nigeria, was the removal of women from public office when the Muslim brotherhoods replaced the traditional kingdoms as local and regional political institutions (Sow, 1985, p. 566). However, Islam did provide certain rights to women that did not exist prior to its incorporation into the culture. In pre-Islamic society there was no regular law system protecting those rights women did possess. Thus, men that had sufficient resources could marry as many women as they liked, and nothing except the power of an earlier wife's family could force the husband to treat her as well as he treated more recent wives. Women whose husbands died or who were abandoned by their spouses became the responsibility of their brothers (or fathers, or maternal uncles or cousins, depending on the particular culture). In some societies, a man was even supposed to marry his brother's widow and care for her.

But should a widow or abandoned wife not be cared for by her brother, brother-in-law, or husband, there was no guarantee that someone else would be responsible for her and often no way such women could care for themselves. They had no wealth unless—and in Senegal this was unusual—they had been very successful in their trade, as they received no inheritance and did not even get to keep their bride price (paid by the family of the husband to the family of the bride). Wives did not own land nor the house in which they lived; all property was controlled by their husbands. In an extended family/subsistence/community system, few if any individuals would be left to starve. Abandoned women would end up, in effect, as servants in a wealthier family compound if their own situation worsened. But the concept of individual rights did not exist. Nothing protected women from being exploited by careless or malicious males in their families.

The subordination of women was very explicit: Wolof women were supposed to find their fulfillment through submission to men. What Islam did, in this situation, was to provide a bill of rights. In so doing it developed a sense of individualism in a way not previously known and undermined the absolutism of the community/family unitary system. For the first time, women were given the right to the money or goods paid for their bride price; they received an inheritance from their fathers, even though they inherited only half of what their brothers did and did not receive land; and they had an explicit right to what they earned themselves. This right they had enjoyed by custom but without the protection of a specific provision to that effect. Islam also gave women family rights they had not had, limiting the number of wives a man might take, giving a mother rights to her children, and obligating the father to maintain them even if under the mother's care. Thus, according to Abdoulaye Bara Diop, Islam had some of the same impact in Africa that it is said to have had in medieval Arabia in providing certain protections for women (Diop, 1985, pp. 15–30).

CHILDHOOD AND MARRIAGE

The socialization of Hausa girls in the Islamic culture of Northern Nigeria (and southern Niger) begins at birth. Girls are assigned domestic duties at about age five; by age six they are dressed in imitation of adult women and begin to be viewed as future wives. In wealthier families, marriage negotiations may begin at this time. Girls go outside their homes only to carry messages for their mothers, to sell food from large bowls carried on their heads, or to go to the markets to purchase ingredients. At the same age, boys are sent outside to play with other boys in their age groups and begin sleeping in the entrances of their family homes rather than with their mothers. By age ten little boys seldom cross the line into female space. They eat with other boys in their father's room(s) and become visitors to their mother's rooms (Schildkrout, 1979). By age eleven or twelve, boys whose fathers are traders or artisans may become apprentices to their fathers. Adulthood means separation, even avoidance, between male and female.

As she grows up, a girl is assigned child-care responsibilities and is made aware that her sex is a potential source of shame and dishonor. She is constantly told that she is inferior to her brothers and that "you are a woman and you are going to someone else's house where you had better know how to behave" (Kabir, 1981). For the overwhelming majority of girls in Hausa Nigeria, it is inconceivable to aspire to any role other than that of wife and mother. Because most girls are married by age twelve (or immediately after the first menses), they experience no time in their life when choices are possible. After marriage at an early age, they are virtually confined to the female quarters of their husbands' compounds for most of the rest of their lives. If a girl is married as young as ten, she will not be expected to cook or have sexual relations with her husband until puberty begins (although it is not uncommon for very young girls to be injured by impatient husbands), but she must enter seclusion and loses the freedom associated with childhood. For all practical purposes, her home is her world. From the time a girl marries until after menopause, she has virtually no freedom of movement or association. Unlike girls, boys do not reach adult status until they become economically self-supportive, usually in their late twenties or early thirties. Therefore, they marry much later than do girls, because Islam forbids men from marrying until they can support their wife (or wives) and children by providing shelter, food, and clothing. Like women, all Hausa men are expected to marry and are not accorded adult status until they do.

Within their own world, women do have a great deal of autonomy. They are secluded, but men are excluded from women's space. Women can visit members of their family once the sun goes down, and, with their husbands' permission, they can receive their friends. Thus, women have access to many homes, men to few. Men never enter the female quarters of nonfamily homes and rarely enter the female sections of the homes of either younger brothers or sisters. However, they may visit older married sisters or the wives of older brothers.

Men and women are seldom if ever together in social situations. Marriages are arranged by families, and the age differential between a girl at first marriage and her husband is generally great. The fact that young girls grow up and then live in a world of women is bound to have profound psychological implications. Although men's overt authority over women is nearly complete, in day-to-day life there is little contact, and hence male authority is actually quite remote. Margaret Knipp found that the educated women in her study in Sokoto in 1984 knew little about their husbands and were unsure even of their ages or their occupations (Knipp, 1987). However, they participate in wide networks through which the most intimate news of large extended families flows. Marriages, naming ceremonies, and other rituals are constant. Women meet, develop connections, and exchange information without any male presence. Through these networks they influence developments throughout their families, which leads some feminist scholars to assert that women wield "power and authority" from behind the walls of seclusion (Mack, 1991).

In Hausaland women move in and out of marriage in a complex pattern of family and patron-client networks that defies simple analysis and is quite outside Islamic prescriptions. For girls of wealthier families, the preferred form of a first marriage is kin marriage (*auren zumunci*). First cousin patrilineal (and less often matrilineal), parallel, and cross-cousin marriages are all common. The overwhelming majority of first marriages end in divorce, largely because the girls are so young and often have difficulty "settling down." Family relationships are not seriously damaged, and property remains basically intact if a girl's first marriage is within the family. For girls, the first marriage is the most important because it is the one around which bride price (*kayan daki*, or the material goods brought to the marriage by the bride), bridewealth (*sadaki*, or the sum paid by the groom's family to the bride's family), and other negotiations have taken place.

Hausa marriage is defined by contract, and the marriage remains valid only as long as both parties feel contractual agreements are being observed. Islam as practiced here does not permit women of childbearing age to remain single. Thus, remarriage is almost a certainty in the case of divorce, and women have little incentive to stay in a bad marriage or in a marriage where there is incompatibility between co-wives, particularly if there are no children. In this society children stay with the father in the event of divorce. Young girls are almost always married to older men who already have one or more wives. Partly because divorce in the case of first marriages for girls is more likely than not, first-child avoidance (*kunya*) is also practiced. Hence, the young girl does not get attached to her first child and can easily leave a marriage if it is not working. Unlike first marriages, second marriages may be initiated by the parties concerned, but the negotiations are a family matter and must be approved by the senior male kin of each family. Without such approval the marriage is not considered valid and is not eligible for the property protections provided by Islam (Callaway, 1986).

Young girls are expected to marry and have children, and no realistic alternatives exist at age twelve, the average age of marriage. A very small percentage of girls now complete secondary school and even get university degrees, but if they think of careers, they think of them in addition to, not instead of, marriage and family. Parents are eager to see girls married early in order that they not be "spoiled" and in order to cement family ties or to form alliances. Girls who are allowed to continue their education must make their marriage arrangements first. In a society where virtually no women remain single (unless they are barren and are forced into prostitution), the social advantages of early marriage outweigh anything else a daughter might do.

Hausa weddings bear little resemblance to marriage ceremonies in the West. When the agreements between the two families concerned have been finalized, prayers are said in the mosque. The groom may or may not be present, but the bride never is. The groom generally celebrates with his friends if this is the first marriage for his bride, but otherwise he only calls on the bride's family sometime during the day. The bride, especially in the case of a first marriage, receives guests and gifts in her home while her sisters, female relatives, and friends prepare large pots of food to feed the visitors and guests. As the guests leave, they take small cakes or kola nuts to pass out in their own neighborhoods to announce the marriage.

Once prayers have been said in the mosque, the marriage is properly sanctioned and the marriage contract binding. The man is obligated to provide food, clothing, shelter, and sexual satisfaction (defined as producing children). If he is polygamous, he must give equal time to each wife in order that each may be assured of equal opportunity to bear children; infertility in either spouse is grounds for divorce. In exchange, a wife is expected to share in household responsibilities, show proper deference to her husband, and be sexually monogamous. A wife is considered "good" if she is modest, obedient, proficient in domestic schools, and fecund. A husband is considered "good" if he is prosperous and generous.

Although most women will be divorced at some point in their lives, most will not be unmarried for more than a few months to a year. Divorced or widowed women generally return home for a short time and then remarry (Schildkrout, 1986). If a woman resists marriage for any length of time, engages in successful economic activity, and begins to become economically independent, she will be labeled a prostitute. The only word for an unmarried woman of childbearing age in the Hausa language is *karuwa*, which translates as "prostitute." A single woman, whether divorced or widowed, of childbearing age is expected to remarry and to continue bearing children until menopause. Divorce for men does not often result in his becoming single because most men have more than one wife.

Women do not normally experience intimacy (other than sexually) with their husbands, but they do form close and intimate relationships with other wives, female relatives, and friends, with whom they are in daily contact. There is therefore a certain element of security and certainty about their lives while they are in marriages. One of the criticisms of "women's liberation" frequently and relentlessly expressed in Nigerian newspapers is the perception that it introduces un-Islamic uncertainty and insecurity into the lives of women.

Much of the socialization of young Wolof girls in Senegal is similar to that of Hausa girls in northern Nigeria. Girls' futures lie in marriage to men who will treat them well and provide them with the social and economic status they (and their families) desire. The early training of girls is largely concerned with domestic tasks and the care of children. They are taught to be obedient and submissive; their value in society and the future of their children depends on their behaving in this way (Diop, 1985, p. 23). Girls expect to be married; they would not have an acceptable social status if they were not. Thus very few Senegalese women, like their Hausa counterparts, remain divorced for very long. Sixty-seven percent of Senegalese women age fifteen or older are married. The majority of those who are single are young and/or in school. Although the Family Code of 1972 (revised in 1989) bans marriage for girls under the age of sixteen, many rural girls marry younger. Fewer do so in Senegal than among the Hausa, however, which may in part explain Senegal's lower divorce rate. Only 3 percent of all Senegalese women were reported as divorced in 1988, although, of course, many had been divorced and remarried but were not included in this figure. The number of divorced women is higher in towns than in rural areas, where only 2 percent of the women are reported as divorced at any one time. Men, of course, are less likely to be divorced because they may have more than one wife; only 1 percent nationally are reported as divorced an any given point in time (RGPH 1988, p. 8).

Most Senegalese are Muslim, which means that men may marry up to four wives. The Family Code of 1972 required men and women to agree at the time of marriage as to whether that marriage would be polygamous or monogamous. The law prescribed a contract between the couple obliging men to adhere to monogamy if such were the initial decision. However, few couples ever sign such a contract—a nationwide survey of 1,000 women in 1991 found only 21 percent of the respondents had done so; of these, 70 percent lived in Dakar (Creevey, 1993, pp. 247–268). In fact, many men do still marry another wife even if such a contract is signed, because there is no provision for punishing them if they do so. Furthermore, women can often be coerced into accepting this change in their status:

Divorce will force them to find another husband, as single women have little place in society, and it may disadvantage them financially, because the man in all likelihood will retain control of all family goods. The wife will only have the product of what she earned and/or invested, and given that she is less likely to be educated, she will probably have a much lower level of income and savings than her spouse. Many educated women complain about the unfairness of this situation but, despite the Family Code, find little relief (Ba, 1986; Sow, 1989, p. 10; *Code de la Famille,* 1979, 1989).

Oddly enough, however, polygamy is not especially widespread. Seven out of ten Senegalese men were in monogamous marriages in 1988. Thirty percent of rural marriages were polygamous, but only 24 percent of urban marriages were (RPGH 1988, p. 9). Of course, more women than men are in polygamous marriages, but they are still a minority. These figures suggest that men and women in urban Senegal, where education is more widespread among women as well as men (see Chapter 4), are turning away from polygamy. However, the major factor explaining this result is wealth. The Quran clearly prescribes that the husband is responsible for family costs, whereas the wife may use the proceeds of her own income as she chooses. In order to be married in the first place, a man has to pay a bride price, which despite government regulation is quite high, especially in urban areas. Thus, as in Nigeria, many men cannot afford to marry until they reach their late twenties or later, and for economic reasons a substantial proportion of these will never have more than one wife.

Like the Hausa, women and men in Senegal interact primarily with others of their own sex in their work and social life, and this is especially so among the uneducated and rural dwellers. Tasks in agriculture and the home are divided by sex, and social organization is divided between women's groups and men's. Thus, there are in some sense two separate social networks having separate authorities. One of these, the men's, ultimately controls the other because it controls most of the economic resources and the forces of national, regional, and local government. In Senegal, interaction between men and women is much more common than among the Hausa, because women are not secluded. But women have their own networks to regulate women's tasks and to arbitrate conflicts over the decisions they make and the goods they control.

Thus, if secluded women among the Hausa have power enabling them to make important daily decisions and influence male behavior both indirectly and directly, so too do the nonsecluded women of the Wolof and Serer, whose social and economic life is also divided by gender. The important factor is that there is such a gender division. On the one hand, this division lends itself to discrimination against women by men based on the latter's control of resources. On the other hand, it ensures some measure of separate power to the disadvantaged group, as men are not involved in, and therefore cannot control, many decisions women make. Equality may only be achieved when major resources, including governmental power, are shared between the sexes and women begin to move in significant numbers into positions of public control. This breakthrough has not yet happened in Senegal any more than it has in northern Nigeria. However, in Senegal, as will be discussed in Chapters 5 and 6, this process is more clearly beginning to get under way.

ON DIVORCE

Islamic law makes provisions for marriages that do not work out. Divorce is common among the Hausa and is rather easily obtained. It is sanctioned for reasons of nonsupport, long absences, and impotency or infertility. There are three forms of divorce: divorce unilaterally pronounced by the husband (*talaq*), separation sought by the wife through an Islamic court (*kuhl*), and mutual dissolution granted by a court after the appointment of an arbiter. Upon divorce, a woman is permitted to keep whatever material goods or property she has accumulated and any gifts given her by her husband. For a specified period of time (*idda*), a woman forgoes social contacts and lives as though in mourning. During this time, her husband remains responsible for her support; if the divorce was instigated by the wife, the husband may seek reconciliation through an arbiter. If there is no reconciliation, a husband's obligations for his wife's support ends at the end of the *idda*, usually a period of six months.

Should a woman become divorced or widowed, she may keep only an infant child (and is entitled to receive support for it), but upon weaning the child may be claimed by the father or the nearest agnatic relative (Hinchcliffe, 1975). Some schools of Islamic law permit a woman to keep sons until puberty or daughters until marriage, but such is not the case in Hausaland. During the mother's period of custody, the father or the nearest male agnatic relative remains the guardian of the child and can make important decisions regarding education or marriage without consulting with the mother. Upon remarriage, a woman generally loses custody immediately.

Although Senegal and some other Islamic countries have repealed laws permitting divorce by *talaq*, it is still the most common form of divorce in Hausaland. Research shows that *talaq* is often provoked by discontented wives (Pitten, 1979; Saunders, 1978; Dunbar, 1991). Once pronounced, *talaq* is simple, quick, and final. If a woman who wants out of a marriage does have to go to court, she is rarely denied (Pitten, 1979). Men generally do not contest divorce—most wives are considered interchangeable, and a discontented one can fairly easily be replaced with a more agreeable one. Any wife seeking a divorce is by definition "difficult," and any man wanting to stay with such a woman is considered weak and the object of pity (Callaway, 1986).

Although women who seek divorce generally get it, many women stay in unhappy marriages because they do not want to leave their children, because of the enormous pressure to quickly remarry should they leave, and because of the near impossibility of either supporting oneself or living a socially acceptable life outside of marriage (Knipp, 1987).

Divorce is viewed as a temporary status. The widespread practice of polygamy greatly increases the chances for multiple marriages for both men and women, although women's marriages must be sequential rather than concurrent. The loss of children is not as traumatic as might be assumed, because once children marry they generally reestablish contact with their biological mother. The widespread practices of first-child avoidance and fostering (lending children to childless or older women) mitigates the impact on children themselves: They are used to living with an assortment of adults on both sides of their families at different points in their lives. If women were given physical custody of children, it would be a disadvantage in their efforts to remarry following a divorce, as men do not normally accept stepchildren, even when marrying widows.

Women in Senegal have somewhat more protection against the disadvantages of the discriminatory divorce arrangements prescribed by traditional Malekite Muslim law. Because Senegal has adopted a family code based on a mixture of Muslim and French law, strict Islamic law is not adhered to even in the area of family matters. This fact is the basis of considerable dissatisfaction among strictly orthodox Muslims, who feel that to water down the prescriptions of the Quran and the *Sharia* is to violate the sanctity of Islam (M. Dieng, 1991, pp. 13–14).

In Senegal the arrival of the Muslim brotherhoods coincided with the arrival of the French, and thus the intermingling of three systems—French, traditional, and Islamic—has been constant. There never has been a time when Muslim law alone was used for the arbitration of decisions, family or otherwise, in Senegal. In the current situation, the revised Family Code of 1989 prohibits *talaq* and requires both men and women to go to a civil hearing to get their divorce approved. Such divorces will be approved only for specific reasons, such as infidelity, nonsupport (by the husband), or unalterable incompatibility. Husbands must pay alimony and child support for a certain period after divorce. Nonetheless, women are still disadvantaged. Men still control family property in a divorce situation and retain authority over their children after divorce (although young children will remain with their mothers). Fathers can determine if the older children remain with their mothers or go to another agnatic relative for schooling. Alimony and child support are not automatic after the first few months; child support will be awarded thereafter only if the mother can prove that she cannot support her family. If she remarries, as society demands, the child resident with her will not get support from the natural father (Creevey, 1993, pp. 219–232).

According to the teaching of some interpreters of contemporary Islam, Muslim law can be reinterpreted, despite what some strict orthodox say to deny this (Esposito, 1982). Reforms in Islamic countries such as Tunisia and Turkey have resulted in revisions to family law to make the position of women more equal with that of men. The real issue is whether the liberal reformers have more or less political power at any one point than do the strictly orthodox. In contrast to Nigeria's Islamic leaders, the leaders of the Muslim brotherhoods in Senegal (who are orthodox and conservative) have resisted changes that threatened Islam, including the Family Code (*L'Etudient Musulman,* 1991, p. 14), but they have been unable to stop the reforms from becoming national law. Their authority and that of Islamic law has not been as deeply rooted as in Nigeria. Brotherhood leaders have accepted a mixed law system, tacitly acknowledging that French law was the ultimate authority. The major marabouts resolved this dilemma by ignoring the Family Code, and the government turned a blind eye to transgressions by their followers in the rural areas in which the brotherhoods are most powerful (Magassouba, 1985, p. 114). The assumption by those in national office is that the Family Code will gradually be enforced as more people are educated and as the marabouts get used to the idea. The radical orthodox, located primarily in Dakar and as yet weak in number and influence, can do nothing to effectively alter the process. In the meanwhile, urban Senegalese women profit from the reforms of the code, which rural women are only discovering. But even urban women still resent the inequities written into the code in family matters: Women continue to be disadvantaged in marriage arrangements and in divorce (see Sow, 1989).

WOMEN AND RELIGION

Behind the walls secluding them from public view, Hausa women have developed a kind of independence, or at least distinct spheres of activity, in two areas: in regard to economic activity (to be discussed in Chapter 5) and in regard to religion, both Islam and Bori. Some feminist scholars of Islam also posit that there are leadership roles for women within Islam (Starratt and Sule, 1991). Several devout Muslim women in Kano now hold positions as teachers, mystics, and social workers within the major brotherhoods (Qadiriyya and Tidjaniyya). Sule and Starratt argue that there is disagreement among Muslim scholars over what legitimate roles women can assume within the religion; furthermore, they note, Muslim scholars are constantly reinterpreting the laws, acts, and sayings of the Prophet and hence are inevitably influenced by local culture and belief. By implication, they suggest that as Islamic societies become more modern, an expanded role for women within the structure of Islam will develop.

Others argue that Islam clearly gives equal status to men and women, especially in terms of religious responsibility and leadership (Yusuf, 1991; Starratt and Sule, 1991; Lemu, 1978). Islam has established a literate tradition, and great respect is given to scholars and teachers. The Prophet Muhammad and the Shehu Usman dan Fodio both taught their daughters to read and to study. It is primarily in the area of literacy and knowledge of the Quran that men and women are perceived as equal. Female teachers well versed in Islamic scholarship have lived in Kano for at least the last century. It is the responsibility of fathers, brothers, and husbands to educate their daughters, sisters, and wives.

Learned women teach privately, generally in the homes of their fathers or brothers. They are an important source of Islamic learning in the large cities of northern Nigeria and are regarded with respect. There are several examples of such women in Kano, Sokoto, and Zaria. They were married young, generally to *mallams*, and continued their studies until they had completed the Quran. Today several such women teach at the Women's Arabic Teachers' College in Kano. Several others run Islamic nursery schools in their homes, where they teach girls appropriate behavior according to the Quran. This is not a common occupation for a woman, but neither is it altogether rare. In recent years women teachers have been very active working with women who go to Saudi Arabia on Hadj (the pilgrimage required of all who are able). Sule and Starratt give examples of several such women in Kano. All the individuals cited married young (at age ten to fourteen), were perceived as devout, and had husbands who either taught them or permitted them to continue their studies of the Quran in their fathers' homes. Now past menopause, they have found a vocation tutoring women going on Hadj as to proper behavior and deportment in the holy places. Several of the instructors also accompany women on Hadj and serve essentially as social workers among them during the long and often difficult pilgrimage to the Holy Land. They care for the sick, seek aid when pilgrims run out of money or food, and generally help to make the experience easier. It is asserted that these women have found appropriate "leadership roles" sanctioned by Islam and serve as role models for younger women. Many of them also run Islamiyya schools (Islamic schools that serve as a substitute for state schools run on the Western model) or schools for married women, teaching them how to strengthen their religious activities. Through these activities, women are teaching each other about their rights in Islam and inevitably developing their own leadership roles.

In recent years, a greater number of devout Muslim women are speaking out against the total subjugation of women to men in the Islamic parts of Nigeria. They write columns in the local press, speak on the radio, and have sparked passionate and sometimes acrimonious debates among male scholars. Women have even declared that the human impossibility of treating multiple wives equally indicates that the Prophet Muhammad was actually warning against polygamy rather than endorsing it (Kabir, 1985; Imam, 1990; Sule and Starratt, 1991; Yusuf, 1991). They argue that law and the courts reflect the values of a given society and that local custom and marriage laws in Hausaland actually distort Islam. These critics call for reform that will correct the imbalance between men and women and make society Islamically more correct (Lemu, 1984). To date this debate is restricted to a tiny educated minority of women activists, but it does illustrate that generalizations about Islamic culture must always be tempered by context.

A further indication of the importance of context in determining the form and expression of Islamic practice is the observation that Islamic injunctions are not so closely observed by Hausa men and women living outside the Hausa heartland. In the Hausa community in Accra, Ghana, for example, women trade outside their homes, go to school at about the same ratio as do other girls in Accra, and work outside the home once educated. Hausa women in Accra marry later than they do in Nigeria, live in smaller polygamous families, and give different definitions of Islamic teachings (Pellow, 1991). Northern Nigeria's strict, sober, homogeneous, orthodox Islamic environment greatly contrasts with Accra's more outgoing, free-wheeling, and heterogeneous urban culture. The contrast between the lives of Hausa Muslim women in these two different settings lends credence to the assertion that environment matters, even within a single culture.

Although Islam is pervasive in Hausaland and women as well as men strive to be devout observers, the pre-Islamic spirit possession cult of Bori continues to flourish (Greenberg, 1966; Echard, 1989). Women have continued to be highly visible in the practice of this cult. In Bori, the spirits have both male and female lineages and reveal themselves by possessing the body of a living human. Those chosen for possession are summoned by appropriate drumbeats, and spectators can then speak about their concerns to the spirits through those possessed. Women in particular turn to Bori to ward off misfortune in their lives. Failure to bear children, concern about the arrival of a new wife, or chronic illnesses are among the problems they seek to address through Bori (Greenberg, 1966). Perhaps more than other acknowledged inconsistencies, Bori has withstood the overwhelming maleness of Islam and preserved a role for women. It has been officially banned by the emirs, yet it is tacitly accepted as an illegitimate but flourishing and effective court of last appeal (Pitten, 1978).

In theory, men and women have equal opportunity to be possessed by spirits and access to leadership roles in Bori (Greenberg, 1966). However, close study of Bori in Niger contradicts the belief in gender equality (Echard 1991). Male adepts are possessed more frequently than female ones and tend to be more important. Female spirits tend to exhibit socially deviant behavior and in particular tend to illustrate insufficiency or failure in the socialization of their sexuality. Hence, in fact, Bori is now a part

of the means by which inegalitarian male-female relationships are reinforced (Echard, 1991). Still, Bori does provide women with opportunities
for achievement and public roles absent elsewhere in the society.

The existence of the Bori spirits is not denied by the Muslim *mallams;*
rather, such beings are identified with pagan spirits condemned by Islamic
doctrine and therefore outside the realm of religion. It is clear, however,
that belief in non-Islamic supernatural beings has survived the adoption of
a monotheistic religion. The open practice of Bori and the acknowledgment of its continued influence demonstrates the gap between professed
belief and actual social practice.

As among the Hausa, women in Senegal were guardians and interpreters of the traditional religions that preceded Islam. Some remained active in these traditional religions long after Islam appeared and continued
to have a certain authority because of their connections with the old spirits, who never completely vanished. In the 1950s, French observers reported this type of activity among Lebou women in the Dakar area (Balandier and Mercier, 1952, pp. 111–119), and in 1960 Lucy Creevey saw
dance ceremonies near Rufisque that supposedly were connected to this
spirit cult (Creevey, 1993, p. 73). Did the spiritual power of women gradually disappear after the arrival of Islam, and did women try to keep these
traditional beliefs alive in part because they had no such role within Islam?
To some extent these suppositions may be true, but the nature of the *sufi*
brotherhoods has to be considered closely before we can draw this as an
absolute conclusion.

Islamic brotherhoods include sophisticated and highly developed belief systems and leaders known to be great scholars. But they were also the
means of popularizing Islam, and they allowed it to soften and absorb the
beliefs and customs it encountered in its spread across the world. Christianity, too, had a popular form as it spread throughout Europe, softening
the stricter moralist form of its origins. As it spread, it absorbed many
cults and belief systems that reappeared as pseudo-Christianity—the elaborate dressing and of statues and something akin to worship of Mary in
parts of Latin America is certainly a reappearance of a female religious ritual. Thus, it seems reasonable to hypothesize that women may in this fashion have preserved many of their spiritual/religious roles within Islam, although we can do no more than suggest that much. Closer investigation of
popular beliefs among Senegalese Muslims would probably show this kind
of syncretism.

Within the formal structure of Senegalese Islam, women's roles are
complex and until recently have been difficult for outsiders to understand.
Some have written that Senegalese women are invisible because they seem
powerless in the brotherhood structure (Creevey, 1991; Cruise O'Brien,
1971, pp. 85–86; Sy, 1969, pp. 201–202). However, most societies, no matter how restrictive, have a female power structure shadowing the public

male structure. Looking more closely may expose the "shadow" structure within the brotherhoods.

Whatever form female power may take within one brotherhood, however, it will not necessarily be consistent in all brotherhoods; hence, the major distinctions among the Senegalese orders must be understood. In Senegal there are four major brotherhoods: the Tidjaniyya, the Muridiyya, the Qadiriyya, and the Layenne. The first two are by far the most important, both in terms of their numbers and their economic and political influence. The idiosyncrasies of the Mourides have already been mentioned—their tighter discipline, their stronger emphasis on work and obedience as the means to salvation, their central role in the introduction of peanut cultivation, and their growing importance in the urban economy, especially of Dakar. The Tidjaniyya brotherhood, however, remains larger than the Muridiyya and is also powerful.

All of the major brotherhoods are split among the lineages of the descendants of their founders and his brothers and chief advisors. The Muridiyya, which operates more often as a unified whole than the Tidjaniyya, has a *khalif* at the apex. This position is sometimes contested upon the death of the incumbent, as the line of succession may be calculated through either the son or the brother (a confusion owing to a mixture of pre-Islamic and Islamic traditions). Individual Mouride lineages may be quite powerful and semiautonomous (although the *shaikh* heading each lineage owes fealty, at least in theory, to the *khalif*). The ordinary *talibe*, or disciple, owes his allegiance to a *shaikh*. Sometimes there are conflicts among the leaders over succession or other issues, which may cause bitter divisions within the order, but ordinarily the Mourides speak (publicly) with one voice to the government, the voice of the *khalif general,* presently Serigne Saliou M'Backe, eldest surviving son of Ahmadu Bamba.

The Tidjaniyya are not unified behind one *khalif* but rather are split among several major families whose original allegiances may have been to the Ida Ou ali-Tidjanis (in Mauritania) or to al-Hadji Umar Tal (from the upper Senegal River area) or even both. (Al-Hadji Malik Sy, for example, had dual allegiance.) Two principal branches still exist and act as separate influences in politics, although with less regularity than the Mourides. The first of these branches was founded by Al-Hadji Malik Sy (1869–1922) and is headquartered at Tivaouane. Malik Sy was a scholar and author of numerous treatises on law, theology, and *sufism.* His center was known for its advanced system of Islamic education, and the emphasis of his brotherhood is still more on scholarship and traditional Muslim virtues, such as prayer and rituals. This emphasis represents a contrast with the Mourides, although the difference is not absolute. *Talibes* of the Tivaouane Tidjaniyya work in the field for their marabouts just as Mouride disciples do, and Mourides sometimes get advanced Islamic education (stressed, for example, by the M'Backe Bousso family). Tivaouane Tidjani leaders also put pressure on government officials, just as Mouride leaders do. The difference lies in the lesser political involvement and power of the Tidjani group.

The second important Tidjani group follows the leadership of the Niass family and is headquartered in Kaolack. The founder, Abdoulaye Niass, died in 1922 and was succeeded by his eldest son, Muhammad. But it was his younger son, Ibrahima, who became the group's most important leader. Although technically owing allegiance to his brother, Ibrahima soon had many more followers than Muhammad and spread his order throughout West Africa. He was very political and actively involved in Senegalese politics until his death in 1975, although he emphasized education and scholarship, as did the Tivaouane Tidjanis, more than did the Mourides. Ibrahima's eldest son succeeded him and proved to be less political and less powerful than his father. The Niassan branch of the Tidjaniyya is today more known for scholarship than anything else (Quesnot, 1963, p. 194; P. Marty, 1917, pp. 175–210; Creevey Behrman, 1970, pp. 61–72).

There is a third section of the Tidjanis made up of a number of major marabouts, many located on the upper Senegal River. These marabouts have traditionally been isolated from national politics but often very powerful locally. Some have been great scholars and others great politicians, such as the late Al-Hadji Saidou Nourou Tal, but this group is not the basis of a national organization as are the two branches mentioned above.

Both the Qadiriyya and the Layenne attract smaller numbers of disciples. The Qadiriyya originally had numerous followers in the Senegal area, especially along the Senegal River. Cheikh Sidia in Mauritania was known throughout Senegal in the nineteenth century for his piety and great learning, and many owed allegiance to him. But by the beginning of the twentieth century, the Mourides began to draw away many of the followers of this group. There are still influential Qadiri marabouts, especially in the southern part of Senegal and north along the Senegal River, but none has particular national prominence to rival the major Tidjani or Mouride leaders. Similarly, the Layenne order has only local importance. The Layenne are members of a subsect specific to the Lebou in the Dakar region, where some of their marabouts have been very influential. The myths of their origin include conversion by the help of a magical fish (the Lebou are fishermen), and the original allegiance is said to have come through the Qadiri (Balandier and Mercier, 1952, p. 110).

Differences among the brotherhoods in organization and outlook might well translate into different roles for women within them. The Muridiyya order, for example, emphasizing as it does discipline and direct obedience to the marabout, might be expected to be harder on women. Indeed, Cheikh Tidjane Sy (Sy, 1969, pp. 201–202) believes that it is more suppressive of women. In contrast, the Tivaouane Tidjanis, with their stress on education, might be more liberal about the role of women. So too might the Niassans, especially because al-Hadji Ibrahima Niass was himself very supportive of educating women in Islam. In contrast, the Tidjanis of the river area, where Islam has been most deeply rooted, might be the most strict of all the Tidjani in regard to women, perhaps as strict as the Mourides, because they would follow the exact prescriptions of the *Sharia*. Most liberal of all to women should be the Layennes; their founder, Limamu Laye, encouraged women in his sect, even permitting them to worship in the mosque (although seated apart from male disciples—ibid., pp. 110–111).

One way these differences in attitude toward women in the brotherhoods might be reflected is in reputed "membership." In fact, women technically cannot be *talibes* in any brotherhood; only men are so designated (Cruise O'Brien, 1971, pp. 85–86). However, whether or not they are technically able to be members, women state that they belong to a brotherhood. Their representation among brotherhood members (52 percent) equals their representation in the population (Creevey, 1993, pp. 64–66). This result is somewhat misleading because the census attributes membership to women based on that of the head of household. However, asking women directly without this bias produces the same result: Most say they belong to a specific brotherhood (Creevey, 1993, p. 69). Indeed, the membership of women in brotherhoods is indicated not so much by which brotherhood is most likely to allow them to join but rather by which ethnic group they belong to and where they live. In fact, none of the brotherhoods is significantly more likely to exclude women than others—membership correlates only with ethnicity and place of residence, not with gender (Creevey, 1993, pp. 67–68).

In all groups, women participate in the common activities that dominate the adult *talibe*-marabout relationship. The leaders of the brotherhoods act as the rural patrons, distributing political, economic, and social favors in return for tribute in the form of work, donations, and loyalty (sometimes shown by the vote of rural followers in relevant elections and referenda). When a follower needs help, he goes to his marabout to ask for advice and/or direct assistance. Women participate in this pattern as well as men, as demonstrated in Aminata Sow Fall's novel *La Grève des Battus* (Fall 1979). Lolli, the wife of the protagonist, Mour N'Diaye, acts as an intermediary with the marabout upon whom her husband's fortunes depend. The marabout communicates through Lolli and discussed her husband's actions with her; she is neither rejected by her marabout nor treated as a child despite her continuing obedience to her husband. More directly, in Abdoulaye Sadji's *Maimona* (1958), the heroine's mother consults the marabout about her daughter to find out what she should do. It is presented as natural and ordinary that she and her daughters would get advice from him, just as a man would do when faced with a difficult decision.

Interviews with Senegalese women suggest that the picture these novels offer is realistic. Women do go to marabouts for advice and assistance. In both novels the women's queries of the marabout were slightly different from likely male queries (which would concern possible jobs or political goals). In the first novel, the wife was seeking help for her husband, not for herself; in the second, she wanted to ensure the best possible future for her daughter. But in both cases the women were participating in the system just as men did. Most marabouts will not shake the hand of a woman or invite a woman to stay and eat with the disciples as they might a man, but they will respond in the same fashion to a request for help. They would expect an offering, and would try to find out how the wish of the woman might be fulfilled and so advise her.

Other aspects of women's involvement in brotherhoods include religious education and even attainment of leadership positions. Despite the teachings admonishing the subordination of women to men, religious education of women is considered important in all brotherhoods in Senegal, although not identically by each one. Most young boys are taught some portion of the Quran, which they memorize from wooden slates while sitting at the feet of their marabout. Young girls are also likely to receive some such training, if not as much. In a 1991 survey in Senegal, 65 percent of those women sampled said they had gone to Quranic school. Mouride girls were less likely to get schooling than girls in any other brotherhood. Tidjani girls were the most likely to get religious schooling. Furthermore, there was a greater gap between men and women in this regard among the Mourides than in any other brotherhood. Ethnic origin also affected the likelihood of schooling. Tukulor girls were more likely than Wolof girls to get this training, and Serer were least likely. However, the brotherhoods seemed more important in this distinction. The Tidjanis, as per their reputation, placed a greater emphasis than did the Mourides on education for either sex and were less likely to deny women access to religious education, among the most devout Muslims (Creevey, 1993, pp. 69–70).

Women seldom hold actual leadership or administrative positions in brotherhoods, although some do, as will be discussed below. However, they do participate on an ever-increasing basis in the religious/social organizations called *dahira,* groups of followers who meet to raise money for their marabout or for some brotherhood cause. The *dahira* became quite common among Mourides in towns in the 1950s as more disciples joined the urban migration. Donal Cruise O'Brien comments that some of the Mouride leaders disapproved of the *dahira* because they included mixed-sex membership, but many were quite pleased with the money thus raised (Cruise O'Brien, 1971, pp. 252–261). Equally favorable were many Tidjani marabouts, as there are many Tidjani *dahira* as well that follow the same principle as those of the Mouride disciples. In general, the leaders of the mixed *dahira* (the president or secretary-general) are men. But there are *dahira* for women only, among the Mourides as well as the Tidjani, which are (naturally) headed by women. Even some of the mixed *dahira* may have a woman in a prominent position, although she may have a male counterpart to cloak her role. The major *dahira* of Sokna Magat Diop (who will be discussed below) is directed by her daughter (Coulon, 1988, pp. 124, 132).

There are various questions about these associations vis-à-vis women. First, is the involvement of women in them a sign of the modernization of Senegal (as opposed to northern Nigeria)? Is this trend a clever progressive move by the marabouts, who see the advantages of appealing to women and also desire women's financial support in a society that has traditionally permitted women to be important producers? Is women's enthusiastic involvement in brotherhood activities a sign that the brotherhoods offer a particularly female religious path by deemphasizing the strict code of orthodox or classical Islam?

In his highly perceptive and interesting article on women in Senegalese Islam, Christian Coulon suggests the latter interpretations (Coulon, 1988, pp. 117, 123). These interpretations seem plausible in the context of Senegalese Islam. Additional reflection, however, may help clarify the picture further. It is important to remember that *dahira* began to proliferate in the 1950s as urbanization progressed. Thus, this particular form of religious cum economic activity was new for men as well as women and became part of the development process in Senegal, where economic growth and change has an impact on religion and all related social and cultural structures. By the 1950s, women were gradually beginning to move into so-called modern economic activities, including both the informal sector and the wage sector (see Chapter 5). Women were already accustomed to acting together in traditional village-level associations that had both a social and an economic purpose. Becoming involved in the *dahira,* even the mixed *dahira*, was a natural step. In this sense, then, the greater visible involvement of women in the brotherhoods through the *dahira* was a product of the development process, but it was equally a new development for men.

The greater public propinquity of male and female in religious activity was a sign of the changing and liberalizing climate in Senegal. It was not, however, necessarily an indication that women were more involved in Islam than before the *dahira* developed, although Coulon does suggest this interpretation (Coulon, 1988, p. 123). As Coulon himself points out, some of the strongest supporters of the brotherhoods in North Africa in the late nineteenth century were women. There is little reason to doubt that this also was true in Senegal when the brotherhoods spread. However, before the economic development process produced the *dahira* phenomenon on such a large scale, the roles of women were hidden behind the formal structure of the orders; now they are out in the open. And the *dahira* phenomenon was possible in Senegal, as opposed to northern Nigeria, because of the country's relatively secular/liberal tradition and its interwoven heritage of Islamicization and European colonialism.

A more difficult proposition to examine is whether or not the brotherhoods attract women because more strictly orthodox Islam is more closed to them. Coulon suggests that the brotherhoods are more open to women because they are more connected to the traditional values transmitted by women (1988, p. 124). The popularization of Islam through the brotherhoods did open the way for some of the beliefs associated with the spirit cults to be included, which permitted women to keep some of their traditional religious functions. However, this interpretation may be too narrow a perception of what the "women's path" might be. *Sufi* brotherhoods popularized religion for both men and women but in the process watered down its intellectual and moral content (although an intellectual elite may be found in most brotherhoods whose beliefs can not be considered to be "watered down" in any way at all).

The question raised by this discussion is whether or not a more intellectual and scholarly Islam can grant women a significant role in society and in religion. Are women confined to the least intellectual, most emotional, and least rigorous form of Islam because the characteristics of the strictly orthodox religion inevitably prevent women from being as involved as their male peers? Most major world religions in their most orthodox forms do subordinate women. But, as in northern Nigeria and Senegal, the form of a religion depends on its context. That should hold true for non-*sufi,* Islam, as well as for countries where Islam is primarily spread through the brotherhoods. It is not necessarily the case that only brotherhoods offer women a meaningful role in Islam; indeed, the reverse may be true in some other parts of West Africa. For example, in northern Nigeria the dominant brotherhood *restricts* women more than any non-brotherhood form of the religion aspires to do—at least publicly—in Senegal. Educated Senegalese women, like educated Senegalese men, are more inclined to disavow membership in a brotherhood because it does not suit their more intellectual definition of what the religion should be. Certain radical reform groups in Senegal (discussed in Chapter 6) do advocate the seclusion and suppression of women, but less radical orthodox groups such as the Union Culturelle Musulmane support educating both women and men and place less stress on controlling and subordinating the former. Many educated women—for example, the devout Muslim women of Kano—remain Muslim without accepting that they should have a second-class position in Senegalese society (interview with Penda M'Bow, July 1991). This too, then, is a "woman's path" in Senegalese Islam, open only to an elite class of women, just as this vision of Islam is only open to an elite class of men.

There is a final but highly significant indication that women have an important (although subordinate) role to play in the Islamic brotherhoods of Senegal: Some highly placed and extremely influential women do hold public religious and political leadership roles. In the 1960s, women were less visibly involved in brotherhood activities, but there were nonetheless Muslim women known to have their own followings in the brotherhoods. One such woman in the 1960s was Sokna Muslimatou, a sister of the reigning Mouride *khalif* (Falilou M'Backe), who resided in her own compound in Diourbel and had her own disciples. Most of them were women, but there were men who also came to ask for her help in regard to various projects or family matters. Her authority came from her position as sister of the reigning Mouride leader, but she exercised authority also in her own right, as descendant of the founder, Ahmadu Bamba. Her followers believed she had inherited some of his *baraka* (grace) and had her own role to play, clearly secondary to that of her more powerful brothers and some other of the founders' favored disciples but influential nonetheless. She had various business interests as well and her own lines of communication with local and regional authorities (Creevey Behrman, 1970, p. 110).

In contemporary times (1990s), Sokna Magat Diop of Thies has even greater influence. Her *baraka* comes from her father, Abdulay Niakhep (also referred to as Abdoulaye Ikyakhine or Abdoulaye Niakhite), who had been a leading marabout in the Baye Fall subgroup of the Mourides. Her mother, Tabara Cisse, also is said to have come from a noble Mandinka family with a strong religious reputation. Magat Diop herself was married first to Sheikh Ibra Fall, founder of the Baye Fall, and after his death to a younger brother of the founder, Serigne Massamba M'Backe. Her last husband was Sheikh Atta M'Backe, son of Ahmadu Bamba's older brother. Thus connected in multiple ways to the powerful *shaikhs* in the Mouride hierarchy, and possessing herself the *baraka* of her father, Magat Diop would have had a certain authority even had she not become the *khalif* of her father's subgroup. This, however, she did upon his death in 1943 (Coulon, 1988, pp. 125–133).

It would have been possible (with precedent) for the headship to have passed to a leading disciple (since both sons of Nakhite were dead), but according to Christian Coulon, Magat Diop's father recognized even before the death of his sons that she was special and should inherit his position. He trained her both in religious matters and in the administration of the brotherhood. Thus, when he died, she became the full leader of her branch of the Mourides. In terms of her authority, Coulon says that she has "the normal powers of a *khalifa*" over her community" (Coulon, 1988, pp. 129–133). She initiates disciples and appoint *muqaddams,* receives the tithe, and has agricultural land that her disciples work and several *dahira.* She is also active in community work, having sponsored the building of mosques and her father's mausoleum, and relates directly to the *khalif* of the Mourides, to whom she has given her oath of submission (*njebbel*). She is also the marabout with the greatest political force in her region, the one to whom the secular administration goes when it needs assistance (Cruise O'Brien, p. 1970, 109; Coulon, 1988, pp. 125–133; Creevey, 1993, pp. 76–79).

Sokna Magat Diop, however, operates with a slightly different style than her male peers. For one thing, she is far more reclusive than they. She is said to live as an ascetic mystic, spending her days praying and reading religious texts. She does not appear publicly, and her son acts for her as spokesperson in religious and political ceremonies. She does not perform marriages or baptisms or go to the mosque. She has a reputation for being holy, and Coulon points out that she has emphasized the *sufi*, or mystic, quality of her authority, in contrast to the more "worldly" and even commercial style of some other Mouride leaders. In addition, not surprisingly, her branch of the Mouride places a much greater emphasis on the role of women in Islam than do other branches. This orientation is reflected in Magat Diop's appointment of women as *muqaddams* and by the fact that women hold key positions in her *dahira* (Coulon, 1988, pp. 131–133).

Sokna Magat Diop belongs to the Muridiyya, the brotherhood that would seem least likely to foster the education of women in Islam. Other *turuuq*—branches of the Tidjani and the Layenne as a whole—have better reputations in terms of their attitudes towards women, but none of them has a more powerful woman than Sokna Maqat Diop. This is not to say, however, that there are no influential women leaders in the other orders. In particular, some of the sisters and daughters of Ibrahima Niass have achieved a reputation for scholarship and become leaders in their own right within the Tidjaniyya. They, too, are believed to have inherited the *baraka* of their father and have gained religious as well as political authority as a result.

CONCLUSIONS

Despite what has been written about their loss of status and power with the coming of Islam, then, women can hold recognized leadership positions in the Senegalese brotherhoods. It seems that the pattern is far more complex than most observers have understood. Women's role in Islamic religious organizations bears a strong resemblance to the role they are reported to have had in the traditional political systems. Ranked below men in terms of overall power, women still retain the possibility of authority. As in pre-Islamic days, the possibility depends in part on their family heritage, in part on their own ability to exert strong influence, and in part on the economic and political conditions in which they find themselves. The situation permits a few women to distinguish themselves even within the religious hierarchy. For the majority of women, the coming of Islam lessened their power as conservators of traditional religions. But this power did not completely disappear; it was hidden within the popular belief structure of the new religion. The statutory political roles for women—the *lingueer* and the *awa* of the Wolof and Serer kingdoms—disappeared and were replaced by the *shaikhs* and *muqaddams* of the brotherhoods, who were generally men. But the role of the *lingueer* was, if not formally recognized, informally accepted, as the female relatives of the major marabouts took on the authority that the female relatives of the kings and nobles had always had. Islam did not publicly acknowledge female leadership roles, but it allowed women of high status to retain their influence in their unacknowledged realm. The net effect was certainly a lessening of status for women qua women politically and religiously, but it was not a complete loss of the roles they had held. Presently women are more publicly involved in brotherhood activities than they were twenty-five years ago. Some observers believe that the brotherhoods are "opening up to women," but it is also possible that the current climate in Senegal encourages certain types of activities, such as the *dahira*, that openly reveal women's power in places where they had always been involved, albeit covertly.

The differences between Muslim women in northern Nigeria and Senegal seem clear. Muslim women in the Islamic areas of Nigeria have many fewer public roles to play outside of their own restricted environment, however important that environment might be. They are as likely to be educated in religious knowledge as they would be in Senegal, and there are women religious leaders in both Nigeria and Senegal. But the overall climate in Senegal is influenced by a distinct process of Western-influenced social and economic development, which is reflected in the religious sphere and allows women to have more open public involvement and authority. In both cases, *sufi* brotherhoods dictate the religious beliefs and behavior of the bulk of the population; the contexts, however, differ. Historical circumstance and present economic and social growth patterns result in different roles and positions of influence for women, even within different branches of the same brotherhood.

4

EDUCATION AND
ATTITUDES TOWARD WOMEN

It is in education that the most dramatic changes can be seen in the lives of Muslim women in West Africa. In all Islamic countries, both men and women assert emphatically that Islam is a learned religion, that according to the teachings of the Prophet Muhammad both men and women are equal before God, and that both therefore should know the word of God. Through the ages Islamic religious leaders have interpreted this axiom to mean that women as well as men should be literate in order to be able to read the teachings of the Prophet and to know its prescriptions for their lives. And, even in Western secular schools, the percentage of Muslim girls (and women) has increased dramatically in recent years.

The teachings of Islam in regard to educating women are not unlike those of other religions. Education is viewed as essential in order that women know how to fulfill their duties as wife and mother. Girls are to study female role models and religious injunctions to learn how best to support male family members. They should learn to please their husbands and to obey them. Their modesty and obedience is praised. Their productivity is measured in the health and well-being of their children and in the satisfaction and success of their husbands and fathers. Reality in most of the developing world, however, dictates that women cannot stay home and fully occupy themselves with domestic tasks. They will also be involved in economic production. Certainly in most agricultural societies, women are part of the labor force, involved in many aspects of agriculture and animal husbandry. Increasingly, too, women are being drawn into the informal sector and eventually into wage labor positions in urban areas. Although they are still a small minority of the paid work force, their percentage in every position level is growing rapidly. Nonetheless, the beliefs instilled by both Christianity and Islam persist—women are primarily defined by their roles at home as wives and mothers. They may engage in work outside the home, but only if necessitated by a shortage of family funds.

If the morally approved role of a woman is to be occupied with domestic chores, then education may be seen as unnecessary beyond the elementary level or some fraction thereof. Education at a higher level may even be seen as a threat to a woman's acceptance of her proper role. Western education, in particular, tends to stress individual rights, individual responsibilities, and individual worth, which may be seen as inconsistent with the view of a woman as subservient to her husband and obligated to meet his, and her children's, needs before anything else. None of the world's major religions directly proscribes education for girls in their principal texts, but various Islamic clerics have interpreted these texts in just this fashion, warning against sending women to school lest they be corrupted by the general decadence of the ideas of Western industrialized societies.

Countering this suspicion of education is the fact that education offers status to girls as well as to boys. The possibility of a girl marrying into a better family is increased by a high level of education. In newspapers in India and Sri Lanka, for example, families describe the attractions of their unmarried children on lists in the classified section in order to find a wife or husband for them, and education is advertised as enthusiastically for the girls as for the boys: "26-year-old Sinhala girl of good family, ABD Oxford. . . ." Her education is considered an advantage, not a hindrance. Furthermore, even where higher education is rare for girls, sensible families have to take into account the ability of a girl to earn money until she is married and perhaps until she has children. A formal education, at least through secondary school, will enhance her earning capabilities.

The first obligation of a girl, however, is to serve her paternal family. When her labor is needed, whether in the fields, with younger children, or in the household, a young girl may be forced to stop school. Similarly, boys are withdrawn from school to help at home, but in general girls will be taken out much more quickly, a tendency enhanced by the fact that girls generally marry younger than do boys. The combination of women's culturally defined roles and their heavy household and family responsibilities leaves girls less likely to receive education than boys the world over. This imbalance will be weaker the wealthier a family is, because child-care and household tasks can be taken on by other family members or servants. But in general, the importance to the family of educating a girl as opposed to a boy is less.

In West Africa, access to education may be the single most important asset available to a girl. Western-style instruction provides the skills and conveys the attitudes that people require to adapt to a modern technological society. Studies of development also frequently point to the gradual spread of mass formal education as the major variable that eventually leads to democratic political behavior—the acquisition of a "political culture" (Almond and Verba, 1962). This culture exists when the general population, women as well as men, believes in its ability and its right and obligation to determine the government. As a girl is educated, she will gain a sense of her own rationality, her own ability to make decisions. She will learn about how the values of her family compare to those of peoples in other regions and other parts of the world, and she will have more skills to enable her to find a position in the wage-paying job market. The more education she has, the more likely she will be to get a good job (although not one equal to that of her male counterpart). Education, then, should lead to a complete change in attitudes and behavior and enable the girl to find her best economic niche.

Throughout Islamic West Africa, Quranic schools offer an extensive alternate system of education. These schools may be simple open-air class-rooms, where young children learn parts of the Quran by rote, or more complex *zawiyas,* where religious ideas, advanced Quranic studies, and even Arabic may be taught. But these schools do not focus on reading or writing beyond the Quran, nor on such subjects as arithmetic, social and scientific studies, and/or the humanities, as do Western schools. Nor are the alternate schools set up in a skills pyramid that leads to the more or less standard levels of knowledge needed for modern business and industry.

Western-style education did not spread widely across West Africa until after independence. The colonialists started schools in the major urban areas, but these were few in number and small. Only a handful of children, for the most part boys, had access to them. In the postindependence period, governments decided to sponsor education throughout the countryside to reach all rural children regardless of sex, as well as all children in the major urban zones. But resources for building, staffing, and supplying these schools were limited; even at present, many children—both boys and girls—never attend school. The percentage of school-age children actually enrolled is increasing steadily, but many still do not attend. Moreover, there is still a significant gender disparity in most countries. The percentage of girls that do not attend school is much greater than that of boys. Attendance figures are the lowest in the poorest countries for all children, as well as for girls as a percentage of the total, indicating that the absence of resources—rather than the attitude of any particular group—is the major deterrent to education for all children and to reducing the gender gap.

Exactly how religious attitudes currently affect the education of girls is difficult to pinpoint. Whatever a cleric may say, people will choose to behave as they feel they must. It is not clear when or why a cleric will prohibit schooling for girls or when families will choose to disobey this advice. In West Africa the majority of clerics are Muslim, although Christian priests and ministers in Dakar, Lagos, Accra, and other large towns can be very influential. Their influence extends beyond even the number of their faithful, as Christian schools educate many non-Christian children. There are also some small, strict Christian groups that might be expected to be

Table 4.1   Education of Girls in West Africa

	Females per 100 males Primary School 1970	1987	Percentage of School-Age Females Enrolled, 1987	Females per 100 males Secondary School 1970	1987	Percentage of School-Age Females Enrolled, 1987
Benin	45	51	43	44	—	9
Burkina Faso	32	24	24	6	4	4
Cameroon	74	85	100	36	64	20
Chad	34	40	29	9	18	2
Ivory Coast	57	—	58	27	44	12
Gambia	—	—	—	—	—	—
Ghana	75	80	63	35	36	32
Guinea	46	45	18	26	31	4
Liberia	49	—	23[a]	30	—	3[a]
Mali	55	59	17	29	42	4
Mauritania	39	70	42	13	44	9
Niger	53	—	20	35	42	12
Nigeria	59	—	24[a]	49	—	3[a]
Senegal	63	69	49	39	51	10
Sierra Leone	67	—	21[a]	40	—	3[a]
Togo	45	63	78	26	32	12

Source: World Bank, 1988, pp. 234, 240.
Note: a. Percent of females in 1965

very conservative on the question of education, but they are not large enough to affect any substantial part of the population. In any case, Catholic priests and ministers of the larger, more conventional Christian denominations are either from the industrialized West or from Africa but educated in the West. Among these clerics, the Western view that education is good for both boys and girls prevails, despite the belief of the more conservative ministers that "a woman's place is in the home." After all, Western education prepares girls to be good mothers, if nothing else. Islam, rooted in non-Western and nonindustrialized cultures, does not automatically recognize the benefits of Western formal education. It remains to be seen whether the negative attitude of Muslim clerics regarding Western education actually blocks the spread of education, especially for girls.

In order for education to be an effective catalyst for change in the lives of women, there must also be changes in male perceptions of appropriate public and private roles for women. If women's lives are to change and if educated women are to have opportunities heretofore denied them in Islamic societies, then men will also have to accept fundamentally different views not only of acceptable behavior on the part of women but also of themselves and their responsibilities. If women are to have a voice on matters that concern them, then men will have to concede that their own opinions are not always beyond question or compromise. Although education makes careers and economic independence possible for women, a salary and a life outside the home does not liberate a woman from the restraints imposed by her culture. Information about the attitudes of both men and women toward women's education and its implications is crucial in seeking to understand education's potential for introducing change into the way women live their lives.

EDUCATION AND MUSLIM WOMEN IN NORTHERN NIGERIA

Secular education in northern Nigeria has lagged dramatically behind that in the non-Muslim south. British colonial policy on education was in keeping with the overall philosophy of Indirect Rule. The British officers acceded to the traditional leaders' wishes that Christian missionaries, whether proselytizers or educators, be banned from working in the Islamic North. This policy effectively meant that there was very little Western education in the north for the first sixty years of this century. As a consequence, very few men and virtually no women received such an education during that time. Because missionaries and their schools were banned, the colonial government did undertake to establish a few schools for the sons of traditional leaders. For the vast majority of northern people, however, there was virtually no government-sponsored education during the colonial era.

Until 1898, no Western schools existed in Nigeria other than Christian missionary schools. As late as 1942, missions controlled 99 percent of the schools and more than 97 percent of the total student enrollment (Coleman, 1960). The vast majority of literate Nigerians owed all or most of their education to mission schools. By the late 1950s, approximately 20 percent of the school-age population in the two southern regions was in school, whereas only .03 percent of northern boys were in non-Islamic schools. The figure recorded for girls was zero (Bray, 1981). The impact of the British policy prohibiting mission work in the North is indicated by the fact that as late as 1954 only *one* Northern Nigerian man held a university degree—and he had converted to Christianity (Coleman, 1960).

However, a system of Islamic education has long existed in the Nigerian North. The British tried to build upon this foundation by urging Muslim leaders to add English and mathematics to the curriculum of higher-level Islamic schools. By the 1950s, northern leaders themselves were expressing great concern about the differences in education levels between North and the South. They recognized the necessity for northerners to acquire Western as well as Islamic learning. As Nigeria approached independence in

1960, both the British and northern leaders were increasingly concerned about the fact that few northerners were qualifying for positions in the modern sector. Education specifically for girls was not discussed in this context. Because the population of the north was approximately one and a half times that of the two southern regions combined, the disparity was even more severe than simple numbers indicate.

The British acquiescence to, even promotion of, the view that Western education was alien and might contaminate Islamic ideas had very serious consequences for both men and women in Northern Nigeria. In contrast to Western secular education, Islamic education is deeply rooted in the Hausa heartland. A school of higher Islamic learning (*madrasa*) was established in Kano in the early seventeenth century and eventually offered Islamic law, theology, philosophy, and Quranic exegesis. By 1913 there were 19,073 Quranic schools with 143,312 students in Northern Nigeria (Hilliard 1957). The tradition begun by *madrasas* and the Quranic schools established a literate alternative to education that is preferred to Western education to this day in northern Nigeria.

Table 4.2 Comparative Educational Development, Northern and Southern Nigeria

Year	Primary Schools North	Primary Schools South	Primary School Enrollment North	Primary School Enrollment South	Secondary Schools North	Secondary Schools South	Secondary School Enrollment North	Secondary School Enrollment South
1906	1	126	n.a.	11,872	0	1	0	20
1912	34	150	954	35,716	0	10	0	67
1926	125	3,828	5,210	138,249	0	18	0	518
1937	549	3,533	20,269	218,610	1	26	65	4,285
1947	1,110	4,984	70,962	538,391	3	43	251	9,657
1957	1,080	13,473	185,484	2,343,317	18	176	3,643	28,208
1965	2,743	12,234	492,829	2,419,913	77	1,305	15,276	180,906
1972	4,225	10,313	854,466	3,536,731	255	964	63,515	337,288

Sources: Haroun Al-Ra'shid Adamu, 1973, p. 51; Federal Republic of Nigeria, 1976, pp. 151–152.
Note: n.a. = not available

There has been little change in the content or methods of Islamic teaching since the sixteenth century. Islamic education is largely Thomistic in approach; spiritual and literary authority, rather than intellectual curiosity, are emphasized. At higher levels theology and law are the basic disciplines, and the emphasis is on preserving the truth, which rests on revelation and interpretation. Thus, for Muslim leaders the sole purpose of education is to learn Islamic doctrine.

The first level of Islamic education essentially involves memorizing the Quran. Study at more advanced levels centers on the sayings and teachings of the Prophet Muhammad to his disciples as he traveled and taught throughout his lifetime (*hadith*). One who pursues Islamic education and memorizes the *hadith* as well as the Quran may ultimately specialize in Islamic law, *fiqh,* and become a *kadi,* or magistrate in the *Sharia* court.

Children enter Quranic school between the ages of four and six and immediately set about learning the Quran, beginning with the first chapter and proceeding straight through. Learning is by rote rather than through discussion and discovery. Fixed sections of the Quran are recited by the teacher and repeated by the students until the texts are learned by heart. In northern Nigeria the school facilities are a roof, a prayer mat, and a piece of slate. Boys attend school for several years, girls usually for shorter periods; both are expected to be sent to school by their parents for basic Islamic learning. Islamic education is noncompetitive, and examinations are foreign to it. The student's educational proficiency is determined by the status of the teacher, not by individual performance. There are no examinations or specific requirements to be met and no teaching materials to bridge the gap between the instructor's knowledge and the wider world (Hiskett, 1975; Hassan, 1975; Gibb and Bowen, 1957).

An effort to combine the Western tradition of learning with the Islamic tradition of memorizing was made in the establishment of the School for Arabic Studies (SAS) in Northern Nigeria's largest city, Kano, in 1947. SAS was meant to function at the level of a secondary school, and the curriculum was broadened to include teacher training as well as the study of Islamic law. SAS was the first secondary school in Kano and was for boys only. It was not until 1978 that a similar institution was established for girls, the Women's Arabic Teachers' College. These schools were established, at least in part, to begin to train teachers who could introduce Arabic and English literacy to the Quranic schools, thus redressing the enormous imbalance in education between north and south in Nigeria.

As independence approached, northern leaders toured other Muslim countries to study Islamic systems of education. They recommended that selected Quranic schools "be organized into classes in accordance with age, year of entry and standard of learning and that the curriculum should be diversified to include arithmetic, reading and writing as well as Quranic study" (al-Rashid, 1973). By 1975 sixty-three such schools, designated "Islamiyya schools," had been established in Kano and today are under the supervision of the Ministry of Education. In 1978, two years after the Nigerian military government commenced the Universal Primary Education program for all children in Nigeria, Islamic Education Centers were established by the education ministries in the Islamic states and given the responsibility of inspecting and registering all Islamiyya schools.

Muslim leaders in Nigeria were quick to endorse Universal Primary Education (UPE), stressing that Islam has always revered knowledge. At that time, only 5 percent of the children in the Islamic parts of Nigeria were in non-Quranic schools, versus 90 percent of the children in eastern Nigeria. The northern state governments began massive education drives, urging parents of both boys and girls to send their children to school. Many of the state governments made education their top priority, establishing Islamiyya and secular schools at an impressive rate. In the mid-1970s, Nigeria was reaping the benefits of an oil boom, and the Nigerian government made massive commitments to the nineteen states for education. For example, between 1976 and 1983 the Kano state government established 3,032 primary schools, 43 secondary schools, 24 teacher training colleges, 3 technical training schools, and 2 commercial colleges. Hundreds of teachers from India, Pakistan, the Philippines, and the British and Canadian "peace corps" were employed. All schools are required to offer courses in Islamic Religious Knowledge (IRK) during which the Quran is recited (Callaway, 1986). The inclusion of IRK as part of the curriculum in the secular schools and the state support for the Islamiyya schools assures that some form of Islamic education will be preserved.

This history is important in evaluating the importance of education for girls and women in West Africa. Educated Muslim Hausa women in Nigeria are most likely to have come through the alternate system of education, and hence their values and perspectives are likely to differ from those of women in other countries who have gone through Western schools. Perhaps the most dramatic impact of education on northern Nigerian women is seen in two recent major developments: the establishment of Agencies for Mass Education, which have targeted adult women for their classes, and the concomitant rise of a radical Islamic women's movement.

The Agency for Mass Education was established in Kano in 1977, and its Women's Division was charged with developing literacy programs for women. In newspapers, on the radio, and in public places, the government repeatedly stressed that Islam gives great significance to learning and that the high rate of illiteracy among Muslim women in Nigeria was "deplorable." Thirty women initially enrolled in the Kano City Women's Center in 1980; the following year the enrollment was 320 women, and by 1982 over 700 women were attending fourteen classes in this center. By 1983, an additional thirty centers, with over 10,000 women students, had been established in the twenty-nine local government areas. They offered courses in basic literacy (in Arabic, Hausa, and English), Islamic Religious Knowledge, and, in some cases, sewing, cooking, and elementary bookkeeping (Usman, 1983). All women attending classes in the Kano City centers in 1982 were or had been married—83 percent by age fifteen and

100 percent by age twenty (Bature, Mahmud, 1982)—and all were required to have the permission of their husbands. Sixty-one percent said they were "sent" by their husbands to the centers because "the Quran says that women should be educated" (Callaway, 1986).

In 1991, Bilkisu Yusuf, a U.S.-educated Muslim woman who edits a major newspaper, stated that 40 percent of the women in Kano benefit from adult education classes (Yusuf, 1991). Catherine Coles stated that 58.7 percent of the women in her 1987 study of another northern Nigerian city, Kaduna, were attending Islamic schools (Coles, 1991). In the ten years since Coles was in Kaduna, nearly all the women had become or were becoming literate, usually in Arabic. Because of the constant reiteration of the high value placed on learning by Islam, few husbands would interfere with their wives' attendance at Islamic school.

This is a dramatic development. It opens the door to literacy and knowledge; it also gives women a measure of mobility that they did not have ten years ago, as they now go to and from school at night. However, with militant Islam on the rise here, as elsewhere, Muslim Hausa women, even little girls, are learning about and adopting the black of the chador as they move about in public. Although the sea of black is depressing to an outsider, it is important to remember that it betokens a new mobility for women who lived in strict seclusion just a few years ago.

In spite of the emphasis on religion, women, whatever their educational background, find it difficult to articulate what Islam means to them. For northern Nigerian Muslim women, their religion is not just a part of their life but is in fact their entire life. Asking them what Islam means to them implies that Islam might mean different things to different people, and religious teaching in northern Nigeria does not allow for this possibility, a fact reflected in women's replies to such questions. Margaret Knipp recorded verbatim responses of the thirty-four educated women she interviewed in Sokoto to the question: "What is the importance of Islam (to you)?" The following responses were typical:

> Most things that you do in life are guided by the religion: whatever you do you do for God's sake.
> Islam is my religion and according to Islamic religion they have five pillars: prayers, fasting, giving alms, holy pilgrimage and witness.
> I should pray every day, five times daily. And, being a woman, I should respect my husband and obey him. If I say yes and he says no, I should be obedient to him.
> It guides one as to how he's going to lead his life. It teaches you about cleanliness and then the way you are going to lead your life . . . rituals, prayers, ablutions, ritual baths, fasting.
> Moral teachings are given including knowing about God, his Prophets. Then, coming to respect your parents, then for the woman, respect your husband and be very obedient to him (Knipp, 1987, pp. 139–140).

Changes brought about by education are real, but it is important to take caution in evaluating their significance. The combination of traditional Hausa cultural practices and restrictive Islamic proscriptions for women places almost unsurmountable obstacles in the path of educated women who want to "make a difference." The fact that a few women have a university-level education and are beginning to work in public positions is a tribute to their fathers and husbands. No one who has done research on Hausa women has found examples of women who went against the opposition of both their father and husband in order to obtain an education. (For that matter, very few women have overcome the opposition of either a father or a husband with the support of the other.) And although more girls now go to school, only a small fraction (about 6 percent) of them go beyond lower-level primary school.

Islamic education is seen as the panacea for societal ills. The vice president of the University of Sokoto suggested that "proper religious education should be made compulsory at all levels of our educational system as a means of cleansing the society of all forms of indiscipline" (*New Nigerian,* May 23, 1984, p. 3). Margaret Knipp reported that when she left the University of Sokoto in 1986, six of the courses in her department (sociology) were to be "turned into 'Islamic sociology,' although it is uncertain just what that means" (Knipp, 1987, p. 214). A girl is still expected to marry, to marry young, and to marry a husband chosen for her; to be submissive to him; and to have co-wives whether or not that is her wish. She will have between five and fifteen children and probably will be divorced more than once. Her belief in Islam will be unquestioning. Leaders of the Muslim women's movement decry the painful initiation to marriage experienced by a girl who is too young—"too young" meaning girls under twelve years of age (*The Daily Times,* March 14, 1991, and *The Triumph,* April 16, 1992). Women still work only with the permission of their husbands. If and how long a girl will go to school is her father's or her husband's decision, not her own.

But the implications of education on any level are great. As women become more educated, as changes in the economy create the demand for a more highly skilled work force, as women expand their range of activities, changes are bound to occur. Many of these will appear small, but any change in this culture is significant and not likely to be reversed. Muslim women now decry the fact that they are being given only minimum literacy skills in order to be able to read the Quran or say their prayers (Yusuf, 1991). They stress that the adult literacy classes and the women's centers offer culturally appropriate education for secluded Muslim women and condemn those husbands who forbid their wives to attend. A small but significant number of highly visible men support their claims (*The Daily Times,* March 14, 1991, and *The Triumph,* April 16, 1992).

The profound increases in women's literacy rates are bound to result in changes in the way women live and the occupations they enter. Within an Islamic context, many paths to achievement are being opened for women—as teachers, as doctors, as social workers preparing women for Hadj, or as counselors who advise other women about their rights within Islam. A number of Islamic organizations have sponsored courses to raise the standard of Islamic education, to enlighten women about their rights and obligations, and to eradicate the non-Islamic tenets of traditional culture. One author suggests that in Islamic countries, women's educational achievement and career choices vary according to the enforcement of Islamic restrictions (White, 1978). However, we know of no explicit comparative statistics to illustrate this statement. Superficially, it would appear that women in northern Nigeria, who are constantly told that "Islam is a total way of life," have less education and fewer choices than do women in West African countries where Islam is more flexible.

The gains in education in northern Nigeria have been impressive and have proceeded on a different path than educational developments in southern Nigeria. In the north, Western secular education has been added on to an Islamic base. It is very clear that Islamic support for the UPE effort launched by the military government in 1976 validated the legitimacy of women's education: "Critics of women [sic] education should stop deceiving themselves and others by opposing women's education from the religious point of view, because God will in the hereafter question them for distorting his words." (Bello, 1983).

As a result of these gains, women are demonstrating creative talents to a degree unprecedented in history of the area (Martin, 1983). In addition, women from all but the lowest social classes now marry into the aristocratic classes through education and occupational routes (Knipp, 1987). At the same time, however, both Hausa culture and Islam stress modesty and uncompetitiveness for girls and women. This, together with the emphasis on early marriage and resistance to planned families, affects attitudes about appropriate education and overall impact. A university student said:

> First of all, the Quran is from one supreme being, that is Allah, the creator of all. He revealed this through his Prophet (peace be upon him) Muhammad, as a guide for mankind. And every single thing, how to enter a toilet, how to greet people, how to stay with others, how to acquire knowledge . . . everything is in the Quran, every single thing (Knipp 1987, p. 277).

Nonetheless, education is the single most visible indicator of change for women. Educational developments in the last decade have been rapid and far reaching. Their impact on the lives of women is just beginning to be felt; the long-term effect on women's perceptions about themselves and their life prospects will interact with deeply ingrained cultural prescriptions. Interview and survey data on aspirations indicate that the practical realities of life as dictated by Islam and the culture, particularly in regard to marriage, have not changed.

In 1986, Margaret Knipp interviewed thirty-four women who were students at the University of Sokoto, twenty-five prominent or professional women resident in Sokoto, and fifteen uneducated women who worked at the university (most of whom were related to each other and from the same village). As it turned out, very few of these women were actually from Sokoto, the very conservative religious center of Islamic Nigeria (Knipp, 1987, p. 86). In any event, the fathers of almost all the university students and of all the "prominent or professional" women were highly educated themselves (at least through secondary school) and had high traditional social status, which substantiates impressions that high paternal education and high social/economic status correlates with acceptance of women's education. These women did not see their mothers as critical figures in their school or professional lives. "I asked each woman to tell me about her mother," wrote Knipp. In most cases women said something like, 'well, she's just a typical mother, she's nice'" (p. 245). Many of the women couldn't tell her anything about their mothers because they grew up in the home of relatives as provided for by the practices of first-child avoidance and fostering. Many of these women felt much closer to their fathers than to their mothers, even though the fathers were fairly remote figures about whom they could relate very little. Most of the women knew their fathers were educated but could not detail where or to what level they had gone to school. Only two women cited their mothers as important in providing encouragement or support (Knipp, p. 246).

In 1982 Barbara Callaway surveyed 572 male and 114 female university students at Bayero University in Kano. Of the 114 female students, 92 were Muslim, and of these nearly half were Yoruba rather than Hausa. Of the 43 non-Yoruba Muslim female students, 25 were from the lower north rather than from Kano State (the Hausa heartland). Thus, in neither the University of Sokoto nor Bayero University were Muslim girls from the two largest northern Nigerian cities well represented. In fact, one-third of the Muslim girls in the Bayero survey had attended Christian schools, reflecting the high percentage of Muslim Yoruba girls among the female students. In contrast, 93 percent of the 572 male students (538) were from Kano State and were graduates of government schools or teacher training colleges in the state.

This survey nonetheless produced some data suggesting that change—slow rather than dramatic, but nevertheless highly significant—was in the offing. Views were solicited on the expansion of female education, the situation of educated women, the impact of education on marriage, the participation of women in the work force, and women's participation in politics. No student, male or female, conceived of life outside of marriage as a viable option. Ninety percent of the Muslim female students ranked "pressure to marry young" as the primary obstacle to girls' pursuing their education, whereas only 50 percent of the Christian female students cited this as an obstacle. The Christian students apparently were not referring to themselves but to girls in general, especially in the north, where the survey was taken.

Table 4.3   Girls' Education—Obstacles
"What is the main obstacle to girls' education?"

| | Female Students (114) | | Male Students (572) | | Totals (686) |
	Christian	Muslim	Christian	Muslim	
Belief it will "spoil girls"	0	7	13	81	101
Cost	11	0	13	180	204
Conservatism	0	1	4	96	101
Pressure to marry young	10	82	2	116	210
Need for girls to do tala	0	1	0	49	50
Religion	1	0	0	0	1
Men's jealousy	0	0	0	0	0
Fear	0	0	0	0	0
Other	0	0	2	17	19
TOTALS	22	92	34	538	686

Source: Based on Callaway, 1987, p. 163.

Since 1976, when the concerted campaign for girls' education (including Universal Primary Education) began, Muslim families have appeared less opposed to Western education for girls. The greatest remaining obstacle is the fear on the part of parents that it will spoil their daughters. However, even if opposition to education per se is less strident in Islamic sections of the country, the pressure for early marriage remains. It is this pressure, rather than outright opposition to education, that now limits the options and life opportunities of most Muslim women in Nigeria.

Cultural differences underscored by religion were evident: Muslim female students cited their fathers as the most important person in their being allowed to pursue education, whereas Christian female students cited their mothers as the influential figure. Christian female students also credited their mothers with supporting them financially while they went to school, whereas Muslim female students gave total credit in this category to their fathers and husbands. However, the Muslim students did cite educated sisters as being important in encouraging them, presumably because educated sisters signaled a supportive father.

Muslim male students felt overwhelmingly that women were not "exploited." Perhaps reflecting the concerted effort on the part of Muslim leaders to stress that education for girls is Islamic, they felt overwhelmingly that boys should not be given preference over girls in access to schooling. However, whereas 87 percent of the female Muslim students stated that it was important to change the status of women in northern Nigeria, only 19 percent of the Muslim male students endorsed this proposition. Both groups of students thought that educated women were "happier" than uneducated women, but a significant subgroup of female Christian students (31 percent) thought that traditional women were happier (perhaps because the students saw more clearly the conflicts in modern life).

The student survey, together with surveys of educated and uneducated men and women in Kano State, suggest that despite acceptance of the importance of minimal education for both girls and boys, the patterns of interaction between men and women in this Islamic culture are not yet challenged. Rising levels of education do suggest the evolution of a more articulate and informed society in the years to come, a society in which women may be more enlightened concerning their rights in Islam, more articulate about their problems, and more effective in influencing public policies that affect them. But there is nothing to suggest that they will challenge the basic teachings of the religion about appropriate roles for men and women, husbands and wives.

It has been stressed that higher education is the most potent force stimulating a reassessment of what roles are appropriate for women (Dodd, 1973; Giele and Smock, 1977). Secondary and university education are credited with expanding women's horizons, thus encouraging them to look for fulfillment not only in the home but also outside it, equipping them with the skills and inclination for employment, and reducing childbearing and the limitations it brings. These assumptions hint at attitudes and practices regarded as Western and unacceptable by religious leaders as well as by both men and women in northern Nigeria. Knipp's interviews with female university students in Sokoto are instructive in this regard:

> A girl should marry when she is young. She will come to love and venerate her husband from a very early age and will become firmly attached to him as she grows up. (cited from Madauci, Isa, and Daura, 1980, pp. 18–19)
>
> I was married at nine and divorced at 11. I couldn't tie a wrapper. I was divorced because of childishness. You just want to go and play with other kids. (p. 100)
>
> I will run, people will run after me and bring me back. They will tell my father and my father will go and give me a nice beating. (p. 100)
>
> Women must obey their husbands unless his demands are in contradiction to Islam. (p. 111)

Table 4.4   The Status of Women

	Agree		Disagree		No Opinion	
"Women are exploited and disadvantaged in northern Nigeria and their status should be improved."						
Muslim male students (538)	103	(19%)	435	(81%)		
Christian male students (34)	20	(59%)	10	(29%)	4	(12%)
Muslim female students (92)	80	(87%)	12	(13%)		
Christian female students (22)	20	(91%)	1	(4%)	1	(4%)
"In education, preference should be given to boys over girls."						
Muslim male students (538)	80	(15%)	451	(84%)		
Christian male students (34)	20	(59%)	14	(41%)	7	(1%)
Muslim female students (92)	40	(43%)	52	(57%)		
Christian female students (22)	5	(23%)	17	(77%)		

"Which women are the happiest?"	Christian Female Students (22)		Muslim Female Students (92)	
Urban educated women	15	(68%)	40	(43%)
Rural educated women	0		10	(11%)
Urban uneducated women	0		5	(38%)
Rural uneducated women	7	(31%)	7	(8%)

Source: Based on Callaway, 1987, p. 166.

> It is the duty of wives to obey what the husband has to say or what he has decided. (p. 112)
> The only women who can go out are any of those old women who are no longer desired by men and whose demeanor and manner of speaking are not seductive. (p. 113)

Every Muslim woman in both surveys said that the decision as to whether or not she would live in seclusion or work outside her home was her husband's to make, and each suggested that only God knew how many children she would have. In northern Nigeria, educated women are as religious as uneducated women. They may be less fatalistic, but they do not challenge the prescriptions to marry, to obey their husbands, and to forever seek greater knowledge of Islam. Alternatives to marriage do not exist; according to Smith, "Until they wed, they remain children, whatever their age" (1959, p. 244). Women's options within marriage are changing somewhat, but the structure of marriage and its expectations do not appear to be changing. Educated women may marry later and start families later, but they still intend to bear as many children as Allah will give to them. Having children, not careers, is central to their lives. All women interviewed believed that the object of marriage was to produce children and were shocked by the notion that some women in other parts of the world might choose to forgo them.

The acceptance of education has exposed many young girls to a wider world than was imaginable fifteen years ago, when UPE was introduced. In school they interact with a much wider circle of acquaintances than was conceivable then. At the secondary and university levels, they meet students and teachers from other cultures in Nigeria and beyond. But thus far very little that challenges Islamic beliefs has been tolerated. Education, even at the university level, is increasingly an exercise in the communication of Islamic values. A memo circulated by the administration at the University of Sokoto in 1986 claimed that single women holding salaried positions (no such women were permitted in the university itself) were contributing to the moral decline of Nigeria (Knipp, 1987). The Imam of the central mosque, speaking to a student group on campus, was quoted as saying: "It is wrong to put women in the top-most part of any organization. . . . Every human being derives strength from the chest, but women have had their own weakened because they have breasts" (*New Nigerian,* May 28, 1984, cited in Knipp, 1987, p. 91).

At the universities in northern Nigeria, objectivity, constructive criticism, and the open communication of ideas are not encouraged; Islamic beliefs about women and their roles are not directly challenged. To the extent, then, that cultural and religious beliefs limit the options for women, those options will remain limited for the foreseeable future.

We can only analyze change for Islamic women within the confines of their actual lives. Dramatic changes have taken and are taking place in the lives of Muslim Hausa women in northern Nigeria. Any comparison with women in non-Muslim parts of Nigeria would be invidious, however. In terms of attendance in secular schools, attendance at universities, presence in any wage sector, life expectancy, infant mortality rate, age at marriage, and overall life choices, Muslim women in northern Nigeria would appear to be severely disadvantaged. Yet it should also be stressed that the formation of the Federation of Muslim Women's Associations (described in Chapter 4), the subsequent emergence of a strong Muslim women's feminist organization and voice, and the changing expectations for girls within Islam itself (education and later marriage) are very dramatic, and it is important to look at these developments within the context of northern Nigerian culture. By comparison with the lives of their mothers, young Muslim women in Nigeria have greater opportunity and more options. Even more significant differences may be seen in the lives of Muslim women of Senegal and Mali.

EDUCATION AND MUSLIM WOMEN IN MALI AND SENEGAL

One of the obvious points distinguishing northern Nigeria from the rest of West Africa is the degree to which Islamic laws are observed. In most countries in West Africa, society was clearly secular throughout the colonial period and remains so today. In the English-speaking areas, this characteristic is generally explained by the fact that the majority of the population was not Muslim (Ghana, Liberia, southern Nigeria, Sierra Leone). In one case where the population was primarily Muslim, Gambia, the British established direct control over the territory in question for various political considerations and did not give independent authority to Muslim rulers. In French-speaking West Africa, a majority of the populations of most countries (except for four coastal ones) is Muslim. The French colonial government followed the standard pattern of top-down administration, with authority emanating from its central officers. Muslim leaders were given privileges and assistance in some countries, especially Senegal, but they were not particularly protected against the influence of Western forces—including education—as were Northern Nigerians. Even Mauritania was governed in this fashion, although this nation, resembling in its population and culture North African states more than the rest of West Africa, did become the sole French African colony to establish a Muslim theocratic state under Islamic law. The conditions in Mauritania, more closely than those of any other state, resemble Nigeria's. Yet even Mauritania's colonial experience was markedly different, as secular rulers made decisions based upon French practice rather than Islamic law.

The contrast between Northern Nigeria and states such as Senegal and Mali, in which Muslim societies are governed in a secular state system without constant reference to religion, is very great. Both of the latter cases are considered briefly here because there is also a great difference between them that illustrates one of our central contentions: Exposure to the West combined with increased access to economic resources will result in rapid and deep changes no matter what the religion of the population.

Mali, which is landlocked, attracts little investment and is significantly poorer than Senegal (see Table 1.1). It has a lower percentage of Muslims in its population and a far poorer record in educating women than does Senegal, which has a higher percentage of Muslims. Education in Mali was not widespread at independence and has not expanded greatly since that time (1960s), although the governments of Modibo Keita, the leftist founding father, and the military and civilian governments that succeeded him have all attempted to spread Western instruction at the primary and secondary levels throughout the country. Nonetheless, education is relatively unavailable to most children except in the capital, Bamako, and even there the majority of girls do not even attend elementary school (only 45 percent do attend). Girls, of course, fare much worse than boys, as Table 4.6 shows.

In Mali, not all ethnic groups converted to Islam simultaneously. As pointed out in Chapter 2, many groups in the central West African area, including Mali, had converted to Islam by the end of the fifteenth century, but other groups converted only toward the end of the nineteenth and beginning of the twentieth centuries. At present Islam is the major religion for the Sarakole, Songhay, Dioula, and Tukulor and for most of the Bozo, Peulh (Fulani), Somono, northern Bambara, Malinke, Bobo, Senoufo, and Dogon. The southern populations of the latter four ethnic groups have remained animist, although larger numbers are continuing to convert to Islam (Imperato, 1989, p. 87). Educational access for girls, however, does not break down on primarily religious or ethnic lines across the country as a whole. Rather, the chief factor seems to be proximity to Bamako (Government of Mali, 1985, pp. 84–91).

Senegal, on which we have much more detailed information, has a quite different pattern of educational access. As in Mali, proximity to the capital, in this case Dakar, is the most vital predictive factor of who is most likely to go to school. As in Mali, attendance at Quranic schools was widespread throughout the country long before colonial control was finally established and has endured and expanded to the present day. Most children, as illustrated by the 1991 survey reported in Chapter 3, do go to Quranic school whether they are boys or girls. But only a few students go on to higher levels of Islamic school—in the same survey, 20 percent of adult male and 11 percent of adult female respondents had attended "Arabic" school (Creevey, 1993, p. 70). In Mali, the only Arabic schools are the Lycée Franco-Arab in Timbuktu and several in Bamako itself, including the Islamic center opened in 1987 (Imperato, 1989, p. 93). The Senegalese have many more options. With funding from the Middle East, they have opened up numerous Arabic schools in Dakar and smaller towns throughout Senegal. Various Senegalese Tidjani leaders have endowed Islamic study centers; even the Mourides have established several Arabic schools and Islamic study centers. But Islamic education does not occupy as central a place in either Senegal or Mali as it does in northern Nigeria. Although most people consider Quranic schooling a normal part of their education, they are quite aware that only Western education, in schools established on the French pattern, will prepare them for the jobs available in the developing modern economy.

At independence in 1960, very few children received formal Western schooling in Senegal. In 1965 only 1 percent of the population was literate; that figure has now risen to 20 percent (Gellar, 1982, p. 101). Literacy in this case, as in the case of Mali, is in French. Arabic is not widely used except by leading Muslim scholars for their publications. Children in most Quranic schools only memorize phrases of the Quran in Arabic without ever learning the language at all.

Facilities for Western education are still not evenly distributed throughout the country. The largest number of schools is to be found in the

Table 4.5   Access to Education for Malian Girls

Primary School		Secondary School		Teacher Training Institutes	Technical Institutes
Children in Primary School (percent)		Children in Secondary School (percent)		Girls in Teacher Training Institutes (percent)	Girls in Technical Institutes (percent)
_1965_ 24	_1987_ 23	_1965_ 4	_1987_ 6	_1985_ 13	_1985_ 12.3
girls in school (percent)		girls in secondary school (percent)			
_1965_ 16	_1987_ 17	_1965_ 2	_1987_ 4		

Source: World Bank, 1990, p. 234; Government of Mali, 1985, pp. 77, 80.
Note: 1 percent of the total age group go on beyond secondary level.

region of Dakar, the only significant urban center. The inequity is more pronounced the higher the level of schooling. Nine of Senegal's twenty-four secondary schools (both technical and general lycées) are in Dakar, five others are in St Louis (the old colonial capital), and the rest are scattered in the larger towns in the other eight zones (Ziguinchor, Diourbel, Tambacounda, Kaolack, Thies, Louga, Fatick, and Kolda). The university is in Dakar (with a secondary university in St Louis). Ninety percent of the children in the seven-to-twelve age group are in school in Dakar, whereas only 41 percent of this age group are in school in the other regions excepting Ziguinchor (Gellar, 1982, p. 3).

Overall statistics from Senegal show that a girl's likelihood of receiving a primary school education has substantially increased since independence. However, in the last sixteen years, the relative proportion of girls among students in primary school has not changed significantly. They remain less than half of the primary school students (although 51 percent of the children), with the best ratio in Dakar and the worst ratios in Kolda and Louga, two of the most remote districts. Ziguinchor has seen the most substantial increase in the proportion of girls among primary school students, but the figure remains less than half (and is still lower than that of Dakar).

Table 4.8 shows the percentage of girls in middle and secondary schools. Here it is important to note that only 15 percent of the relevant school-age population in Senegal is in school; of that 15 percent, only 10 percent is female. Less than 3 percent of college-age Senegalese go to the university (World Bank, 1990, p. 234).

Distribution by region should help explain which factors have the most influence on whether or not a girl goes to school. For example, the primate status of Dakar, the concentration of resources within its metropolitan area, and its consequent exposure to all manner of Western influences lead one to expect that it should be most able to fulfill its announced policy of providing equal schooling for both sexes. In fact, although equal schooling is not yet available, girls are more likely to be educated here at all three levels—primary, secondary, and university—than in any other region.

Other variables that might be relevant include the percentage of Catholics in the population and the presence of Catholic schools in the region. Table 4.9 shows the percentage of Catholics in each region and the percentage of middle school students in Catholic as opposed to lay middle schools, as well as the percentage of girls in Catholic schools. The data suggest that Catholicism has a fairly important positive influence on the likelihood a girl will receive an education. In the first place, Catholic schools provide a significant part of middle school education, out of all proportion to the number of Catholics in the population at large, even in solidly Muslim regions. This fact is a striking demonstration of the missionary educational tradition, which has continued from early in the colonial period to the present. Second, the ratio of girls to boys is higher at

Table 4.6   Primary Education by Sex (percentage of students)

Regions	1970		1980		1986	
	Boys	Girls	Boys	Girls	Boys	Girls
Dakar	54	46	55	45	54	46
Ziguinchor	73	27	69	31	61	39
Diourbel	67	33	64	36	65	35
St Louis	63	37	61	39	61	39
Tambacounda	69	31	66	34	66	34
Kaolack	62	38	62	38	61	39
Louga	—	—	64	36	67	33
Fatick	—	—	—	—	61	39
Kolda	—	—	—	—	71	29
Senegal	62	38	60	40	60	40

Source: Situation Economique du Sénégal 1988, p. 48.

Catholic schools than at lay schools in most regions. The fact that the numbers of girls and boys are not equal does not necessarily reflect the policy of Catholic schools but more likely stems from the availability of students—that is, the willingness and financial ability of families to allow their children to continue in school. Catholic schools are open to both sexes without a quota restricting the number of girls. However, the percentage of Catholics in the population does not predict the percentage of girl students in middle school. In fact, Ziguinchor, the most strongly Catholic region in the country, has the second-lowest ratio of girls to boys in Catholic middle schools, followed only by Louga, where there are very few Catholics.

Interpreting this situation is complicated by the history of French-speaking West Africa and its relationship to France. It was not until independence that Senegal or Mali had many interactions with countries in the Middle East and North Africa. Thereafter, Muslim countries began to provide aid to Senegal (and to a lesser extent to Mali), but in general they did not provide aid for the formal education system. In large part, they withheld such aid because that system was modeled on the Western system as introduced by France, and the language of instruction was French. French aid supported, and still supports, numerous teachers, especially in the middle and high schools and the universities. Muslim countries have provided large amounts of money for the construction of mosques, helped establish a number of Arabic schools (providing religious and language instruction),

Table 4.7   Middle, Secondary, and Technical Schools
(percentage of students by sex and region, 1987)

Region	Middle		Secondary		Technical	
	Boys	Girls	Boys	Girls	Boys	Girls
Dakar	56	44	63	37	66	34
Ziguinchor	63	37	80	20	—	—
Diourbel	66	34	66	34	96	4
St Louis	57	43	76	24	90	10
Tambacounda	65	35	83	17	—	—
Kaolack	59	41	77	23	70	30
Thies	59	41	70	30	—	—
Louga	93	7	84	16	—	—
Fatick	66	36	73	27	—	—
Kolda	63	37	89	11	—	—
Senegal	59	41	70	30	70	30

Source: Government of Senegal, 1988, pp. 61, 66, 68; United Nations 1990, p. 51.

and paid for scholarships for a significant number of university students to go to the Middle East for their education. But the efforts have had little impact on the gradually expanding system of mass education for Senegalese children, or, for that matter, Malian children. Hence, although there are relatively few Catholics in both Mali and Senegal, they have had a greater impact than Muslims on the education system, modeled as it is in the Western image congruent with their cultural prejudices. Catholic priests and missionaries started the first schools, which were established in the colonial period. Despite more than thirty years of independence and independent African governments' lack of support for the church and its activities, Catholic schools remain a significant part of the educational system of Mali and Senegal. The model they established, slightly modified to suit the more secular and technological tenor of the day, still remains.

The difference between the two countries, so clearly demonstrated in the tables put forth here, is that Mali has not had the resources to spread education as widely as Senegal has. In both cases, religion does not seem to significantly impact access to education, but proximity to the capital does, so it is interesting that the gap between girls and boys is so much wider in Mali than Senegal. Here again, the answer seems to be clearly an absence of resources rather than any policy adopted in Mali or the more conservative nature of its regimes, especially following the fall of Modibo Keita.

Table 4.8   Catholic Middle Schools: Percentage of Middle School Students and
Percentage of Girls in Catholic Schools

Region	Percentage Catholic	Percentage Students Catholic Schools	Percentage Girls in Catholic Schools
Dakar	6	31	50
Ziguinchor	31	61	36
Diourbel	<1	40	30
St Louis	<1	24	49
Tambacounda	3	52	42
Kaolack	1	36	49
Thies	5	38	43
Louga	<1	77	8
Fatick	8	45	31
Kolda	4	0	—
Senegal	5	37	43

Source: RPGH 1988; Government of Senegal, 1988, p. 61.

Keita himself supported education for girls, and his successors have been eager to attract Western help, so their public pronouncements encourage women's education. It is simply a legacy of the colonial regime that in a poor country where education was offered first to boys and secondarily to girls, recent efforts to improve the position of women have had only a gradual impact. There simply are too few resources to support any kind of change in the system. Traditional society is likely to condone keeping girls at home. Muslim society, especially in its most old-fashioned, strictly orthodox aspect, is even more likely to keep the girl at home and away from exposure to Western education. The incentives of a rapidly growing and changing economy and exposure to current Western thinking help alter traditional views on what options should be made available to women. The actual existence of schools helps alter perspectives. The latter conditions were met in Senegal but not in Mali, and the result in educational opportunity for girls and women is very clear.

EDUCATION AND CHANGING ATTITUDES IN SENEGAL

Surveys in northern Nigeria indicate that women are very gradually seeking more equal treatment—more education, the right to work, even a more equitable share in decisionmaking power (Callaway, 1986; Coles and

Mack, 1991; Pitten, 1979). But at present women in northern Nigeria still largely accept their subordinate role as defined in traditional Islamic texts. A different study in Senegal (the 1991 Senegal Survey) also tried to ascertain what women thought of their status and what factors made them move to take more modern—that is, self-assertive—positions. In particular, the impact of Western education as opposed to religious affiliation on changing attitudes and expectations was analyzed.

This survey was based on the assumption that the more responsibility, exposure to outside ideas, and actual personal independence a woman has (or thinks she ought to have), the more "modern" she is. Respondents were asked if they were married, single, divorced, how many children they had, and whether or not they were the head of their family. If Muslim, they were asked:

- if they had co-wives or had signed a contract insisting upon monogamy at marriage;
- if they read books or newspapers or listened to the radio;
- whether they wished to work if it was not economically necessary;
- how much education they desired for their boy and girl children;
- whether they wanted their girls to work even if it was not economically necessary;
- who should be the family head—the husband or both husband and wife together;
- whether they, their husbands, both they and their husbands together, or some other family member made such decisions as

  - how to spend the respondent's salary;
  - what kind and amount of education would be provided for their sons and/or daughters;
  - whether or not the respondent actually worked outside the home, and if so what kind of job she had;
  - where the family lived; and
  - how family property was used.

As a contrast, the survey also inquired as to who actually paid the family bills: education, housing, clothing, food, health costs, and social events (including parties, marriages, baptisms, and funerals). Answers to the latter questions were presumed to reflect the actual state of the respondents' marriages, although it is clear that women sometimes responded to this kind of question in terms of what they thought they and/or their husbands ought to do rather than what was in fact done (Creevey, 1993, pp. 96–116).

Listening to the radio and reading are clearly modern, as is believing that husband and wife are equally heads of the family, but the assumptions about the other factors need to be defined. Being single or divorced is considered here modern (whether or not desirable), because traditionally women's status is determined by being married. Having two children or less is also seen as modern, because traditional society expects women to produce as many children as physically possible. Actually being the family head is modern (although again not always desirable), as men are traditionally the family heads. Having no co-wife is seen as more modern than having one and, of course, signing a contract for monogamy is as well.

Interpreting the other questions is more controversial. For this study, the desire to work and to permit one's daughters to work even if not economically necessary is selected as the more modern attitude. (Given the independent work patterns of traditional women, though, the latter may be less of a step forward than in societies such as northern Nigeria, where women were traditionally more secluded.) Wanting equal education for girls and boys is seen as more modern, although this factor is difficult to weigh, as the very existence of formal education is in itself a nontraditional phenomenon. The other factors, all pertaining to family decisionmaking and responsibility, are difficult to read because different ethnic groups would certainly not have had identical traditions. However, certain assumptions were made based on a common pattern (understanding that it actually varies somewhat by group) to facilitate interpretation. Both husband and wife in each of the Senegalese ethnic groups would have had certain obligations toward the family and certain areas in which they would have been expected to make decisions. It was assumed that women would have a say in the education of girls but not boys and would not have been allowed to decide whether they should get a paid job themselves (this would have been their husband's choice), but they would have been allowed to decide on the use of whatever money they earned. They would not have any say over the use of family-owned goods, however; this would have been their husbands' prerogative. They would be subject to their husband's decision on where the family should live. In regard to actual financial responsibility, men would have had the major share, but women would have been expected to pay for (in money or kind) the family social costs, to provide their daughters' (but not their sons') education, to procure part of the food, and to provide part of their own and their children's clothing. Modern attitudes would extend the decisionmaking power of women and also their financial responsibility for the family.

In the actual results of the Senegal Survey, 80 percent of the respondents were married, and 85 percent had more than two children. Only 21 percent of the Muslim women had signed a contract to have a monogamous marriage, and more than 61 percent of those who answered the question had co-wives. Only 20 percent of the sample were heads of their families, and 62 percent of the women felt their husbands, and not they, should be the head of the family. Thus, the overwhelming majority of the respondents followed what we have defined as traditional patterns in their marriages.

Significantly, the only variable that related strongly to whether or not a woman was married was education. Women with some education were substantially more likely to be single or divorced than those who had none. Although women in Dakar were slightly more likely than women elsewhere to be single, this relationship was not significant. Age and ethnicity did not affect marital status, nor did religious preference. In terms of the number of children women had, it was again education that had the largest impact, although the relationship was not strong. Again, no other variable had any significant effect, including religion.

Education did not determine whether or not a woman was in fact the head of her family; in this instance, ethnic background appeared to explain why some were and others were not. The Dyola were significantly more likely than other women to be heads of their family, followed by the Tukulor and, more distantly, by the Wolof and Serer. An understanding of the different traditional patterns of work and family for women in each ethnic group would help one understand the results of the survey, but this is too detailed a subject to include here (see Creevey, 1993, pp. 141–152). The only point we can emphasize is that religion, age, and education had little or no effect on whether a woman was head of her family.

Whether or not Muslim women had co-wives related significantly to education—those with schooling were less likely to have a co-wife. It also related to residence, as women in Dakar were less likely to have a co-wife than women elsewhere, with Dyola women less likely than women of the remaining groups to have a co-wife (followed by Serer women). Age significantly related to this question: Older women were more likely to have co-wives. All of these factors were close in weight, although none determined more than 20 percent of the variance except education, apparently the strongest determinant.

As for the contract to be monogamous, few women had signed one. It might have been expected that women in Dakar would have been better informed about this possibility, but residence had no effect. Nor did age—younger women were no more likely to have a contract. However, two factors did seem to have significant influence: education and ethnic background. Educated women were more likely to have such a contract, and Dyola women were much more likely to have one than women of any other group. In fact, ethnic background explained more of the variation than did education.

In regard to Senegalese women's view of their position in the family, education again seemed to be the major determinant of whether women believed themselves equal to men. Better-educated women were significantly more likely to say their husbands were not the family heads, that they had an equal role. In this case, however, religious preference did make a difference: Catholic women were much more likely than Muslims to assert their equality. This influence, however, was not as strong as that of education. Nor was it as strong as the impact of where a woman lived. Women in Dakar were most likely to take the more assertive position, followed by those in Ziguinchor. Education, however, still seemed to have the strongest impact.

Senegalese women are more independent-minded when it comes to the media and their attitudes about themselves and their daughters at work. Only 6 percent of the women said they did not listen to a radio some of the time, and more than 70 percent said they listened to it often. More than 50 percent said they looked at newspapers and magazines, although a quarter of these said they did so rarely. Most women (93 percent) wish to continue working and expect that their daughters will do so regardless of economic necessity (94 percent). Virtually all the women (95 percent) want their daughters to have education beyond secondary school if possible, only 2 percent less than the 97 percent who hope for this level of education for their sons.

Education, naturally, was the major factor in determining whether or not a woman read newspapers or journals and how often. Clearly, the more educated a woman was, the more likely she was to read. Religion had a slight but not significant relationship: Catholics were more likely to read than Muslims. Given the possibility that this finding might reflect the somewhat greater likelihood of a Catholic woman being educated, a sample of those without education was tested. Here, religious preference was an even stronger predictor of the probability of a woman reading a newspaper: Uneducated Catholic women were much more likely to do so than Muslim women, and the gap was wider than in the full survey. However, when only educated women were considered, religion had no bearing on the likelihood of a woman reading a newspaper or journal. A more significant variable was where a women lived: Women in Dakar and environs were much more likely than other women to read, probably reflecting the availability of schools and reading material in the urban zone. Tukulor women were least likely to read newspapers or magazines, and Serer women were the most likely to do so. But this ethnic variation disappeared both in the sample of educated women and of women in the Dakar zone.

Education was not the determining factor in predicting whether or not women listened to the radio. In this case, the only significant variable seemed to be availability of radios, and, not surprisingly, only region of residence reflected this. Women in the most remote rural zones of Tambacounda and Kolda were much less likely than women elsewhere to listen to the radio. Ethnicity seemed to have some effect, although this was a less strong predictor than residence. Wolof and Serer women were significantly more likely than Tukulor and Dyola women to listen to the radio, but the significance of ethnicity disappeared when only the Dakar sample was considered. Women of different ethnic groups in and around Dakar were equally likely to listen to the radio.

A different pattern emerges when we analyze the survey data on economic decisionmaking and responsibility. Most women (56 percent) said they decided how to spend the money they earned—the only significant variation was between women in wage positions and those in agriculture or the informal sector. The former were more likely to claim independent control over their salaries. Religion appeared to be an irrelevant consideration in this regard. In regard to who decided if a woman should work and what type of jobs she might take, religion's impact was statistically significant but not great enough to support or refute the hypothesis that Islam would restrict women's choices. Catholic women were more likely to make decisions about whether (and at what) they should work with their husbands, whereas Muslims were more likely to say they made these decisions independently. Muslim women were also more likely to say their husbands decided alone (31 percent), although this group was much smaller than the group of Muslim women who said they decided with their husbands or by themselves and was not very much larger than the percentage of Catholics who acknowledged their husband's authority in this matter (21 percent).

Two factors seem most relevant in interpreting this data. First, Catholics are in monogamous marriages, and most Muslim women are in polygamous marriages. The monogamous ideal calls for joint decisions, whereas the polygamous situation permits independent decisions because women often live alone in their own compound or apartment (with their children). Western women's journals and movies and even modern Muslim family counseling urge joint decisions in Muslim households as well as in Catholic, so the group of Muslim women who selected "joint" as their option was not insignificant. Overall, however, Catholic women are less independent in this important matter, even though (as noted above) they are more likely to see themselves as equal.

Catholic and Muslim women split the sample again, but somewhat differently, on the question of who decides where the family lives and how family goods are used. Muslim women were more likely than Catholics to acknowledge their husband's right to decide these matters (54 percent). Catholics adhered to the joint decision ideal (45 percent). The relationship was weak and still did not explain much of the sample variation, but it did suggest a religious impact.

Religion had no significant impact on predicting who assumed most family expenses. The definition here was that taking on some or all of this responsibility reflects a "modern" attitude; however, this survey showed women as more likely to say their husbands paid even for those things that by tradition had been primarily the responsibility of women—such things as the education of their daughters, part of the cost of the food, and social costs. More than 50 percent of the respondents said their husbands paid for all children's schooling and for food, housing, and health care. A more even sharing of responsibility was found in provision of clothing for both children and wives and for social events, with about a quarter of the sample saying that men alone should pay for these things. Interestingly, a larger percentage of Catholic women said that they, or they and their husbands together, pay for everything, including traditionally male responsibilities such as rent and family food. Muslim women, in contrast, appear to follow Islamic prescriptions, which direct that the husband is responsible for family expenses. But the relationship between religion and any variation in opinion was very slight.

Because expectations for women's behavior differed across ethnic groups in traditional Senegal, the impact of ethnic origin on women's perceptions of their status has to be studied and compared to the influence of religion. Analysis is complicated by the fact that different ethnic groups in Senegal converted to different branches of Islam because they encountered Muslim proselytizers from different brotherhoods during different historical periods. However, it can be concluded that the impact of ethnic origin on women's attitudes is not stronger than that of religion. The results do shed some light on religion's influence. The Wolof, who are largely Muslim, had the highest percentage of women responding that they take most of the responsibility for decisions about the use of their income and about whether or not they will work. They are the second most likely (behind the Dyola) to decide either independently or jointly with their husbands on education for their children and second least likely (again behind the Dyola) to say their husbands alone decide upon their residence or the use of family goods. Although Wolof husbands are responsible for paying most of the family expenses, they are less likely to be *solely* responsible for expenses than those of any other ethnic group.

Dyola women respondents are the most likely to say they have independent or joint decisionmaking power over the use of their own salary, the use of family goods, and where they will reside. They also are the most likely to say they decide independently on boys' education and the second most likely to make independent decisions on girls' education. Yet when it comes to paying for all types of family expenses, Dyola women have either the highest or the second highest percentage of respondents saying this is their husband's responsibility.

Serer and Tukulor women have a different pattern, one that seems to show a strong tendency toward dependency and subordination, as predicted above. They are less likely to say they decide how to use their own salaries and more likely to say their husbands decide whether or not they work, what the boys' education should be, where they live, and how family goods will be used. More Tukulor women than any other group decide independently on their daughters' educations, or say their husbands decide on their daughters' education (instead of deciding together or having another family member make the decision). In terms of expenses, the Serer and Tukulor attribute to their husband the responsibility for all expenses except food, social costs, and clothing, which the spouses share.

Factors other than religion seem to play a significant role in determining female attitudes of independence. This conclusion is reinforced by analysis of the importance of residence. This factor predicts much more strongly than religion or ethnic group as to whether or not women's attitudes have changed. Not surprisingly, women in the urban area of Dakar, which is mostly Wolof, have more of a role than women elsewhere in decisionmaking and in helping to support the family. Ziguinchor, which has a population of 394,680 (only a quarter of the population of Dakar) and a plurality of Dyola, has an even stronger tendency in this direction. The peculiar character of the Ziguinchor relationship seems to result from a combination of traditional matrilineal cultures not found in the rest of Senegal, with a consequent authoritative role for the woman in the traditional family, and from an urban effect that reinforces the independence of females. Women in St Louis (and Tambacounda and Kolda), who are predominantly Tukulor, adhere to a more distinct traditional pattern in which they make more independent decisions than women in any other region on most matters. However, they are still the most likely to indicate that their husbands have decisionmaking power (and the obligation to pay) and are by far the least likely to say they make joint decisions with their husbands.

Contrasting education with these three other variables (religion, ethnic origin, and residence) raises again the question of the primacy of formal education in bringing about change for women. If education is the decisive factor, then its impact on these attitudes and opinions should be much stronger than what has been so far described. Indeed, when the sample is divided between women with no education and those with some, the results are striking. Education supplants residence and ethnicity in importance except in regard to the decisions on the education of children, and it seems to have more influence on all other decisions. Education does *not* relate significantly to whether women or men assume family expenses, as most women say their husbands pay for rent, food, and so on. A relationship does emerge that suggests a tendency for educated women to be more likely than uneducated women to acknowledge that they pay or share in the payment for all the items surveyed—education, rent, food, clothing, and health and social costs. The pattern appears to be more or less uniform. (See specific statistical comparisons on impacts of residence, ethnic origin and education in Creevey, 1993, pp. 111–116.)

CONCLUSION

The relative impact of religion and education on the changing roles and attitudes of women is still a complex and difficult question. This study indicates a number of important relationships. First, in a secular state where both the leadership and the population are Muslim, Islam does not appear to be a barrier to the education of girls. Far more important in both Nigeria and Senegal is the inequity of the distribution of resources, the split between the urban and rural areas. The availability of education is the best predictor of whether or not a girl will go to school. Young girls in the more remote rural areas in both countries will be much less likely than urban girls to go to school and highly unlikely to ever receive more than a partial primary school education.

Second, the urban/Western influence also seems to be a strong factor in changing women's attitudes and behavior patterns. Women from all regions and ethnic groups who come to Dakar or Lagos are exposed to a more cosmopolitan, Western set of ideas that affect what they think and how they act. This influence is less strong in larger northern Nigerian cities, where the Western influence has been weaker, although even there it is not missing altogether: Educated men and women read magazines, watch television, and listen to the radio, suggesting that Western ideas penetrate even there. But education is a stronger predictor of changes in attitudes and lifestyle. The more education a woman has, the more she will see herself as equal to her husband, able to make family decisions on her own and to take responsibility for family finances.

Religion does play a role in determining the level of education for girls, but it is closely interlinked with ethnicity and economic status. The continuing significance of ethnic origin in determining opportunities for girls as well as the attitudes and behavior they adopt is clearly shown in this study. The various ethnic groups still socialize their girls differently, and these differences still emerge despite the influence of the West or the available educational opportunities.

In Senegal, at first glance it seems that the role of religion varies according to whether women in a particular ethnic group are Muslim or Catholic. Christianity, linked to the French in Senegal, was a major sponsor of Western formal education for girls as well as boys. Indeed, Christian missionaries started schools in the major towns and still play a significant role in education. In the 1991 Senegal Survey, Catholic women were slightly more likely to be educated; furthermore, women of the two most heavily Catholic ethnic groups were more likely to be literate and to read newspapers. But the fact remains that these two ethnic groups were in the majority Muslim, so the strength of the independence of these women cannot be explained by their religion. Clearly, there is a strong ethnic factor apart from religion. Finally, it appears that the type of Islam (in this case brotherhood affiliation) may be extremely important in explaining the role Islam plays. This relationship is curious. Tidjanis in Senegal were more likely to be educated than Mourides, yet Tukulor women, who are 95 percent Tidjani, were less likely to be educated than women of any other ethnic group. The explanation may be found by further studying the divisions among the different Tijaniyya groups—there are conservative ones and more liberal ones. It must be reemphasized, though, that distance from Dakar is more important than religion or brotherhood in predicting either access to education or changes in attitudes toward the roles women play in society.

Perhaps the most interesting (because it is most unexpected) pattern to emerge from this study is the contrast between Catholic and Muslim styles of female independence in Senegal. Education has an impact in the predicted direction; the more a woman has, the more she asserts her equality and increases her responsibility for her family. But Islam's influence is more ambivalent. Islamic women in some ways adhere more to traditional patterns than do Catholics. They certainly are more likely to attribute family leadership to men and to believe that husbands should decide where the family will live and how family goods will be used. Catholic women see themselves as equal to their husbands and are much more likely than Muslim women to say decisions are made (and costs are paid) by husband and wife jointly. In these ways, this study supports the hypothesis that Catholicism fosters modern attitudes in regard to women that Islam does not. However, in actual fact Muslim women are more likely to make decisions independently of their husbands than Catholic women. Thus, although in some ways Muslim women are more traditional (i.e., less modern), in other ways their traditional patterns are more independent (i.e., more modern) than those that characterize Catholic women. Men are often a remote presence in Muslim women's lives, and in day-to-day household matters they are rarely consulted. Ironically, however, the importance of this difference is undermined by the influences of education and urban Westernism, which promote the ideal of joint and equal marriages.

Finally, contrary to the notion that largely Islamic societies devalue female children, the sample strongly demonstrates the importance, for all Muslim women in all ethnic groups, of their daughters and their future. Virtually all of the women did believe in equal education for their sons and daughters despite the fact that in the sample a significant number of women have less education than their spouses, although most are on a par with their husbands. Women also want to continue working, and they wish this for their daughters also, even if the income is not needed to maintain the family. Almost all women cling to the control of whatever revenue they earn as well. These things underline the traditional independence of all West African women regardless of religion, education, or residence.

Yet there are differences revealed in the surveys between northern Nigerian and Senegalese women. The northern Nigerian women still expect to live in seclusion and work only with their husband's permission, and they do not believe men and women are equal other than before Allah. What might explain the more conservative, less modern, more fundamentally Islamic perspective of even educated Muslim women in northern Nigeria? Again, the date of conversion to Islam, the traditional political system in the northern Nigerian Hausa states (which combined the features of a secular state with Islamic law), the political prominence of a conservative Islamic elite, and the lack of exposure to Western education promoted by a pro-Islamic British colonial policy all combined to create a different socialization profile for Hausa Muslim women than for Muslim women in Senegal. Both societies are Muslim, but this can mean quite different things. In the Nigerian case, the elite in the northern states used Islamic themes and teachings to support secular government while opposing southern non-Islamic political movements led by non-Muslims. In Senegal, after the original French conquest, Islamic leaders never saw themselves as directly threatened by the modern secular state. Hence, the power of militant political Islam was diluted in its interaction with liberal Western institutions in Senegal. Currently there are some signs of liberalization in the perceptions of proper roles for women in northern Nigeria, even among men and even among men in power, but there is still a wide gap in outlook on appropriate roles for women here as compared to Senegal or Mali. The culture of Islam developed over the centuries in northern Nigeria has informed and altered traditional culture so that women do not express their independence and equality the same way their sisters in southern Nigeria would certainly do in a similar survey. But Muslim women in Senegal are no less Muslim because they live a different life-style than do Muslim women in northern Nigeria. The differences are more attributable to the historical context than they are to the impact of Islam per se.

As far as education is concerned, clearly it does have a major impact on outlook, expectations, and options for all West African women, whether Muslim or Christian. Women gain the ability to move into the modern sector on increasingly equal terms with men the more education they receive. That impact is similar in all countries if one basic condition is met: The quality of education (its content and standards) must be equal for both men and women. If Western education incorporates religious training to the point that rigorous and objective standards of scientific inquiry and analysis are abandoned and only the received word is venerated, students will take longer to develop independent minds and acquire technological skills. Yet the case of northern Nigeria suggests that even in the latter situation change will occur; it simply will happen more slowly with more ambivalent results than in West African countries where formal education is not so constrained.

5

WOMEN IN THE FORMAL
AND INFORMAL ECONOMIES

Over the course of the past two decades, the changing status and roles of women, combined with the rise of modern feminism, has prompted concern with the meaning, significance, and explanation of gender. After twenty years of feminist scholarship, there is a general consensus that gender is a fundamental organizing principle in all societies and that, like class and race/ethnicity, it is a source of inequality. In many societies women are defined as unequal by both law and custom.

At the same time, women's crucial role in economic production is widely recognized, although it is often ignored in national statistics. Whether in the formal labor market, the informal sector, the agricultural sector, or the home, women contribute as producers of goods and services, as consumers, and as household managers. The essence of women's distinctiveness lies in the multiplicity of their roles. Most women, in addition to being involved in economic production, take prime responsibility for the care of children, the elderly, and upkeep of the home. In West Africa, as in most developing countries, much of this contribution is unremunerated; in the agricultural sector in particular, women provide substantial amounts of unpaid labor, producing crops for use by the household.

Throughout history, changes in the structure of the economy have been followed by changes in the composition of the work force, thus affecting family structure and fertility and mortality rates. Sociologists, demographers, and economists have studied these phenomena and linkages. Marxist feminists in particular, building upon Engels (1884/1922), have explored the sexual division of labor and theorized about its interrelationships with the state, property rights, and the process of socialization, including cultural understandings about appropriate sex roles.

Ester Boserup, in her landmark study of women's economic roles, noted that women seemingly lost status and relative material well-being with every economic "advance" made in the name of "modernization" (Boserup, 1970). In more recent times, West African governments have launched programs of "structural adjustment" in order to qualify for debt refinancing and other forms of economic help from the World Bank and the International Monetary Fund (IMF). These programs also acutely disadvantage women.

In the 1980s, most developing countries experienced rising indebtedness and suffered substantial loss in the value of their exports, which led to setbacks in their growth and development. In some cases economic contraction and declines in living standards reached astounding proportions. Both Nigeria and Senegal have experienced significant declines in per capita income and overall standard of living over the past ten years. The response of the developed countries through the World Bank and the IMF has been to provide for short-term debt relief in exchange for long-term economic restructuring through stabilization and adjustment of lending policies. Although the resulting loans have different maturities, come from different sources, and are used in different ways, they all have policy conditions attached to them that have a direct impact on women's lives, work loads, and incomes. The main thrust of IMF stabilization and structural adjustment programs has been to cut back on expenditures through controls on credit and government programs and cuts in public sector employment and wages. In addition, these programs include measures to encourage resource reallocation to more productive uses in the international trade sector through devaluation of currency, price deregulation, and the removal of subsidies, especially for food. These programs clearly have implications for women as producers, consumers, household managers, and care givers.

Such programs in fact greatly disadvantage women who must produce the food and income to sustain the family while the domestic economy contracts and government subsidies cease. As long as women carry a double burden—unpaid work in the service of their families, plus work outside the home to support themselves and their children—they will be unable to compete with men in the open market on equal terms. They are particularly disadvantaged because domestic arrangements are almost always structured by unequal gender relations. If women are to benefit from economic restructuring, they need public sector services such as water supplies, electricity, waste disposal, public transportation, health care, and education to lighten the burden of their *unpaid* work and enable them to acquire the skills they need to enter the market economy. Structural adjustment programs, however, do not target the public sector infrastructure for development, so women are not likely to benefit from the reduction of state activity in the economy and an increased role for the market. They need restructuring of the public sector *and* the private sector to make both more responsive to women's needs as producers and reproducers. In fact, the structural adjustment required in the public sector may be not simply a reduction in expenditure and costs but a change in priorities in relation to the users of public services.

The impact of stabilization and structural adjustment policies on women is rarely taken into consideration by policymakers. Women's varied economic activities remain largely invisible and ignored, a peripheral factor in discussions of macroeconomic issues. Yet evidence shows that in key respects women are more seriously affected than men by the ongoing economic deterioration in their countries. The poverty-inducing aspects of structural adjustment programs result in downward mobility for middle-class women and an even more serious decline in the standard of living for poorer women and children. Constraints on government spending curtail programs and services that helped integrate women into the economy and increase their employment and income opportunities. Poor women become poorer, more women become poor, and women are poorer in relation to men, as even the World Bank recognizes (World Bank, 1990).

The decline in per capita income so closely associated with the debt crisis in West Africa has disrupted virtually all aspects of women's lives, forcing them to shoulder extra burdens to keep families alive. Women have to work longer hours, go farther for work, and earn less. It is women who must cope and devise survival strategies when household incomes fall and prices rise. Under structural adjustment programs, there has generally been an increase in food prices and in the prices of the things women have to buy to invest in their own ventures. The drain on women's time, resources, and energy inhibits their ability to participate in political life in order to change those policies that affect them so adversely. The crisis has diminished educational opportunities and economic possibilities for young women, thus affecting their future ability to contribute to society on an equal basis with men.

Gender is inescapably inscribed in all policy, whether this be deliberate or unintentional, detrimental or beneficial to women. Gender relations have acted as an obstacle to women's gaining equal access to productive assets, capital support, and employment. As a consequence, women have not benefited to the same extent as men from development policies. Their work loads have not been reduced and continue to be greater than men's; their incomes have neither grown nor become secure. Policymakers have yet to be persuaded of the benefits of increasing education and employment opportunities for women, of making equity a national goal. It is within this context that we must analyze women's role in economic growth (or decline) in West Africa.

WOMEN'S ECONOMIC ROLES IN WEST AFRICA

In West Africa as a whole, industrialization was introduced from the outside by European colonialists in the relatively recent past and superimposed on the preexisting subsistence agriculture cum trading system. The old classes and the old values have not totally disappeared. Indeed, the new classes, consistent in the Marxian sense with the industrial era—the wage-paid workers, the middle class, the government functionaries—are still a minority in most countries of the region; the peasant farmers still predominate. However, the peasant farmers are hardly untouched by the changes economic modernization has introduced. There has not been a replacement of one class structure by another but rather a mixing of traditional and more modern classes. Eventually, industrialization may fully take over; the majority of the population will be urban, and the numbers of those remaining in rural areas will be small. At that time the urban class structure may become the only relevant one. For the time being, however, relatively few people can find permanent, full-time, wage-paying jobs in the urban centers, and a majority of the population still relies on farming for at least part of its subsistence. Another very large subgroup relies for survival on petty trading and the informal sector, either alone or together with farming and wage-paying jobs. Women, who have more difficulty finding wage-paying jobs, are central in agriculture, especially in food production, and in the informal sector, where they produce, among other things, food, beer, clothing, other basic commodities, and crafts and provide such services as hairdressing and catering (Robertson and Berger, 1987).

Women's economic standing has a lot to do with their material well-being, their independence, and their social status. This is true despite the tendency of Western economists and sociologists to consider the economic and social status of women as being determined by that of their husband or male family head. Studies on household budgets and intrafamily economic roles clearly document the inequity of the distribution of assets, income, and obligations between men and women. Furthermore, these inequities are to be found within the family itself and are responsible for an intra-family conflict/bargaining process, wherein husbands, wives, daughters, and sons struggle with each other to increase their access to assets, their income, and their overall power. Indeed, as N. Folbre argues, it is inconsistent of economists to accept as given the normal selfishness of individuals in the marketplace and ignore the same natural tendency in the family system (Folbre, 1988, p. 980). Economic roles are defined by gender and family position in most cultures, and these are the subject of struggles, negotiations, and redefinitions as economic change progresses (Bruce, 1989, p. 980). Thus, a West African woman is not necessarily well off if she marries a man in a good position or badly off if her spouse has a low-paying job or is unemployed.

Most women in West Africa work, whether in agriculture, the informal sector, a wage-paying job, or some combination thereof. The proceeds of this work are used to supplement the family budget, often providing a major part of the revenue. Given the importance of their work for family well-being and the rapidly rising incidence of female-headed households resulting from divorce or migration, examining the economic roles of women is essential to understanding their position in society. Women are moving out of subsistence agriculture into the modern economy but at a different rate and following a different pattern than are men. If women are consistently being held to second-class positions and receive lower salaries than men, they will remain inferior in status and also will be deprived of the material gains open to their male counterparts.

In traditional pre-Islamic subsistence agricultural systems, especially in polygamous societies, women had a right to use the proceeds of their labor. Families kept separate budgets, each adult having some kind of work and income tally. Traditional expectations determined how any profit might be used. Women were obligated to grow and prepare food for the family, provide clothing, and assume other household expenses. Men also had family obligations that involved expenses. Indeed, their degree of responsibility to the family was greater. But men held the only available resource—land—and they had the right to the labor of the women on the family plots, which they controlled (although the women were often paid in money or kind for this work). Women in West Africa retain a degree of control over their salaries, especially in polygamous households, where separate budgets continue to be a necessity because of family structure. As more families become members of the urban middle class and live monogamously, family budgets may unify; of course, the increasing rate of divorce may contrarily lead mothers and children to become the basic family unit. At present, however, married women and men still maintain separate budgets in West Africa, and women are quite aware of what they earn and how they wish to use this money. Also, at present women may be found in every sector of the economy in most of the coastal countries, including southern Nigeria. They are a small proportion of the wage earners in business and industry, but the proportion is growing. They are moving into the public sector, taking jobs that only men held until a few years ago, but they are primarily in the lowest positions. Aside from a sprinkling of directors and other political appointees, most women are found in clerical positions. Their representation in the wage sector is much lower in the landlocked countries of the North, which are also the areas most solidly Islamic in their religious persuasion. In the rural sector, where most families are still located, women do not own land; they rapidly are being further disadvantaged in this regard, as laws passed to allow private registration of land principally apply to the male family head only. And women are taking on more work and responsibility as the male family heads migrate to find work.

Table 5.1 shows the involvement of women in West African economic production according to United Nations statistics. However, in the official records of almost all countries, the activities of women are severely underestimated. Women's involvement in agriculture (aside from paid labor)

Table 5.1   Women in the Work Force in West Africa

Country	Economically Active Women (thousands)		Estimated Rate of Economic Activity (percent, 1990)		Women Percent Total	Administrative, Managerial	Clerical	Labor	Agri. Hunt.
	1970	1990	Females	Males		(females per 100 males)			
Benin	649	986	77	89	48	—	—	—	—
Burkina Faso	1,251	1,742	77	93	46	—	—	—	—
Cameroon	1,048	1,344	41	87	33	6	26	9	82
Chad	293	387	23	90	21	—	—	—	—
Côte d'Ivoire	947	1,459	48	88	34	—	—	—	—
Gambia	92	121	58	90	40	17	48	7	118
Ghana	1,411	2,224	51	80	40	10	292	81	90
Guinea	830	1,128	57	90	40	—	—	—	—
Liberia	164	253	37	88	30	—	—	—	—
Mali	283	408	16	90	16	—	—	—	—
Mauritania	83	140	24	87	22	—	—	—	—
Niger	1,046	1,512	79	93	47	—	—	—	—
Nigeria	8,099	13,624	46	88	35	—	—	—	—
Senegal	686	1,112	53	86	39	—	—	—	—
Sierra Leone	384	451	38	84	32	—	—	—	—
Togo	311	455	47	88	36	9	206	61	78

Source: United Nations, 1991, pp. 104–105.

is frequently considered just a household duty; the informal sector is ig-nored, and women are generally subsumed under the category "housewife" and not considered economically active no matter how many hours they spend in the field daily.

In West Africa the economic position of women is rapidly changing as the economy develops. The pattern is very complex, and the overall trends are not completely clear. Women are increasing their involvement in the modern wage-labor force but decreasing their involvement in agriculture because that sector is shrinking. Thus, the participation in the work force of females over fifteen years of age is reported to have gone down in the period 1970 to 1990 in the more rapidly industrializing countries (United Nations, 1991, p. 105).

NORTHERN NIGERIAN WOMEN

The economic activities of Hausa women have been described by a num-ber of researchers, but no one has discovered a hierarchy of roles or work chores for women related to class and status, although status for men, based on class and occupation, is clearly defined (see M. G. Smith, 1962; Barkow, 1972; Bashir, 1972; Hill, 1977; Schildkrout, 1978, 1979, 1981, 1982; Jaggar, 1976; Tahir, 1976; Coles, 1988; Frishman, 1991). Women acknowledge each other's abilities, skills, and economic success, but this recognition does not translate into socioeconomic status. That is deter-mined first by the status and class of a woman's husband and second by the social status and class of her father. Hausa society's emphasis on the "Islamic way of life," which stresses the importance of marriage for women (and of proper behavior in marriage), obscures the very interesting economic activities of women. Differences among women in terms of their economic roles and the factors upon which they base occupational choices are related to age, class, childbearing activity, marital status, and of course education. But because their socioeconomic status is determined by their fathers' and husbands' standing, women do not think the success of their own work affects their status.

Men are required by the teachings of Islam to provide for their fami-lies, and in the 1970s and 1980s it appeared they were able to do so. Thus, the incomes women produced were theirs alone to invest or spend. But by 1990, with Nigeria well into its program of structural adjustment, there ap-peared evidence that Muslim women had joined their non-Islamic sisters in providing essential support for the household.

In 1985, Catherine Coles returned to Kaduna, a large governmental center in northern Nigeria, to trace the 125 women she had studied in 1981. She located 79 of them. Their lives had changed a great deal in a very short period of time. In 1981, all the women were engaged in income-earning activity, and they regarded the proceeds as theirs to use as they pleased. By 1985, 90 percent of the seventy-nine women were spending their money primarily on food and clothing for their children. Seventy percent admitted they were contributing money to their husbands for their very subsistence, and 40 percent said they were paying for part of their children's education. In 1981 the women had asserted that all these things were the obligations of their husbands (Coles, 1991, p. 183). Coles estimated that in Kaduna, women were providing 25–50 percent of household income by 1985 (p. 190). Thus, between 1981 and 1985, when the Nigerian economy was greatly contracting in response to structural adjustment, Hausa women, like women everywhere, responded by contributing more to their family's basic needs.

Much had changed in terms of women's role in the household economy, but the structure of the household itself had not changed. It was still the case that women in Kaduna were married between the ages of eleven and fourteen and then secluded. Although the responsibility to provide for their families still belonged to men, women were responding to economic reality, apparently with their husbands' blessings. In this instance, economic reality appeared to be undermining Islamic teaching. It is conceivable that economic necessities may increasingly push Hausa Muslim women out of their homes and into the work force, but at the present time most women still work from behind the walls of seclusion.

In theory, women in seclusion are wholly dependent on their husbands for food, shelter, and support, but in fact they are very active economically. Historically, only wealthier men could keep their wives in seclusion; poorer men were forced to rely on wives' labor outside the home to contribute to the support of the family. Today virtually all Hausa families, rural or urban, rich or poor, endorse seclusion, and many wives are secluded even when it is clear their husbands cannot support them adequately. As a practical matter, then, wives must engage in some sort of remunerative activity at home in order to sustain the family.

Just as women in subsistence agriculture traditionally had a right to use the proceeds of their labor, so (at least theoretically) do urban women in northern Nigerian cities. These women had and have the right to use any income they generate in any way they choose, and at the moment they are "choosing" to contribute to basic household expenses. In point of fact, women's income was largely invested in the marriage system itself, at least until recently, when men found it increasingly difficult to provide necessities for their families. At marriage, a young girl brings to her husband's house her dowry, or *kayan daki*. The contents of the *kayan daki,* usually large numbers of brass or enamel bowls, a bed and linens, and jewelry, are the responsibility of her mother. Hence, most women used any income they could generate to invest in *kayan daki* for their daughters in order to help secure good marriages for them. In the event of divorce, a portion of the *kayan daki* could be sold in order to generate cash, which might be needed in the transition between marriages.

The definitions of appropriate economic activities of men and women have not changed, but the realities have. Whether or not these new realities result in changes in women's relationship to the means of production (land and wages) remains to be seen.

The Wage Sector

Unlike southern Nigeria and many other countries in West Africa, northern Nigeria has few women in wage positions in either the public or the private sectors. A few very highly educated women of high social status are increasingly found in the upper echelons of the civil service or work as physicians, providing medical services to women. Educated women also teach in girls' schools and women's colleges. But they do not work as clerks or secretaries in the lower ranks of the civil service, they seldom work in hospitals, and they certainly do not work alongside men in factory jobs. In Lubeck's surveys of factory workers in Kano in the 1970s, and Frishman's surveys in the 1980s, very few women were to be found, and *none* of them were Hausa/Fulani.

If and where a woman works is her husband's decision, not hers. Women are not found in the lower ranks of the civil service because they will have too much contact with men in these positions. In more highly exalted or senior positions, they can generally be protected, having contact with no more than a few men of equal social status. In 1980 Alan Frishman combed both the traditional walled city of Kano and the newer industrial and market sectors that have grown up around it seeking the ninety-three businesses run by women he had studied in 1973. He did not know the ethnic origin of the women in the original study. Most of their firms had been in the non-Hausa *sabon gari* section of Kano. Frishman wanted to know how many of them, if any, were actually run by Hausa women. He found sixteen of the original ninety-three firms, but only one of them was owned by a Hausa woman, and she was a Christian who had returned to Kano from Ghana (Frishman, 1991). One of Frishman's students at Bayero University retraced the steps of Paul Lubeck from a decade earlier (Lubeck, 1975) trying to document the number of Hausa women in factory jobs in the new industrial estates just outside the city. None were to be found. At the same time, students from Ahmadu Bello University "surveyed" the streets of Kano trying to measure income produced by indigenous firms. Frishman admitted that their procedures were haphazard and their data questionable (Frishman, 1991, p. 199). Nonetheless, he reported that of the 1,457 firms recorded, sixteen (or 1.1 percent) were owned by Hausa women. Of these sixteen, only three were located inside the city walls. All the women involved in all sixteen firms were older, divorced, barren, or widowed.

Although there are a few women employees in the factories of northern Nigeria, virtually none of them are Hausa. One postmenopausal woman in Schildkrout's study in the 1980s had shocked her family by announcing that she wanted to work in a factory for a set wage. She died, however, before she could carry out her plan. As in the rest of West Africa, unskilled labor positions are largely reserved for men. Educated women, who for lack of professional education or other qualifications cannot work as administrators, managers, teachers, pharmacists, or doctors, generally do engage in income-generating activity from behind the walls of seclusion. They do not hold positions thought of as "female," such as clerks or nurses, because contact with the general public is required. As was indicated in Chapter 4, university-educated women will work in higher-level civil service jobs or as teachers or other high-level professionals if their husbands give them permission to do so and if the requirements of their employment do not require contact with the general public. Otherwise, they do not work in the public sector. Secondary school–educated women generally do not work outside the home, and elementary level–educated and illiterate girls generally do not work in the wage-labor sector at all.

Clearly the impact of religion on the economic activities of women is very different in northern Nigeria than it is in most of West Africa. Pellow has suggested, on the basis of a very small case study in Ghana, that Hausa women's lives are very different outside Nigeria—their economic activities elsewhere are not so different from those of women around them in the host country (Pellow, 1991).

National statistics are not useful in looking at the employment of Muslim women in Nigeria. In fact, such statistics do not differentiate between Muslim and Christian women. The overall pattern for Nigerian women is quite like the one that emerges in other countries, but such statistics do not record religion. We know from microstudies conducted in the major northern (Islamic) cities that women do not work at all in the sectors for which statistics are gathered (Hill, 1969, 1972; M. G. Smith, 1955; Mary Smith, 1981; Simmons, 1976; Pittin, 1976, 1979; Remy, 1975; Jackson, 1978; Schildkrout, 1979, 1982, 1983; Coles, 1983; C. Martin, 1983; Knipp, 1987). The reason, of course, is seclusion. Women are secluded because Muslim northern Nigerians believe this to be the teaching of Islam. Hence, here religion is the fundamental and critical variable.

Why is religion such a different variable in Nigeria than in most other West African cases, including settings (Ghana) where Hausa immigrants live and work? Several factors seem to suggest themselves. First of all, until recently Muslims were a minority in Nigeria and were particularly sensitive to the disadvantages they suffered in the modern sectors of the state, disadvantages largely resulting from educational differentials among the various regions of the country. As explained in Chapter 4, the exclusion of Christian missionaries from the Islamic North left that region cut off from the educational opportunities they offered. The northern elites constantly extolled the superiority of Islamic versus Western (Christian) education and, by implication, the superiority of Islam over other religions. Hence, Islamic consciousness is much greater here than in countries such as Senegal, which is 95 percent Islamic. The second explanation flows from this fact: In Nigeria, Islamic law is critically important in defining and defending the religion, and Islamic law is inherently conservative.

Another factor that might be relevant is the existence in many West African countries of a class of Westernized Africans educated and socialized in European customs and influential in the politics and society of the colonizer. In the French colonies there was even a small class of "assimilated" Africans who held French citizenship. The British in Nigeria, in contrast, protected the traditional rulers from metropolitan influences. No Muslim northern Nigerian ever aspired to become "English," nor was such a thing ever expected to be possible. Hence, there is a fundamental religious/national consciousness in Nigeria that appears to be lacking in Senegal and other West African cases.

Limited educational opportunities and the fact that a very small percentage of women (less than 1 percent) are now graduating from the universities of northern Nigeria have made it possible for a few young women to have high-level careers in the wage sector as teachers, midwives, or even as commentators on radio or television. But in the Islamic sections of Nigeria, women must have the permission of their husbands to work, so any look at national statistics that records entry-level information for the various sectors is irrelevant. Islamic women only work when their husbands give permission, and in most cases positions are offered through the husbands's contacts, not through a woman's own efforts.

Agriculture

We cannot compare women in agriculture in northern Nigeria to those in the rest of West Africa because Hausa women have not been significantly involved in farming in Nigeria in over half a century. Scholars have speculated that the reason Hausa women do not work on farms is related to the fact that this was an area in which the use of slaves predominated before the British arrived (M. G. Smith, 1959). Women who were secluded no longer had to work in the fields. Hence, one consequence of the end of slavery and the seclusion of women is that female labor disappeared from what became the agricultural sector. To this day, very few Hausa women are involved in either small- or large-scale agricultural activities.

The most common occupation for women is the preparation of food items for sale by young girls hawking on the roadsides, often accompanied by their grandmothers or other postmenopausal women. The trade in ready-to-eat food is an important component of both rural and urban household earning and spending patterns. In a survey of 294 women (all of whose husbands were primarily farmers) in the village of Malumfashi in Kano State, 89 percent were engaged in income-earning activity, but not one of them was engaged in farming. However, 36 percent cooked and sold food for a major meal, 12 percent cooked snacks, 16 percent were involved in some other sort of food processing (i.e., pounding grain or yams, shelling peanuts, making bread, removing the hull from rice, or pounding for other women), and 64 percent were involved in some sort of food preparation. In all cases, monthly earnings were low.

Table 5.2   Incomes of Secluded Women in Malumfashi

	Number of Women	Percent of Women	Average Monthly Income (N)
Preparing a main dish for immediate sale	107	36.39	10
Preparing snacks (bean cakes, kake)	36	12.24	5
Other food processing	47	15.98	5
Trading	30	10.20	4
Spinning, cap making, embroidery	33	11.22	4
Weaving and mat making	10	3.40	5
Other	2	.06	7
None	29	9.86	0
TOTAL	294	99.35	5

Source: Based on Callaway, 1987, p. 74.
Note: The minimum wage in Nigeria in 1982, when this research was conducted, was N150.00 ($213.00) per month, or N1,800.00 per year.

In September 1987, the Nigerian military government announced the Better Life Program for Rural Women with the aim of "raising the status of Nigerian rural women by stimulating, mobilizing and empowering their income generating creativities" (*The New Nigerian,* September 20, 1991, p. 1). The president's wife, Maryam Babangida, is the chairperson of the program. Nigeria has allocated N5,000,000 (naira) to this effort, establishing a People's Bank and providing seed money for women's cooperatives and income-earning schemes. By October 1991, 7,635 cooperatives, 997 cottage industries, 1,751 new farms and gardens, 487 new shops, 419 women's centers, and 163 welfare programs had been established nation-wide under the aegis of the Better Life Program (Bilkisu Yusuf, *Citizen Magazine,* October 28, 1991, p. 7). In Haska, a village in Kano State, women with small loans from the People's Bank were able to establish three cooperative organizations, one each for condiment farming, ground-nut oil producing, and pottery making. The women farmers had access to a regular supply of fertilizers and improved seeds, and the potters bene-fited from a loan to purchase a glazing machine and build a kiln. The groundnut oil producers bought an oil pressing machine, which relieved them of the process of hand-squeezing the oil (*The Democrat,* November 28, 1991, p. 3). The problem, of course, is that the market for the women's products is limited because of the great financial dislocations caused by Nigeria's program of structural adjustment.

Each of the Nigerian federal states has undertaken a Better Life Pro-gram for Rural Women. In Kano State, each of the forty-six local govern-ment areas has established such a program. Before Kano's Better Life Pro-gram took off in 1988, the state had only one women's cooperative. By 1990, with help from loans provide by the People's Bank, there were seventy-two registered cooperative groups. A "corner shop" had been es-tablished in Kano City to sell the products of the cooperatives, but it, too, was having difficulty developing a market for the products. Because women have not farmed for a long time in Kano State, they do not have access to the land and must grow their staple food crops within the walls of their compounds. Thus, the state's Better Life central committee re-quested that each of the forty-six local government areas set aside land on which only women could work. The Better Life central committee has ear-marked N45,000 to be used by women for farming when the land is set aside, and it has requested that the Ministry of Agriculture and Rural De-velopment send extension staff to train women in modern farming meth-ods. Each women's center is expected to offer programs in vegetable gar-dening, animal husbandry, food and nutrition, food packaging and preservation, literacy, and, of course, Islamic Religious Knowledge.

In 1990 N100,000 had been given out to women's groups and indi-viduals under the Better Life Soft Loan Scheme. By 1992 the women had begun repaying their loans on schedule, although none of the groups had yet turned a profit. Additionally, each of the local government areas was given the sum of N5,000 to disburse to women for small-scale production. Approximately 200 individual women entrepreneurs benefited. In the city of Kano, 700 women had received loans from the People's Bank, which represented about 60 percent of the loans distributed. The women's repay-ment was deemed "absolutely satisfactory" (Annual Report: Better Life Program in Kano State. 1991, pp. 1–10). Finally, the Better Life Program in Kano State has assisted in mass immunization of children and partici-pated in nine nutrition workshops and in workshops seeking to deal with the problems associated with "constant childbirth, early marriages, neo-natal deaths and so on."

It is not known whether or not the Better Life Program will survive the military government and be supported by the civilian government due to assume power in Nigeria by the end of 1993. But the program clearly has made significant inroads, and rural women all over the country have been encouraged to raise their sights and aspire to diversify and increase their productivity. It is too early to tell whether or not these efforts will be more successful than others to involve women in the development process, but the national effort to provide resources and credit to rural women is definitely raising national consciousness about the role of women in the economy and lifting the standards of health and nutrition in the country-side. As a part of the Better Life Program, women's centers have been of-fering instruction in credit, record keeping, marketing, sewing, and health and nutrition. The endorsement of the program by leading religious lead-ers as well as by public officials has given it visibility and legitimacy. To date, Muslim leaders have lauded its efforts to improve the quality of life for rural women and children.

The Informal Sector

Whereas in some other West African countries, large surveys and national statistics are available to provide information on the economic situation of women, in northern Nigeria we must rely on micro studies for data on women's economic activities in the informal sector. It is clear that most women work in the nonwage, or informal, sector in northern Nigeria, as indeed they do in most countries of the Third World. Several microstud-ies in recent years have sought to document the nature and structure of such work, as well as the income generated (See Hill, 1969, 1972; M. G. Smith, 1959; Mary Smith, 1981; Simmons, 1975, 1976; Schildkrout, 1978, 1979, 1982, 1983; Coles, 1983, 1991; C. Martin, 1983; Knipp, 1987).

Women play a particularly crucial role in the urban economy of most African countries, and northern Nigerian women are no exception. How-ever, they are constrained in their degree of participation and choice of ac-tivity by the teachings of Islam. Women are engaged almost entirely in those things that may be seen essentially as extensions of their normal household activities: preparing and selling cooked food, doing laundry, sewing, hairdressing, taking care of children, weaving straw floormats, pounding grain, chopping up ingredients for each other, or making char-coal or incense. Older women may develop a small-scale trade in such items as soap, kola nuts, or cloth; a few will be midwives. Wealthier women may engage in the trade of jewelry, shoes, or imported wax prints. In all cases, though, the activity is essentially carried on from behind the walls of seclusion.

Because income-generating labor is often hard to distinguish from regular domestic (unpaid) labor, precise studies are problematic. Many scholars have drawn attention to the linkages between productive and domestic/household labor (Edholm, Harris, Young, 1977; Beneria, 1982; Beneria and Sen, 1992). Qualitative analysis of this type of work is difficult. Census data is either lacking or inaccurate, and economic statistics focus on the formal sector and do not take account of income-generating activities that are conducted primarily in the home (Fapohunda, 1978; Beneria, 1982). This omission produces inaccurate views of women's work.

Only through microstudies such as those carried out by Enid Schildkrout and Polly Hill in the 1970s or Renee Pitten and Catharine Coles in the 1980s can we get a handle on investment and profit. Polly Hill lived in a Hausa village for a year, collecting day-to-day data on income-earning investment and activity. Enid Schildkrout lived in Kano and kept daily diaries on the activities of eighty-nine women in two wards of the city over a two-year period. Schildkrout demonstrated that within the informal sector there were differences in the types of income-generating activities in which women engage. These differences reflected status, albeit status determined by the standing of the woman's husband. They also reflected a long history of male occupational specialization within the two wards, and this male specialization was mirrored in the organization of women's work (Schildkrout, 1979, 1981).

Kurawa, located immediately behind the Kano Central Mosque and the emir's palace, traditionally was the home of learned men and *mallams*. Today, most of the men living in Kurawa are civil servants working for state and local governments, teachers, Islamic judges, or *mallams*. Women live in seclusion, and most engage in embroidery and small-scale trade in gold and cloth to earn incomes of their own (see Table 5.3). Most young girls attend both Western or English-speaking schools, as well as the traditional Quranic schools. Sending girls to school is a recent development, but the "learned men" here point out that the new emphasis on education for girls in fact reflects Islamic values. Usman dan Fodio, the leader of the Fulani *jihad,* stressed the importance of Quranic education for all women. Today, Shehu dan Fodio's concern for appropriate education for girls provides a rationale for accepting the Western model as consistent with the ideals of Islam. Among elite families in Kano City, educated girls are becoming an indicator of high status. However, as Schildkrout has explained in detail elsewhere, because girls are now in school, women have less help in their income-generating work (Schildkrout, 1979, 1980, 1981, 1982). Girls are now available only a few hours a day to go shopping or to deliver materials and goods to customers for their mothers. Women in Kurawa engage in work for which there is increasingly low return, and although they fret about their small profits, they do not yet think in terms of alternative strategies. Their main concern is to generate funds for an appropriate dowry for their daughters, and increasingly, a high level of education is seen as a component of dowry. Therefore, it is now a wife's responsibility to raise enough to educate her daughters.

Table 5.3   Occupations and Incomes of Secluded Women in Kurawa

Occupation	Number of Women	Percent of Women	Average Monthly Income (N)
None	4	7.5	0
Sewing men's caps	9	16.98	5.80
Knitting, embroidery	4	7.50	5.00
Machine sewing	3	5.66	5.00
Hair plaiting	2	3.77	5.00
Selling cooked food (without children hawking)	5	9.43	11.25
Selling cooked food (with children hawking)	8	15.09	12.81
Trade in gold	10	18.86	6.80
Trade in cloth	8	15.09	5.50
TOTAL	53	99.88	6.35

Source: Based on Callaway, 1987, p. 71.
Note: Naira (N) = $1.42

Kofar Mazugal is one of the oldest wards in the city of Kano, predating the settlements in Kurawa by several centuries. It is the home of small traders, butchers, and other men of traditionally lower social/economic status. Trade continues to be the principal occupation of men in Kofar Mazugal, although there are a few who now work at the lower levels of government or who have branched out into businesses of their own, such as minor construction or contracting. Women here are almost exclusively engaged in the preparation of cooked food. They are dependent on female children to shop for ingredients for them and to sell their products from house to house or on the streets. Many fewer girls go to school here than in Kuwara, but the women earn more from their food enterprises than do the women in Kurawa from their embroidery and sewing (Table 5.4).

Data collected by Hill in 1977 and Callaway's students in 1982 suggests that in rural areas there is little relationship between the scale of a woman's trade and the economic (not social) standing of her husband. In

Table 5.4 Occupations and Incomes of Secluded Women in Kofar Mazugal

Occupation	Number of Women	Percent of Women	Average Monthly Income (N)
None	0	0	0
Sewing men's caps	6	17	5.80
Hair plaiting and sewing caps	2	6	9.50
Machine sewing	3	9	7.50
Pounding grain	2	6	7.50
Selling cooked food (without children hawking)	3	9	14.00
Selling cooked food (with children hawking)	19	54	25.66
TOTAL	35	101	17.74

Source: Schildkrout, 1981, p. 92; and Callaway, 1987, p. 72.
Note: Naira (N) = $1.42

the city this was not so clearly the case, as the work of Schildkrout indicates. Women in Kurawa married to men of higher status tended to engage in trade yielding smaller incomes; women in Kofar Mazugal earned nearly three times as much from their trade in cooked foods. In the villages, however, there was little difference in type of work or income level between wives of richer husbands and wives of poorer ones.

The food distribution network is indicative of the complexity of Hausa social patterns and economic networks among women. The case of a seventy-five-year-old widow is not unusual. She lives alone in her late husband's house and receives food daily from the wife of a married son who lives nearby, from her late husband's two brothers' wives, and from a married daughter. Whatever food she doesn't eat or redistribute to others around her she sells in order to have a small income for herself. She is not technically a producer, and she is not economically self-sufficient, but she does not think of herself as living in a state of dependency, either. She expects food to be sent to her, and it is accepted that she will sell some of it in order to earn the money she might need for other essentials (Callaway, 1987).

This rather involved pattern is repeated, with variations, in most families. Traditionally, husbands provide an allowance to wives for the purchase of food and household essentials. Men eat three meals a day, but hardly any women actually cook three meals a day for their families. They do, however, spend the day cooking, but most of this food will be sold.

Men will eat their main meal at home but will generally purchase snacks from street vendors throughout the day. In this way, men support their wives' entrepreneurial activities (Schildkrout, 1982).

The practice of wife seclusion assumes that the household is a unit of consumption, not production, and that women are dependent consumers. However, women are in fact independent producers who generate income of their own by diverting cash provided by men for domestic consumption into domestic production. The separation between men's and women's incomes and the pattern of monetary flow between them presents yet another instance in which relationships between men and women are more complicated than they may at first appear.

The overall impact of women on the Kano economy is substantial. Frishman estimated that over 100,000 women were economically active in the five wards of the city in which he worked in 1987 and that the average income was N135 (Frishman, 1991, p. 198). By comparison, the average salary for step one on the civil service scale for men was N161. Women's N135 was about one-third of total family income and quite significant in determining the family's standard of living. The poverty level in Nigeria in 1985 was set at N310. In Kano, 52 to 67 percent of the population was classified as below the poverty level (Frishman, 1991, p. 198). Seventy percent of the wage-earning male labor force in Kano was employed in the lowest grades, or SSI sector, earning income in the poverty category. If 100,000 secluded women earned N135, their combined income would be N13.5 million, which, combined with the income of non-Hausa women working in the markets or other sectors, makes women's earnings comparable to the total industrial wage bill in Kano (Frishman, 1991, p. 203). Clearly, women's hidden economic activity was sustaining families. Their roles are crucial and indispensable to the urban economy and must be taken into account in developing an appropriate economic strategy for growth and development.

In both rural and urban areas, a girl's socialization into the world of work begins early. As noted in Chapter 3, all girls are given child-care responsibilities early in life. From age five or six they begin to receive gradually increasing responsibilities; they shop, run errands, deliver messages, help in the preparation of food, and in many homes sell. Thus, girls learn early to be involved in economic activity, and they learn that their world is separate from that of men.

As more girls go to school and the level of their education rises, some girls may begin to enter professions. The first northern Hausa Muslim woman to go to medical school began her internship in 1983. As more women undertake such careers, their incomes will more overtly help support the family. However, the marriage ethic is so strong that it is unlikely women will see having incomes of their own as a means to independence outside of marriage. It may be, however, that substantial incomes for women may create the foundations for change in the nature of marriage relationships. Government policies and Islamic teachings that encourage education for women may prove more revolutionary in the context of Islam than overt challenges to it.

Structural change may be occurring already. As more and more children spend more and more time in school, they are less available to help their mothers in income-earning activities. Although some women can afford the drop in income this occasions, others may be forced out into the visible economy. Such change would indeed be revolutionary in this culture.

Education may thus be creating new expectations about marriage and work that may require changes in the division of labor by age and sex and a consequent change in expectations within the family. This transformation will not occur by direct challenge to Islam, and women will continue to play economic roles that generate incomes for the support of the family while giving lip service to their dependence on men. However, there is likely to continue to be a self-limiting quality to women's economic activities. Women's work remains fitted around their domestic roles. Seclusion and physical separation from men has underscored economic separation. Some version of seclusion is likely to endure, and this will restrict the nature of women's work basically to small-scale house-based trade. But it is also true that by not cooking three meals a day for household consumption, women have set a precedent for freeing themselves from household routines in order to engage in productive and paid activity. And however limited their incomes, they are an important part of the cash economy.

Clearly, throughout West Africa, education is the crucial variable in determining which women work and what they do. Without education, women cannot work in the salaried sector. Ten years ago, university students at a northern Nigerian university indicated that they overwhelmingly endorsed education for their daughters, although only 20 percent of the male students expected them to continue to university, whereas 87 percent of the female students expected their daughters to continue and, with their husband's consent, to work (see Table 5.5).

In Hausa society, overt competition between men and women is unacceptable, and their worlds seldom if ever intersect. Women have their own exclusive sphere within seclusion and have relative autonomy so long as they stay within it. Financial success does afford some security and a modicum of freedom and decisionmaking power, but such independence is severely limited, and not only because of the restrictions that frame the institution of marriage per se. Because 75 percent of Hausa women will divorce, and because the average number of marriages per woman is three (Saunders, 1978), women are essentially transients in the homes of their husbands. Their economic security is based on their own efforts, but their economic autonomy is severely limited by the cultural beliefs about marriage, which are reinforced by religion.

Table 5.5   Education and Marriage

Answers

Question	Husband alone		Husband and wife together		The wife alone		The girl herself		The girl and her parents		The girl and her husband-to-be	
	M	F	M	F	M	F	M	F	M	F	M	F
1	201	28	20	10	0	0	6	5	8	15	8	7
2	115	83	89	15	0	0	0	0	329	15	39	18
3	91	2	85	2	0	0	6	21	225	82	107	7
4	118	20	325	20	99	19	0	5	0	0	30	50

Source: Survey by Barbara Callaway, 1983.
Notes:
Questions:
1. Who should decide who a daughter should marry?
2. Who should decide when a daughter should marry?
3. Who should decide to what level a girl will be educated?
4. Who should decide whether a wife will work?
N = 686 (F = 114, M = 572); does not account for "other" or no answer

Nonetheless, changes in the structure of women's economic activity have taken place. Although such changes do not in and of themselves negate the constraints of a patriarchal society buttressed by conservative Islam, they do suggest the potential for further alteration in the nature of submission, seclusion, and economic opportunity open to women.

Income-generating activities are almost always initiated by women themselves. As women's skills, interests, and resources change with increased education, so may the things they do to earn income. It is already clear that over the course of their lifetime, Hausa women change occupations many times. As women develop their skills and abilities, as they acquire training through the Better Life Program, from the Centers for Mass Education, or in secondary schools and universities, they will be better equipped to respond to economic change. Already, Hausa women are beginning to work as teachers, as doctors, in state ministries, in the civil service, and in other wage positions (C. Martin, 1992), albeit in small numbers. We must be careful lest our cultural blinders obscure for us the tremendous changes that can take place—and are taking place—within an Islamic culture.

Islamic writing on the subject of sex roles often stresses "complementarity," which essentially means that women obey and serve men and perform all domestic tasks. Therefore, working Hausa Muslim women are finding themselves concerned with the same problems as Western women—child-care arrangements and the pressure of the double day in the workplace and at home. The difference in northern Nigeria is that women do not feel that confronting men to discuss a different allocation of responsibilities in the home is a legitimate option. Still, choices are expanding, even if most women cannot yet take advantage of them. It is increasingly accepted that girls should be educated; new employment opportunities are opening up; women can vote; and there are Islamic women's activists calling for reforms. Radio and television are expanding awareness, and books and magazines are increasingly available, all of which present alternative ways of life. The Better Life Program is creating possibilities for greater income capability.

To predict that change in economic roles for women will be slow is not to deny that change will occur. The interplay between these pressures and entrenched cultural norms will often be contradictory and unpredictable. Hausa mores, Islamic teachings, men's attitudes, and the association of women's liberation with Westernization circumscribe the dimension of possible change. The cognitive and emotional dissonance created by the expansion of education on the one hand and strong, culturally imposed norms of subservience on the other leaves an opening for an Islamic women's movement to tap a wellspring of support, and dramatic changes could occur. In fact, that time may be now.

SENEGALESE WOMEN

It might be argued that northern Nigeria is unique because of its relative isolation from modernizing currents in other Islamic cultures and because strictures on personal behavior called for in *Sharia* law are actually observed there. Hausa women are only gradually emerging from seclusion and are only beginning to assert some level of equality and independence. They are only now, and only at the upper status levels, entering the wage labor sector. They are virtually excluded from commercial agriculture, and their enormous contributions in the informal sector in the urban areas are still invisible because women are unseen and unheard publicly. No other predominantly Muslim country in West Africa presents quite this situation.

Between the case of Senegal on one end of the spectrum (which we will discuss below) and the case of northern Nigeria on the other, a wide range of conditions prevail that influence the role of Muslim women in the economy. In Chad, for example, which is a military state ruled by Muslims (but not governed according to Islamic law), few women are to be found in any paid jobs—but then, neither are men. The proportion of women in wage-paying jobs is less there than in Senegal, but this situation seems more related to a lack of development than to religious prohibition. Women are not secluded. Indeed, one observer has suggested that Islamic women in Chad are in a better position than their non-Islamic sisters because Islamic law protects certain rights for them, including the right to whatever money they earn, the right of inheritance, and the right to keep and spend their bride price (interview, William Foltz, 1992).

A study of Niger in 1991, as another example, shows a substantially lower development of small-scale enterprises nationwide than in Senegal and a markedly smaller proportion of women in them (interview, Richard Vengroff, 1991). Furthermore, there are many fewer women in either the public or the private sector holding wage positions. In Mali there is somewhat better representation of women, but a substantially lower proportion of them have entered the job market or developed small-scale enterprises than have men. Contrasts between Mali and Zaire have led one observer to attribute the slow development of small enterprises and the low involvement of women at least partially to the restrictive influence of Islam (Prindle, 1991). Yet that conclusion must be tempered after we analyze the case of Senegal.

The Wage Sector

Seventy-four percent of those in the employed category in Senegal are male. Women constitute 32 percent of the unemployed (RPGH, 1988, Table V.1). Those that do have jobs work in private industry and in government jobs, but they are substantially fewer in number and preponderantly in lower-status positions (for a fuller discussion of women in the wage force in Senegal, see Creevey, 1993, Chapter 4). Table 5.6 below illustrates women's participation in the major enterprises of the private sector.

Close examination of this table shows a curious twist, echoing the situation in northern Nigeria. Rather than entering as laborers, skilled or unskilled, it seems that women are more able to compete for upper-level jobs (which, of course, are fewer in number than worker positions). Women have their best representation at the second- and third-position levels in private industry as administrators, managers, secretaries, and clerical workers. Unskilled labor positions are filled by men, which is consistent with the picture presented above of the majority population in West Africa, where women without education or training are relegated to agriculture, the informal sector, or both.

Table 5.7 illustrates the improving job situation for women in Senegal by comparing the percentage of women versus men at every job level in service, industry, building, and commerce positions in 1982 and 1987. The table indicates an overall growth in the number and proportion of women in most categories except seasonal work. The highest growth was in the upper cadres and at the management and administration (and secretarial)

levels. The percentage of women in skilled and unskilled labor actually decreased. In all, the data indicate a net improvement for women. Seasonal
positions are the most marginal in the economy, and worker positions are
the most poorly paid of the ranked jobs. Women therefore not only have
increased their proportions of the job market but also have bettered their
overall position in it. They remain, however, a small proportion of those
employed.

Many of those employed in Senegal are not to be found in the private
sector. The government is a major employer, especially in the urban regions. Table 5.8 adds information to the employment pattern by looking at
public sector employees. In all, 68,537 people, or 3 percent of the total
work force, are government workers. The proportion is substantially
higher in Dakar, where 12 percent of those employed work for the government. Women are 15 percent of the government employees nationwide.

In the health and education ministries, women are often named as un-
derministers or even ministers because of their alleged "female" nurturing
attributes. They are employed in significantly lower proportions in the
armed forces, that traditional male preserve, and in the powerful ministries
of the economy and the interior. (For information on the position of
women by rank, see Chapter 6.) Perhaps more significant is the fact that
although women are still a minority in *all* ministries, including health and
education, they have markedly increased their proportion throughout the
civil service. At independence thirty-two years ago, there were no women
employed by the government of Senegal except foreigners working as secretaries and technical assistants.

The representation of women in the civil service is very similar to
their presence in the private sector. Only in the two "female" ministries
are women significantly better represented than in the private sector, and
this is not true if we only consider the private sector jobs traditionally construed as female, such as service and hotel or restaurant employment. The
result of this comparison is somewhat surprising; after all, government
policy advocates hiring women, whereas no such policy guides private em-
ployers. However, government interest in increasing female representation
is a very recent development. Only the annual reports of the last five years
—since the end of the UN Decade for Women—show this tendency. Moreover, the government does do better in comparison with overall private sector employment—15 percent of its labor force is female, whereas only 7 percent of the combined private sector labor force is made up of women.

Assuming that the trend to increasing numbers of women will continue and perhaps even accelerate in both civil service and private sector
positions, the question remains as to what factors increase the likelihood
of individual women in Senegal getting these jobs? The first, most obvious
factor seems to be education. Women do much better relative to men in
getting jobs at the higher positions where education above primary school

Table 5.6 Women in the Private Sector in 1987
Percent Female Among Senegalese Employees

Position	Textiles		Industry (gen)		Building		Commerce (lg)		Commerce (sm)	
	Total	Percent F	Total	Percent F	Total	Percent F	Total	Percent F	Total	Percent F
Manager Director	58	7	283	4	71	4	125	6	85	27
Technical/ Administrative	108	>1	688	7	83	4	332	5	168	16
Clerical	444	5	3,837	5	547	10	1,126	11	515	19
Workers	3,740	2	8,393	4	2,336	5	2,343	9	1,642	15
Total	4,350	2	13,201	5	3,037	6	3,926	9	2,410	16

Position	Transportation/ Telecommunications		Service		Hotel Restaurant		All enterprises General	
	Total	Percent F	Total	Percent F	Total	Percent F	Total	Percent F
Manager Director	271	4	184	7	94	13	1,355	7
Technical/ Administrative	1,107	8	280	21	193	21	3,356	9
Clerical	4,510	6	651	26	918	17	14,718	10
Workers	4,061	5	3,316	10	1,603	12	39,260	7
Total	9,949	6	4,431	13	2,808	14	58,689	8

Source: Situation Economique, 1988, pp. 29–37.

Table 5.7   Proportion of Women in the Private Sector
(Percentage by Rank, 1982 and 1987)

| Sector/ | 1982 | | 1987 | | Ratio |
Rank	Total Employees	Percentage Female	Total Employees	Percentage Female	1987:1982 (1982 = 100)
INDUSTRY					
Permanent	31,940	6	32,109	7	166
Manager	393	3	525	4	135
Technical/					
Administrative	1,236	4	1,193	6	139
Clerical	6,727	4	6,451	10	218
Workers	23,584	7	23,940	7	—
Seasonal	9,678	3	14,505	11	380
BUILDING					
Permanent	6,245	1	3,037	6	0
Manager	42	0	71	4	—
Technical/					
Administrative	88	3	83	4	106
Clerical	564	5	547	10	200
Workers	5,551	1	2,336	5	460
Seasonal	2,695	<1	3,060	0.0	0
COMMERCE					
Permanent	6,162	9	6,335	12	130
Manager	114	5	210	15	279
Technical/					
Administrative	341	7	500	8	115
Clerical	1,186	12	1,641	14	117
Workers	4,521	9	3,984	11	133
Seasonal	912	1	872	4	373
SERVICE					
Permanent	12,592	7	17,208	9	135
Manager	193	5	549	6	123
Technical/					
Administrative	474	11	1,580	12	100
Clerical	2,375	13	6,079	10	78
Workers	9,550	5	9,000	8	163
Seasonal	1,602	3	4,012	2	89

Source: USAID 1991, Table IV.6

Table 5.8   Women in Government Service
              (Five Largest Ministries)

Position	Army		Interior		Economy/ Finance		Education		Health	
	No.	Percent	No.	Percent	No.	Percent	No.	Percent	No.	Percent
Total	14,021	>1	8,749	4	4,262	13	21,222	24	5,894	35

Source: DTAI/MEF, 1989.

is required. This fact does not mean that the more education a woman gets, the better she will do in a competition with her male peers for positions; top-level positions still seem to be male dominated. It is likely that, as happens in other countries, the return on each year of schooling for a woman will be less than for a man in terms of jobs acquired, although the statistics presented here cannot prove this supposition.

The 1991 Senegal Survey supports the contention that education is the best predictor of economic success for women. Women with education were significantly more likely to get a wage-paying job than women without. Conversely, almost half of all women with no education reported that their income came from agriculture or the informal sector, and few had wage-paying jobs (see Creevey, 1993, pp. 130–132). Level of income (which of course is itself strongly related to type of job) was also determined by education: Women with no education were almost all in the lowest income group (86 percent). Women who are educated had a plurality among those in the highest income group (41 percent), followed by a smaller group (35 percent) in the middle category.

Although education is strongly significant in determining a woman's chances of getting a better-paying job and moving out of the traditional sector in Senegal, other variables also have an impact. Certainly residence is important. National statistics show that the highest concentration of the highest-paying positions is in Dakar, although only 15 percent of the wage-earning population is in this region. They also show that Dakar has the highest level of unemployment (30 percent), followed by the next largest urban region, St Louis, with 16 percent. No other region has more than 9 percent unemployment, but this is explained by the relatively low numbers seeking jobs in the largely rural/agricultural regions.

Table 5.9 shows the national distribution of salaried employees according to their sex and level of position. Domestic workers are excluded. What is particularly interesting in this table is that although more women find jobs in the Dakar region, at all levels, than anywhere else, there does not seem to be any strong evidence that if a job were available one would be more likely to get it in Dakar than in any other region. Zones more remote from the modern urban nexus of Dakar might be expected to be more traditional in their attitudes. Or, contrarily, the region in which the Dyola live might be expected to be more liberal than any region but Dakar in its employment of women, as Dyola women are apparently more independent (see Chapter 4). However, neither hypothesis is borne out by this table. There is no obvious pattern of discrimination against women by region in the data. Apparently those who set up modern companies and employ salaried workers share the same, or more or less the same, policies toward female employment.

The 1991 Senegal Survey reinforces the importance of residence in finding a salaried job. Women living in Dakar are significantly more likely (71 percent) than women in other regions to hold a salaried job and least likely to be in agriculture, whereas women in the most remote zones are unlikely to hold salaried jobs and most likely to be engaged in the agricultural sector. Residence also related directly to income level. Women in Dakar were most likely to earn above $1,333 a year (more than 61 percent did so) and least likely to fall in the lowest income group, whereas more than 92 percent of those in the most remote zones were earning less than $333 a year (see Creevey, 1993, Chapter 4).

Ethnic origin might also be expected to affect what jobs women fill. The Wolof, as the largest ethnic group located in the central zones of Senegal, may be expected to dominate salaried positions. Differences among groups in traditional definitions of women's work roles also might cause adaptation to the modern job market to take place at different rates or even predict different types of positions taken. The results of the survey do in fact show ethnic variation for the entire national sample. Wolof and Dyola women were more likely than Serer or Tukulor (or Peuhl) women to hold a salaried job. There was a slightly weaker relationship between ethnic group and income: Wolof women earned higher incomes than any other group, especially Serer or Tukulor/Peuhl women.

Table 5.10 shows the distribution of Wolof and other ethnic groups in Dakar, the distribution in the Dakar sample, and the survey sample distribution in regard to whether or not their revenue was primarily derived from a salaried position, their income levels, the type job they held, and the position in the job hierarchy they occupied.

The Wolof are disproportionately represented in the sample but they do not dominate the high-level positions or the high-income category. They do have a significantly different pattern, however. The Wolof are more likely than members of any other ethnic group to be found in salaried positions. They are least likely to be involved in agriculture, but in this they match all other groups, for whom—not surprisingly in this urban zone —agriculture is not a common major source of revenue. Wolof women are

Table 5.9   Distribution of Private Sector Salaried Jobs
             Percentage Female by Level and by Region

Region	Executives		Skilled Workers		Unskilled Workers		Apprentices	
	Total	Percent Female	Total	Percent Female	Total	Percent Female	Total	Percent Female
Dakar	8,803	11	9,550	13	4,787	5	30	0
Ziguinchor	541	7	704	13	473	3	29	0
Diourbel	353	2	521	5	391	1	0	—
St Louis	1,919	7	2,333	2	5,211	1	0	—
Tambacounda	28	21	502	1	190	0	0	—
Kaolack	967	11	869	7	861	1	12	42
Louga	268	3	114	9	48	8	11	0
Fatick	147	5	224	6	86	13	0	—
Kolda	219	1	439	1	332	0	0	—
Thies	1,783	7	1,588	7	740	6	0	—
Senegal	15,228	9	16,853	10	13,119	3	82	6

Source: RGPH 1988.

significantly less likely than women of other groups to rely on the informal sector. In regard to income and level of position, however, there is not a significant difference between Wolof women and women of other ethnic groups. One possible explanation might be that skilled women from other ethnic groups and not originally from the Dakar region might have migrated in for specific jobs and therefore might have more luck than some of the untrained Wolof women born in the zone. Interestingly enough, however, the Wolof and Tukulor women, who hold the higher-level positions, are equally likely to have been born in Dakar (75 percent and 76 percent, respectively). The Serer and Dyola women are more likely to be migrants than they are to be originally born in Dakar (63 percent and 67 percent, respectively). This distribution suggests that the latecomers are moving into the lowest-salaried positions—as domestics, in most cases. Wolof women in Dakar, then, do not seem to have a monopoly on economic privilege. They are not disproportionately favored in jobs or level of position. Wolof and Tukulor women, however, do seem better off in the Dakar job market than do Serer or Dyola women. Looking at the results of the national sample and the Dakar subgroup together suggests that ethnicity is much less significant than residence in determining job status. The

Wolof are the majority group in the Dakar region; the greater likelihood of a Wolof woman's holding a salaried job is doubtless a reflection of where they live rather than of some cultural distinction between them and other groups.

The impact of religion on the economic position of Senegalese women appears to be very weak from the results of this survey. Religion does not significantly relate to whether or not a woman has a salaried job, what level of income she reports, the type of salaried job she holds (in the public or private sector), nor the level of her position. The data show that a smaller proportion of Catholics than Muslims are in agriculture. They also show a larger proportion of Catholics in the highest income group, but these results are not significant and explain little of the variation (see Creevey, 1993, Chapter 4). Only when the subsample from Dakar is analyzed does any significant correlation emerge. Here there is still no significant relationship between religion and either income or type of job. However, religion does impact the level of position for salaried workers. A larger percentage of Catholics than Muslims falls into the highest management category (17 percent as opposed to 2 percent) and the workers group (33 percent as opposed to 19 percent), whereas Muslims are most likely to be secretaries (55 percent as opposed to 28 percent). Table 5.11 shows the distribution of women by religion in Dakar according to national statistics and the 1991 survey results, indicating the percentage of people in each religious group that gain their major source of revenue from a salaried job, agriculture, or the informal sector, and the percentage of each found in every level of position of those in salaried jobs.

Being Muslim (as opposed to Christian) in Senegal does not seem to relegate one to worse jobs in either the salaried or nonsalaried areas. Nor does it imply a lower income. In the Dakar area, Catholics are in the highest- and lowest-paid positions, which may be as well explained by ethnic as by religious factors. The Dyola and Serer are more likely to be found as workers than the longer-resident Wolof or Tukulor. So few women are in the category of director (a total of eight) that particular personal circumstances may explain the rise of Catholics as opposed to Muslims in this regard. In any case, better-educated women of either religion and any ethnic group will be in salaried positions. Breaking the Dakar Muslim sample into Mourides, Tidjanis, and women having no brotherhood affiliation provides further information. Again, it is possible to predict in two ways with the brotherhoods. Mourides, known for their commercial involvement, might be expected to be more adept in acquiring salaried jobs and therefore in earning income. In contrast, Tidjanis, especially Wolof and Serer Tidjanis, might be equally skilled: The ethnic orientation might override whatever original brotherhood differences there were, or the Tidjaniyya brotherhood, because it came later to the Wolof and Serer areas, might have brought less of the reformist/orthodox cast than it brought to the Tukulor.

Table 5.10 Distribution of Women by Ethnic Origin and Occupation in Dakar (percentage)

	Actual Total (thousands)		Sample			Type Job (percent)			Salaried Position (percent)				Income (percent)		
	Number	Percent	Number	Percent	Salaried	Agricultural	Informal	Director	Administrative	Secretarial	Worker		Low	Middle	High
Wolof	766	54	161	79	75	67	78	80	88	75	67		50	83	75
Serer	165	12	16	8	13	0	3	0	4	12	20		17	7	12
Tukulor/ Peuhl	263	19	21	10	7	33	17	75	12	8	6		17	7	13
Dyola	67	5	6	3	4	0	3	0	0	6	8		17	4	1
Other Casamance	37	3	0	—	—	—	—	—	—	—	—		—	—	—

Source: Creevey, 1993, p. 136

Table 5.11 Distribution of Catholic and Muslim Women by Occupation and Level of Position in Dakar

	Total (Thousands)	Percent	Survey Number	Percent	Source of Income (percent) Salaried	Agricultural	Informal	Level of Salaried Job (percent) Director	Administrative	Clerical	Worker
Muslims	670	93	188	88	67	5	28	2	24	55	19
Catholics	48	6	25	12	89	0	11	17	22	28	33

Source: Creevey, 1991, survey

In any event, an interesting pattern emerges. There is no significant relationship between membership in a brotherhood and income, position in the salaried ranks, or whether or not the job is public or private sector. Neither is there a difference in these regards between the Tidjani and the Mouride. There are, however, significant differences in regard to whether one holds a salaried job, and these differences explain more than a quarter of the variation in the sample. Women with no brotherhood affiliation are most likely to be in salaried jobs (61 percent). Women in brotherhoods are more likely not to have a salaried job, but the Tidjanis are more likely to hold such jobs than the Mourides. Table 5.12 compares women's source of revenues to their brotherhood affiliation.

Table 5.12   Source of Revenue
(Mouride, Tidjani, and Women with No Brotherhood)

	Salaried (Percent)	Agriculture (Percent)	Informal Sector (Percent)
No Brotherhood	68	14	18
Mouride	21	28	52
Tidjani	32	33	34

Source: Creevey, 1991 survey

The Mourides are shown in this table to be the traders and merchants that their reputation suggests they would be. This data may also explain why the Mourides come out with a larger percentage in lower income categories, as the informal sector appears to produce the lowest income in the Dakar region (see Creevey, 1993, for fuller discussion of wage sector and survey results, especially Chapter 4).

Agriculture

The complexity of the changing economic situation for women in Senegal is most clearly apparent in the agricultural sector. Focusing on the modern wage sector permits us to ignore the actual changing intrahousehold roles for men and women. In agriculture, however, different factors have to be considered.

In the first place, income may not be the best means of assessing women's economic position. Many subsistence farmers of both sexes will be unable to state what their income is. Or, just as likely, their income will be below poverty level, but they will have access to commodities such as food, which they produce themselves or gather wild. The specific resource they do have, or at least have access to, is land. In some cases they own the land outright—since the Loi de Domaine Nationale (Law of National Domain) was passed in 1964 and revised in 1972, farmers have been able to register land in their own name. Many farmers do not own land outright but have its usufruct through customary allocation to their family from those who originally controlled it (in the old days the higher-caste families and nobles or kings). Family members' access to the usufruct of the land depends on their role in the family and their sex. The authorities monitoring this allocation are the patriarchs—the head of the extended family, the *chef de carré,* and under him the head of the immediate family, the *chef de ménage.* Adult women are allocated land apart from the main family plot. How much land they receive, and whether they get land at all, depends on the ethnic group from which they come. Each ethnic group has a slightly different definition of what tasks women perform, what crops they grow, what animals they raise, what their responsibilities are to the male production system, and what obligations are owed to their production by the men.

In a brilliant article looking at Mandinka women farmers in neighboring Gambia, Judith Carney and Michael Watts demonstrated the major problem in relating the traditional economic status of women to a definable current pattern of change: Change has been ongoing throughout time and is often irregular. Traditional agricultural patterns, including the gender roles in production, have never been etched in stone. They were altered in response to different influences both within the culture and from outside. In the Gambia, from the initial incursion of the Europeans (even before the formal establishment of the colony), outside stimuli produced changes in the agricultural system that significantly affected the roles women played. However, they did not affect all women equally, as the European influence was not equally spread throughout the area.

In general, though, traditional agricultural obligations were very strictly defined for Mandinka men and women. Rice was produced by the women and corn and sorghum by the men, and all of these crops were used for food and traded when a surplus occurred. Women worked in plots allocated to them and controlled the product of their labor. Men assisted, primarily by clearing the land; likewise, women worked in the male-controlled family fields, the product of which also was controlled by the men. The introduction of peanuts, a cash crop, led the men to convert their fields for cultivation of this product. Less food was produced as a result, and heavy pressure was placed on the women to provide more rice, which now had to fill consumption needs of the Mandinka population. Food shortages and even famines resulted. The Europeans tried to get men involved in rice production but at the time of the Carney-Watts article had not succeeded. Instead, in various projects introduced to increase rice production, Mandinka men tried to get control of fields formerly held by women and redefine them as family fields in order to gain control of the product of the women's labor. Women fiercely resisted this tendency. In some cases they succeeded, but in others they did not, and as a result women began to sell their labor either as individuals or in work groups (Carney and Watts, 1991, pp. 651–681).

Similar struggles between men and women must have been stimulated by the presence of the French in Senegal and the surrounding areas. As a result, some phenomena, such as the increased amount of land recently allocated to Tukulor women in the St Louis area, may appear to be moves toward bettering the agricultural position of women. In fact, however, they are only improvements relative to the last few years. The economic position/status of women may have been superior in the precolonial period, before changing trade patterns destroyed the market for the products women produced (Sow, 1991).

It is impossible without doing a thorough historical study of each group over time to understand exactly how economic status has changed for women still primarily in the agricultural sector. We will thus examine some basic information on traditional economic roles and expectations as they have changed in the present century for the four largest ethnic groups in Senegal: the Wolof, the Serer, the Tukulor, and the Dyola. Thereafter, we will look at available information on the current economic status of women of all four groups in the rural sector (see Creevey, 1993, pp. 142–150).

Wolof. Traditionally the Wolof had a complex system of economic interdependency. There was conflict among all family members involved in some manner in economic activity on the family-controlled subsistence farm. Each contributed labor to the collective enterprise, and each had to produce specific commodities and perform services for the family. Thus, for example, men had to provide lodging, and women made clothing for themselves and their children. Tasks and obligations were strictly defined by gender and position in the family. Women never inherited land, the only resource, but they had acknowledged rights to its use. Male family heads controlled land allocation. Conflict arose over division of the limited resources available, including labor time; each actor in the family system would use whatever power he or she had to increase production of those resources over which he or she had direct control. Doing so would necessarily impact others, perhaps removing labor or land access from other members (see for discussion Venema, 1978; Diop, 1981; Diop, 1985; Creevey, 1986, pp. 81–94; Gastellu, 1981; Gravrand, 1989; Gamble, 1957; Waterbury and Gerskovitz, 1987). Currently, Wolof women are also given plots to cultivate for themselves. Men clear the land, and the women plant the seeds, weed, and help harvest the crops—the same things they do on the family-owned land.

The introduction by the French of the first cash crop, peanuts, in the 1920s distorted the traditional pattern of crop production. Men began to grow peanuts on the family fields, resulting in a decrease in the amount of food being produced. Today men still produce the principal food crop, millet, but in lesser amounts, contributing to the growing need for food imports in Senegal. Women have switched from growing rice in their plots to producing peanuts for the income this will yield. They intersperse some millet in their plots as well, as they are obligated by tradition to produce a certain amount of food for the family (although men have the major responsibility in this regard). Women also have begun to grow increasing amounts of vegetables such as tomatoes, chilies, and onions in plots close to the wells, as the market for them has grown both in rural areas and in the expanding cities. Historically diets included meat of wild animals, provided by the men, and certain wild plants (such as the products of the baobab) collected by women. As such wild resources dwindled, the women substituted vegetables from their small plots and used the income to purchase some meat, fish, and canned or other store-bought items occasionally. Increasing numbers of women raised chickens, guinea fowl, and small ruminants to supplement the family diet and to sell for extra income.

It is unclear whether Wolof women have always been involved directly in the production of food crops. What seems possible is that they, like Tukulor women, were not much involved in such production in the nineteenth century. One interpretation, by Bernhard Venema, suggests that Wolof women earned income by selling dyed cloth woven from the cotton they produced in a communal field. They were also apparently allowed to own cattle and slaves, which would substantially increase the income possibilities for wealthier women. However, the introduction of mass-produced cloth by the Europeans destroyed the market for locally produced cloth. Because men and women had set obligations to fulfill for the family, a woman needed this revenue. In addition, any surplus was hers to use as she chose, just as with the cloth she sold. This need—which may even be seen as a right of the Wolof women—was recognized by men and women alike, and the result, as the cloth market declined, was the provision of plots of land to the woman to use to grow her own crops. Initially she grew rice, but as the market for peanuts expanded she substituted the latter and added vegetables as the market for them increased (Venema, 1986, pp. 84–88).

Serer. The obligations of rural Serer women are quite similar to those of Wolof women, and an equal amount of confusion reigns over what changes have taken place since the 1800s in what might be called their traditional economic role. Part of the confusion is due to the fact that the

Wolof and Serer intermarried and otherwise influenced each other. In his intensive study of the Serer, Gastellu wrote that the Serer subgroups are very different from each other and sometimes are more similar to other ethnic groups with whom they are living (Gastellu, 1981, p. 18). As mentioned in Chapter 2, the Serer and Wolof are both considered to be bilineal, meaning that both the father's and the mother's families have important roles.

Serer women, like their Wolof counterparts, reside in their husband's compound. They are given a parcel of land (by the male family head) to cultivate, over which they have total control. The products of this parcel are used for food and to pay for family expenses, such as the purchase of clothes for the woman and children. Whatever residual exists may be used by the woman as she sees fit. As Gastellu states, "The budgetary autonomy of the Serer woman is total," although her husband has the right to "advise her" (Gastellu, 1981, p. 105). Serer women also work on the male-controlled family field and do all household and child-rearing tasks. According to Gastellu, in the old days, before peanuts were important, men grew cotton, which women made into thread. This material was then given to the low caste *griots* (singers) of the village, who turned it into cloth in return for millet, which the women grew on their plots. Serer women could use the cloth for the family or sell it.

Traditionally, Serer men contributed "gifts," which were actually payments for the work of women in the fields and in the household. These gifts of millet could augment the profit of the women or help fulfill family obligations. As peanuts became important, Serer women started to grow them in place of millet (and, of course, the production of cloth stopped as well). Men no longer give gifts of grain but instead supply labor on the women's fields, sometimes using mechanical equipment to help the women in clearing, sowing, weeding, and harvesting the crops (Gastellu, 1981, p. 108). Gastellu's interpretation here of the Serer's transition from production of millet/rice and cotton/cloth to peanuts may also apply to the Wolof; in fact, it may be as plausible for describing the Wolof as the one suggested by Venema above. In any case, Serer women, like Wolof women, grow mainly peanuts, whereas Serer men produce the food crop, millet. In this regard there is some difference between Wolof and Serer men; the latter are more likely to grow millet than peanuts, whereas Wolof men, although also primarily responsible for providing the family staple food, grow mainly peanuts.

The problem of defining traditional economic role expectations in modern times can be dramatically highlighted by considering Serer women who have migrated from Sine Saloum to Senegal Oriental (now Tambacounda). Women from traditional Serer families came with their husbands and children in response to an offer of land. Pressure for migration had become severe in the zone of origin, the Sine Saloum (now Diourbel and Fatick). The Serer had practiced an intensive form of cultivation, using animal fertilizer and growing *Acadia albida* (a nitrogen-rich local plant) to revitalize the soil. But the spread of the cultivation of peanuts, the growing population, the drought, and the fragility of the soil left a decreasing amount of arable land available to family members. Serer families who went to Senegal Oriental were given ten hectares of land per family, a relatively large amount. This land was cleared for them by tractors. They received credit to buy tools and equipment and money to buy or build lodgings.

This was relative wealth, and it had an immediate impact on Serer economic practices. For one thing, the Serer began to cultivate *extensively* rather than *intensively,* as they had done in the Sine Saloum (Trincaz, 1979, pp. 19–36). The advantages of having more land were clear to the Serer family members, who found more revenue available. As a result, their intrafamily relationships began to change slightly. Young boys who would not have been able to have land now had their own parcels, which gave them a separate income and more status and led to increasing struggles over authority with their parents. Wives, too, had much more land (and therefore income), and quarrels developed: Family heads argued their wives were spending too much time in the fields and not enough on household and family maintenance duties (Trincaz, 1979, p. 29). Perhaps most striking of all, the wives who collaborated with each other in carrying out family duties, cultivating their own parcels, and working in the main family field became aware that more labor power would increase the amount of land they could cultivate. Therefore, according to a 1983 study by P. Trincaz, the wives urged their husbands to marry more wives to strengthen their work pool. Many Serer men and women were Catholic and had to convert to Islam, but this did not seem to be an insuperable obstacle. The number of Muslims and the rate of polygamy among Serer in the zone of migration rose significantly (Trincaz, 1979, pp. 19–36; 1983, pp. 199–201). Whether the women wished this transition to polygamy or the men urged it on them, the whole family power system, based on the economic division of labor by gender and position, was shifting.

Tukulor. Fatou Sow writes that women among the Tukulor were severely subjugated and controlled by male family heads in a system tightly regulated by Islamic law, conservatively interpreted. Following a strict reading of the *Sharia,* Tukulor women were excluded from property rights and did not have the political influence enjoyed by women among Sahelian groups such as the Wolof, Serer, or Lebou. Other scholars do not make this strong a differentiation between the Tukulor and other Senegalese ethnic groups (see Robinson, 1975, pp. 5–27)—after all, neither Wolof nor Serer women could own land, either. But it does seem that Tukulor caste structure was much more clearly defined and important in determining what a person could do than that of the Wolof or Serer. Furthermore, in the beginning of the nineteenth century, Tukulor women apparently did not have the same agricultural roles as other women did. They did not work in the family fields and did not use their small plots for personal income. Only recently have they begun to have the same level of agricultural involvement as the Serer or Wolof. As Sow observes:

> In contrast to peasants of other ethnic groups, notably the Wolof, . . . (Tukulor women) were scarcely involved in growing family grain. Their agricultural activity was essentially dedicated to their personal garden on the edge of the family field. . . . There they grew vegetables necessary for family consumption such as sweet potatoes, squash, gumbo. (Sow, 1990, p. 45)

Unlike the Wolof or Serer, by the early twentieth century Tukulor women did not traditionally get an income from their gardens. Where they obtained revenue, it was from spinning cotton, making cloth and dyeing it, and selling other crafts. They also sold food products, including those made from cereals or vegetables, meat, and milk. These revenues were theirs to use as they chose—to buy jewelry and clothes, to beautify their home, or to give to their children. Their maintenance was completely provided by their husbands. As the trade to the north dried up in the late nineteenth century and the demand for local cloth was destroyed by European products in the early twentieth century, this source of revenue for Tukulor women began to disappear. At the same time, the economy was monetarized. Increasingly, money was needed for the purchase of domestic items, food, and clothing, whereas Tukulor men were disappearing to Dakar and then, in ever larger numbers, to France. Furthermore, the economy of the Senegal River area was dramatically altered by the building of dams and by the introduction of large-scale mechanized rice production in the 1960s and 1970s. Tukulor women, who had not worked in the family fields before except to help sow the grains, were not included in the large-scale rice schemes.

By the 1980s, Tukulor women were often in perilous economic circumstances. The migration of males is shown by the relatively high number of female-headed households—30 percent in St Louis in 1988 as compared to 12 percent in neighboring regions of Fatick and Diourbel (RGPH 1988, Table 2.01). Women were now frequently responsible for feeding and maintaining the family. The result was much greater involvement in agriculture for women, and this has accelerated in more recent years. A survey of the river region in 1979 showed only 19.2 percent of the women engaged in agricultural work. By 1990 that figure had become 59.8 percent. Interestingly, none of the women in either of these surveys owned the land they cultivated, despite the Loi de Domaine Nationale of 1964, which technically permits any adult to hold land in his or her own name. All the women had land given them by their husband, husband's family, or their own family. Less than 9 percent of the respondents worked in a collectively owned women's field. The absence of ownership is, of course, consistent with the *Sharial* proscription mentioned above (Sow, 1990, pp. 50–52).

Dyola. The Dyola, living principally in the southern region of Senegal in the Casamance, are like the Tukulor in being cut off from the urban region of Dakar and somewhat marginalized from the concerns and activities of the central zones. In other ways, however, their circumstances are as unlike those of Tukulor women as is possible in Senegal. Indeed, they may represent two different ends of a spectrum in terms of the traditional independence of women. This observation does not mean that Dyola women had more authority in the family than did the males. Among the Dyola, too, there was a male family head, and polygamy was common. Women played the supportive roles; they prepared the meals and did not eat until after the men and adolescent boys had finished. However, Dyola women's place and social status was apparently higher than that of Tukulor women. Originally, rice was the staple food and major crop of their area. Women and men cultivated rice in their separate fields, and women had their own granaries, which was seen as a symbol of power. Women could and did leave the husband's home and go off to live with other women for short periods of time. They could pass on to their children what they had earned or acquired. As Louis-Vincent Thomas writes, women had a relatively large amount of independence, although they were not equal to men: "In brief, the diola family is an association based on equality; but in the realm of dignity, the role of men is preponderant" (Thomas, 1958, p. 253).

Land was traditionally not owned by individuals but was used according to custom. Men usually controlled the land, but women could expect to receive tracts for their rice cultivation. Dyola women from those groups that had a more predominantly matrilineal base of organization could in fact own or control rice fields. Other Dyola groups situated on the left bank of the Casamance River were organized more patrilineally and did not permit their women to own or inherit land, but these women still could own rice granaries in their own names (Thomas, 1958, p. 281; see also Journet, 1981, pp. 117–138).

Three major influences began to undermine the position of rural Dyola women, especially in the postindependence period. The first of these was the advent of peanuts, a crop introduced to men but not women. As peanuts were the major source of cash in a rapidly monetarizing economy, the cultivation of rice was devalued. The status of the women's separate rice granaries was lessened and, because they had less access to cash, women's dependence on male family members increased. Second, men began to migrate to Dakar, leaving women responsible for the family. However, this was less of a problem for the Dyola than it was for the Tukulor: Even in the late 1980s, only 16 percent of the households were headed by women (RPGH 1988, Table 2.01). Third, whereas Thomas could write in 1958 that the essential Dyola religion was fetishism, in 1991 this had completely changed (Thomas, 1958, p. 68). Many Dyola, especially those closer to the town of Ziguinchor, had converted to Catholicism or Islam. Indeed, in the 1991 Senegal Survey, 53 percent of the Dyola were Muslim and 45 percent Catholic. Only 2 percent reported being animist.

Common Themes. In the 1990s, there seem to be more similarities than differences in the situations of rural women in the major ethnic groups. The economy is monetarized; no region is far enough away from the pull of the urban nexus to be untouched. Men began migrating to the cities long before independence. Now women of all groups are migrating as well, although a significant proportion remain behind in the rural areas, where they are responsible for the entire maintenance of the family rather than just their traditional share. Migration is heaviest in the Senegal River areas, but it is also a factor in the south. Where the women of separate groups have had widely differing degrees of involvement in agricultural production and concomitant differences in degree of independence, those discrepancies appear to be lessening. Perforce, Tukulor women are more independent and more involved in agriculture than they were, whereas Dyola women have lost some of their economic importance as the value of rice has lessened in society. Serer women, like the Wolof, have been pushed to modify their patterns of production as men respond to the demand for cash crops, as wild crops and animal products become less available, and as their early sources of revenue disappear. All of these women have more responsibility for food production and for earning revenue themselves to supplement the family income than they formerly had.

In the long run, it seems clear that the importance of agriculture in Senegal is declining, and women gradually will migrate to cities or will find wage-paying jobs in the rural areas as more opportunities expand. Traditional land tenure patterns are also changing. Since the 1964 Loi de Domaine Nationale, land has been registered, gradually at first but more and more rapidly in recent years. Around cities, especially around Dakar, traditional usufruct rights are being replaced. Pressure on traditional lands increases yearly as population grows and alternate uses of the land give it real monetary value. Formerly pastoral peoples such as the Peuhl have been squeezed out of grazing lands and forced into sedentary farming, and agricultural people try to prevent land they have held for generations from being usurped. Other special projects increase pressure on land in different regions. For example, areas near the *barrage,* the dam on the Senegal River, are being forcibly registered, as the government is claiming lands that are not registered for its large-scale agricultural program in the region. To register land, one must have some kind of agricultural work in progress with a building present, even if only in the form of fences and impermanent storage sheds. People in this region, afraid of losing the land they have always controlled, are rushing to have their holdings registered in their names. As they lose land, more people migrate to the towns or the city in search of other kinds of work.

For those women who remain in the rural agricultural zones, the world is gradually changing around them. The question is how these changes affect their status and their living conditions. It does seem clear that women do not necessarily benefit from the changes that are taking place. Few of them, for example, can or do register land in their names; the land they work is registered in the name of their husband or father or, if they are in a matrilineal group, their uncle or brother. A study in 1984 found that, following the administrative reform that permitted registration, land was being quickly given individual title, but no women had land registered in their names (Fana Bana, 1984, p. 108).

The household farming system has changed in Senegal in the post-independence period. For example, in most ethnic groups, the *chef de ménage* has taken on more authority relative to the *chef de carré*. These changes, however, do not generally indicate that men and women family members are equal. In modern Senegal rural families still live together in compounds. An extended family, comprising as many as five households, may live together under the direction of a *chef de carré*, but the members of each household will follow the lead of their individual *chef de ménage* in most day-to-day economic decisions. The *chef de ménage* allocates the land to his family members. In general, the smallest plots of land lying the furthest from the dwellings (and therefore the least convenient) are allocated to women for cereal and peanut production.

The modernization of agriculture has not generally improved women's relative economic position. As pointed out in Chapter 2, training and tools came from the West, and as a result the agricultural needs of women were ignored. Training was geared to men, and credit and tools were made available to them rather than to women. It was assumed that whatever advantages were made available to men would also benefit the women of their households. To some extent, there was a trickle-down effect of this kind; however, women did not gain equally. At times they gained from the greater demand for their labor (for example, when the area under cultivation in the family field increased). Or they may have profited from the new equipment, fertilizer, and seeds, as men would share them once the main family fields were taken care of. But women got the least, and they were the last to receive these advantages. As a result their productivity often lagged behind that of the men. Table 5.13 indicates the small size of plots given to Serer and Wolof women and their low rate of production in those fields relative to the male-controlled family fields.

Some positive changes have definitely occurred, especially in the last few years. For one thing, the government of Senegal has taken a public position that rural women have been disadvantaged and that it is important to

Table 5.13   Household Division of Land and Production

Status	Peanuts (percent of plots)	Average Size (hectares)	Yield (kg/ha)	Millet (percent of plots)	Average Size (hectares)	Yield (kg/ha)
Chef de carré	25	2.4	1,292	73	1.6	1,165
Chef de ménage	8	1.6	1,078	13	0.9	1,196
Women	29	0.7	985	8	0.8	551
Unmarried men	24	1.3	1,067	5	0.9	781
Migrants	13	1.3	1,071	1	0. 3	504

Source: Waterbury, John, and Mark Gersovitz, eds. *The Political Economy of Risk and Choice in Senegal,* 1987. London: Frank Cass, p. 50. Reprinted with permission.

assist them, both for the overall growth of the economy and for the relative position of women in society. In 1982, following the beginning of the UN Decade for Women, the government of Senegal initiated a program of reforms and incentives to help rural women. Chief among these was the formation of Women's Promotional Groups (Groupements de Promotion Féminine) related to a variety of economic activities. These village-based associations were to be the basis of training and were to receive credit, tools, and equipment. Senegal had begun a program in the 1960s to encourage farmers to form cooperatives for production and marketing. Initially, women did not participate in these; they were dominated by the *chefs de ménage,* the marabouts, and the relatively wealthy males. By the early 1980s, few women had joined cooperatives, even among the relatively independent Dyola (Gellar, 1987, pp. 123–159).

The 1982 women's groups were a different matter. Women in all ethnic groups had always collaborated, traditionally in age-based or family-based groups to help with each other's field or domestic labor. They formed village mutual aid societies to save money for recurring expenses, such as celebrations or funerals, or for unforeseen catastrophes. The Women's Promotional Groups, then, were a further development in a familiar line of women's cooperative work and promised several new benefits. Registered *groupements féminins* could receive credit, usually unavailable to rural women having no collateral, and they also were eligible for government assistance for specific projects they undertook. By 1987 there were 2,500 such groups officially registered. The actual impact of these groups may not have been as far-reaching as intended. Fatou Sow points out that some of them are groups in name only; many tend to promote only small projects and some, she says, encourage "to the limit mediocrity" (Sow, 1990, pp. 6–9). The existence of the groups and their proliferation, however, suggests that women are responding to incentives that promise to provide resources and improve economic opportunities.

The fact that there is a wave of economic reorganization among small farmers, including women, in former subsistence areas throughout the country is borne out most strongly by a recent study of the newly forming economic interest groups. The Groupements d'Intèret Economique (GIE) register according to a law passed in 1984 to become eligible for credit from the Agricultural Credit Office (Caisse Nationale de Crédit Agricole), plus other grants and resources. The 1990 study suggests that a proliferation of GIEs resulted after the law probably because of the credit made available and the withdrawal of the former Regional Development Societies, which had lost their resources.

By 1990 there were 4,745 GIEs registered nationwide. Some of these were in urban areas, but the majority were in primarily rural sectors. Significantly, a plurality—1,618—were in one region, St Louis, where the effect of the dam had obviously placed new pressure on land tenure and caused the greatest dislocation of traditional practices (Vengroff, 1990, p. 24).

In an initial evaluation of the GIE study, the authors pointed to the lack of women members in the economic groups. Of the groups surveyed, 71 percent had a primarily male labor force, and only 25 percent had predominantly women. This imbalance, they argued, existed because "women's groups are distinct from men's groups and are hardly represented despite the phenomenal development of G.I.E. witnessed in recent years" (Vengroff, 1990, p. 39).

Furthermore, few women were employed by the GIE according to the survey data. Only 25 percent of permanent employees were women.

Reinterpretation of these data, however, suggests that an alternate perspective may be more appropriate. Women were scarcely represented in the cooperative movement of the 1960s, and they have traditionally always had a second-class position in the modernization of the rural sector. Men got the training and tools, went first to the training programs, and became the first extension agents (prepared, of course, to work primarily with men). The 1982 rural development effort also established more programs for women and centers to train women extension agents. But all these are recent efforts. It is perhaps more surprising how *many* women are involved in these economic groups, rather than how few are. In fact, most of the *groupements féminins* are registered as such rather than as GIE. There are 2,500 women's economic groups, and almost a third of the membership and employees of the other registered economic groups, the GIE, are also women. Sixty-two percent of the GIE did have women in them, reflecting the phenomenal growth of women's participation in economic ventures beyond their subsistence work in agriculture.

Despite the growing similarity of conditions for rural women discussed above, there remain strong variations in living and attitude patterns.

Some of them join economic groups or act as individual entrepreneurs in their own right. Some do not and remain in a very traditional living pattern at the lowest end of the economic scale. The question is: What stimulates women to change? Specifically, does religion have an important role in determining what women do?

The 1991 Senegal Survey does provide some suggestions as to what is happening (see further discussion in Creevey, 1993, Chapter 4). To begin with, most women say they do belong to some economic or political association or a functional literacy group (excluding traditional village groupings, which were not seen by the women as an association). None of the major determinant variables for other types of change predict whether women join economic groups or functional literacy programs. Religion has no impact, nor does family or personal income, education, land ownership, or the receipt of credit. The only factor that does predict, which is also consistent with the GIE survey above, is that women involved in agriculture are much more likely than women not in agriculture to join an economic group. Looking only at the subsample of those who are in agriculture, we see that women from families with lower incomes are more likely than others to join an association as a way of bettering their economic position. Again, no other factor, including education, religion, or ethnicity, explains why women join associations. Nor are association members more likely to say they received credit than private individuals or that their personal incomes are higher. So far, it appears that the disadvantaged join these economic groups to improve their positions (see Creevey, 1993, pp. 156–161).

Of those women who are in agriculture, the most salient differences among them seem to be related to their ethnic background. In regard to their work and economic production, all groups seem to be following traditional patterns. Wolof and Serer women provide the labor for the family fields controlled by their husbands but work long hours in their own plots as well. Tukulor women work less in the family fields but are beginning to work long hours in their own plots, which have become their only source of independent income. Faced with a heavy outmigration by males from their zone, they are compensating by their increased agricultural role. They remain very traditional in their views of themselves and marriage and their position in the family. The Dyola are much more independent and less likely to distinguish themselves as providing labor for a male-controlled family field. They still grow rice, and they still control the sale of their product. They are poorer, especially in comparison to the Wolof, and faced with a growing problem from migration, but they have not lost their independence in the process. The Serer seem to be the most subordinated in their work and in their attitudes.

The final factor here has to be the impact of religion on these women. Most of them are Muslim, but there are Catholics as well in the agricultural sample. The results are indeed interesting: In many ways, it appears, traditional rural women were quite independent. Neither Islam nor Christianity completely destroyed this independence; in fact, each reinforced it in slightly different ways. Rural Muslim women are probably more independent from their husbands in their living patterns than Catholic women. They are much more likely than Catholic women to own land, the only valuable rural resource. Whether or not they own land, Muslim women are much more likely to farm their own plot of land than are Catholics. Yet, as Chapter 4 indicated, Catholic women are more likely than Muslim women to view themselves as equal to their husbands. The traditional Muslim view is that men have the authoritative and decisive role in the family, whereas Catholics say husband and wife are equal, an outlook more akin to the modern Christian stance on family structure. Hence, Catholic women are more likely to view land as family land, whatever the legal technicalities.

Despite these differences, however, religion does not appear to empower or disempower rural women in most major ways. It does not predict to their being the head of the family, nor does it affect the likelihood of their being married or single (or divorced). In the end, then, this sample suggests that the motor of change for rural Senegalese women is simply the spread of education and the increase of job opportunities in relatively accessible locations. To some degree, women of two ethnic groups —the Dyola and the Wolof—have some advantages in utilizing whatever resources become available. The former are advantaged by their traditional independence and the latter by the relative economic privileges of the Wolof as opposed to other groups. Association membership is also a way for low-income women to try to improve their economic position, and increasingly women are joining such groups. Religion in itself does not seem to be a major variable in this situation at all. (For a fuller discussion of differences among rural women, see Creevey, 1993, Chapter 4.)

The Informal Sector

There is no reliable nationwide data for Senegal on how many informal sector businesses exist or where they are located. Casual observation suggests a large and vibrant sector in both urban and rural parts of the country. A 1990 survey of informal sector businesses conducted in eleven Senegalese cities and towns provides some more concrete information. This study provides basic data on the activities and employment patterns of the businesses and their managers' perceptions of the constraints they face in their work. It also gives some interesting indications of the role of Senegalese women in these activities. However, as the research director suggested himself, the type of enterprise that is liable to be identified using this approach will not necessarily be typical of the majority of informal activities: It will be larger, better organized, more profitable, and closer to the formal sector than the average small-scale entrepreneurial activity. Because women may be found disproportionately in the smaller and less organized activities, these results may not in fact indicate the overall extent or type of women's involvement in the informal sector. Furthermore, although this survey was conducted in all the major cities and towns in Senegal, it did not include an equally representative sample of rural areas, which provided only 20 of the 114 businesses studied. Thus, agriculture-related enterprises have a much lower representation than they would in a more random national sample. It is, however, still valuable to look at the role of Senegalese women in the larger urban informal sector enterprises revealed in this study.

The study found that 28 percent of the businesses had female employees. Only nine percent of all workers in these enterprises were female, most of them in the lowest-level positions. Twenty-two women were managers or administrators of their businesses, but they only accounted for 17 percent of the total group of managers. However, women were much better represented in some types of enterprise, as Table 5.14 illustrates.

Women in the informal sector, at least in these larger enterprises, seem to face the same conditions as those employed in the formal sector. They are best represented at the upper levels and, except in the service sector, worst at the unskilled worker level. They are most active in the service sector and, surprisingly, industry and mines, and least active in commerce and agricultural businesses. The largest percentage of the women employees (37 percent) were rural, followed by Dakar (26 percent). Forty-six percent of those in management were in Dakar; the rest were distributed across the nine other cities, with a plurality in the "other" sample. Fifty-six percent of the women workers were in the rural sample, but only 28 percent were in Dakar, again suggesting that unskilled employment in urban areas discriminates heavily against women, more so than jobs that require some education or training.

The 1991 Senegal Survey approached the position of women in the informal sector from a different perspective: It asked women what revenue-generating activities they primarily carried out. Fifty-one percent of the women surveyed admitted to receiving income from economic activities or employment. Here, because there is no bias toward any size enterprise, a large percentage of women claimed to be in the informal sector. Indeed, more than a third of those earning revenue were to be found in this sector. Residence, of course, had an important effect on the likelihood of a woman's earning money from such activities: Those from the remote agricultural regions, such as Tamborcounda, were least likely to earn income from informal sector activities. In Dakar, where women were most likely to have salaried employment, approximately a third (36 percent) were in the informal sector. In relatively populous and accessible rural places, such as Diourbel and Kaolack, however, women were significantly more

Table 5.14   Women Employed in the Informal Sector

Position	Total		Agricultural & Agricultural Processing		Service		Industry and Mines		Commerce	
	Number	Percent Female	Number	Percent Female	Number	Percent Female	Number	Percent Female	Number	Percent Female
Permanent	778	10	190	4	284	18	297	8	97	10
Part-time	8	0	0	0	3	0	1	0	1	0
Seasonal	177	9	120	0	11	100	47	0	1	0
Manager/ Administrative	133	17	24	8	52	23	39	21	35	14
Clerical	13	31	2	50	8	25	2	50	1	0
Professional	3	67	0	0	2	100	1	100	0	0
Technical	41	0	3	0	34	0	3	0	1	0
Worker/Other	779	9	282	5	207	21	298	7	63	6

Source: Vengroff, 1990 survey
Note: The 114 firms sometimes had more than one major activity. As a result there is some double counting in the specific activity columns.

likely to be in the informal sector than those in Dakar. More than 50 percent in both regions reported that they did some informal sector work.

Religion played a role here as well: Catholic women were far more likely to be in the informal sector than Muslim women and far less likely to be in agriculture. More important, ethnicity predicted significantly to informal sector involvement. Dyola women (50 percent) and Wolof women (45 percent) were much more likely than Serer women (33 percent) or Tukulor women (30 percent) to be in the informal sector (see Creevey, 1993).

Looking at the characteristics of women in this sector as opposed to those in other sectors, we can discern a transition. Women in the agricultural sector are the least educated and the poorest. Women in the informal sector have better education and higher individual income. Not surprisingly, women in salaried positions have the best record on both counts. In terms of family independence, women in the informal sector have more individual responsibility and more resources than women whose revenue comes from agriculture. Salaried women are most likely to be single or divorced, followed by women in the informal sector. Predictably, being unmarried closely relates to one's being a family head. Unmarried women and those who are family heads have significantly higher individual incomes than do married women. Perhaps more important, women in the informal sector are far more likely than either salaried women or those in agriculture to own land in their own names. Finally, women in the informal sector are much more likely than women in either other revenue category to receive credit.

Within the informal sector, certain variables predict differences for women. Not surprisingly, the best predictor of income for women in this sector is place of residence: Women in Dakar are far more likely than those of any other group to earn more than $333 a year from their activities. Cost of living is also higher in Dakar, so the value of being in the urban central zone is somewhat mitigated. However, education again emerges as the significant factor, explaining almost a third of the variance. More than 50 percent of the educated women are in the highest income group, whereas 75 percent of the uneducated fall in the lower category. The only impact of religion that emerges is in attitude: Catholic women in the informal sector are significantly more likely than Muslim women to see themselves as equal to their husbands in the family. This factor is even stronger than education, although educated women also are more likely than uneducated ones to say they are equal to their husbands. But religion does not predict level of education: Catholic women in the informal sector are not more likely to have gone to school. Nor is income for women in the informal sector affected by whether or not they are Catholic or Muslim.

The economy of Senegal has been called stagnant, and many have pointed to its inability to live up to the expectations of the 1960s. Senegal was devastated by repeated droughts in the 1970s and 1980s, and its economy never took off in the postindependence period. The market for peanuts, originally the major cash crop, fell off dramatically after independence, and the export agricultural sector shrank. Industry has fared better but still has not been very successful. Overall industrial production was lower in 1988 than in 1982, although phosphates, the major mineral export, had in fact increased substantially. The service sector, including tourism, became the largest source of national income, but then it clearly overexpanded, with a significantly lower percentage of beds occupied in 1987 than in 1986 or 1985. Senegal's total external debt in 1988 was $3,019,000,000 or 64 percent of its GNP (as compared to 1970, when the external debt was only 16 percent of the GNP).

Nonetheless, Senegal is teeming with modernization and change, despite its huge national economic problems. Virtually no one is untouched by the process, even in the most remote areas of the country. It does seem that the traditional economic sector—subsistence agriculture and trading—is rapidly disappearing. The society is largely monetarized; every family has to respond by seeking ways to create or increase its revenue. Traditional social roles have been assaulted with the dramatic effects of multiple outside influences and internal changes. As they are challenged, they alter in response, resulting in a variety of new definitions of responsibility and privilege. Women are moving into new positions, taking on new economic roles.

There is still a substantial degree of independence for women. Almost all groups traditionally have expected women to be involved in economic production and allowed them to keep the proceeds of their own labor time. Despite having this degree of economic independence, women were viewed as inferior to men in subsistence society, a view that was at least as strong in modern industrializing Senegal at the outset of independence. At this time, people didn't seem to consider economic options for women important, either for themselves or for national economic development. Now there seems to be new growth in women's economic involvement, fueled both by increasing need and increasing awareness of opportunities. Although still handicapped, both by their traditional past and by the intervention of the French on the side of male economic dominance, women are moving steadily into the modern wage sector and informal enterprises and beginning to organize themselves or join other economic groups in the agricultural sector. They hold weaker, less important, less well-paid positions than men, but they are moving up. Factors that seem to lead to this progress include primarily education and the increasing rate and level of industrialization. Undoubtedly, the tenor of politics in a country still seeking economic help from the West pushes these changes forward. What does not seem to be significant in a major way in this process at present is religion. Should Senegal opt for a closer affiliation with more conservative

Middle Eastern countries, this might change. But Islam is not currently a major factor blocking the move of women to greater economic equality.

CONCLUSION

Analyzing the place of women in the economies of northern Nigeria and Senegal suggests that there is a set of common factors that interact in all West African countries to determine the economic position of women and the role of Islam in that determination. These factors include: (1) economic incentives and degree of economic growth; (2) residence, particularly proximity to a modern urban center; (3) ethnic origin; (4) nature of governmental institutions; (5) education; and (6) religious emphasis (conservative versus "liberal" Islam).

In a rapidly changing economy, strong incentives are offered to women, pulling them out of their traditional subsistence agricultural work to either the informal sector or the wage sector. Sometimes these incentives are positive—for example, the possibility for increased income that may have led many Senegalese women to form *groupements* or join *GIEs*. At other times the incentives are negative, as appears to be the case for Hausa women in Nigeria and Tukulor women in Senegal. The contracting Nigerian economy is forcing Hausa women to play a larger role in the family economy even from within their secluded residences. Tukulor women have been pushed into agriculture as the market for their traditional production has disappeared, as migration has removed male support from their families, and as new land tenure laws have threatened their family holdings. Where the economy is developing very slowly, as in Chad or Mali, women receive fewer incentives and move less quickly out of their traditional situations. At the same time, the gap between them and males remains larger. It takes the shock of more rapid and intense change to begin to eliminate the inequity between the sexes.

Proximity to a modern urban center is a second vital factor in determining women's employment, especially in Senegal. The closer a woman is to a city, the better the likelihood of her earning from the informal sector or the wage economy. Dakar has the monopoly on all major infrastructural and service facilities, including schools, roads, and health care, and the majority of wage positions and largest (wealthiest) market for the informal sector is also there. Moreover, Dakar attracts many foreign African and European businesses. A woman in or near Dakar is exposed to more options and choices than women in many other societies have. Dakar, then, has an effect in itself that goes beyond mere wealth. Kano, however, is an urban industrial center but a more homogeneous one. It is a very metropolitan city, but because of its geographic isolation and its standing as a Muslim center of learning it does not have the cosmopolitan effect of

Dakar. Conservative views of proper roles and behavior for women are pervasive. Kano's modernizing urban economy provides a large market for Hausa women's goods, produced in the seclusion of their homes. The connection between women's traditional income-earning activities and the modern economy of Kano is not simple. The incomes women generate from within seclusion are nearly equal to those earned by men in the industrial wage sector. As women become more educated they are moving into the regular wage sector, but at the higher rather than the lower end of the scale. Most West African capitals are more like Dakar or Lagos in southern Nigeria, or Bamako in Mali, than they are like Kano. Of course, the larger and more economically vibrant centers, such as Lagos and to a lesser extent Dakar, have more of an impact than slower-growing smaller towns such as Bamako.

Ethnicity is the third factor influencing women's economic position. We have shown, for example, the relative independence of the Dyola in Senegal and the greater incomes of Wolof women. Residence and religion both have a strong interactive effect with ethnic origin. Ethnicity is important in all countries in West Africa where precolonial and pre-Islamic customs will have an important impact on the ability of women to move into the modern sector. How this ethnic factor operates is still difficult to understand, however. There is some suggestion that matrilineal societies gave women more power and influence in all aspects of their lives than did patrilineal ones (although women still did not have power equal to men). However, as we have shown, ethnic group patterns changed over time and were never stagnant and fixed. Many factors, including economic changes, wars and conquests, and even natural disasters, have caused groups to adapt and alter their living patterns and organization. Therefore, there is not just one ethnic variable for each group: Custom and interpretation change to suit whatever conditions arise.

The nature of the government, its policy and outlook, is obviously highly significant in all West African cases. The Nigerian military government, like Senegal's civilian government, has taken a public position that improvement in the economic status and position of women is a national priority, particularly in the rural areas. The Better Life Program in Nigeria is an effort to implement this policy, and Muslim women are responding in large numbers, although the results so far are limited. Still, women are being pulled into the economic mainstream, however ineffectively. Just as significant is their involvement in adult education and literacy classes. The question is: Will the male Muslim elite in Nigeria tolerate a true modernization of women's position? The evidence is mixed. Different forces are at work in Senegal, where the tone of the government, although avowedly Muslim, is far more liberal and even secular than in Nigeria. This difference has to do with the kind of elites that dominate politics. Senegal's appear to be less socially conservative than Nigeria's and more aware of, and responsive to, the need to improve the position of women as a part of economic revitalization. This awareness may in part be due to the stability of Senegal's democratic governmental institutions—by contrast, there have been five military coups in Nigeria. But Nigeria's military has been more willing to extend rights to women than civilian governments, which have shied away from these issues. It was the military in Nigeria that extended the right to vote to Muslim women in the northern sections of the country, developed a program of Universal Primary Education, and today supports the Better Life Program for Rural Women.

In Senegal, a much smaller country than Nigeria, the elite is concentrated in and around Dakar and more directly exposed to influences from Europe and the United States. The economy also is more directly dependent on aid from Western countries than is Nigeria's. In Nigeria, the northern traditional elite still dominates national and regional politics and holds the associated economic power. That elite identifies itself very strongly with Islam; it is very dependent on conservative religious support in its regional base and hence is careful not to offend it. In Senegal, the marabouts are conservative as well, but they do not have the same political impact. Thus, change for Senegalese women is easier as long as the marabouts are not directly threatened. The technocrats governing Senegal know well how to offer increased economic benefits and avoid many direct confrontations.

Across West Africa, education is the key to the movement of women out of the traditional sector into the wage-paid labor market. Education relates directly to women's ability to get jobs in both the public and private sectors. No other factor is as important or as determinant. Education is here defined as formal Western education emphasizing the development of individual skills of thinking and analyzing, as well as fundamentals such as reading, writing, and arithmetic. Where education is constrained by religion, of course, its impact will be less and change will be slower, as the northern Nigerian case illustrates. Yet all West African governments have publicly stated their intention to educate both men and women. In most cases, the factor preventing them is the lack of resources to open or staff schools in the most remote rural areas. Education remains most accessible to those living in or close to urban centers and to women from families that are relatively better off economically. In the northern Nigeria case, the conservatism of the ruling elite, the prevailing conservative social orientation of the populace, and the emphasis on the development of Islamiyya schools inhibits the spread of modern secular education to girls. But even here a growing number of girls are attaining ever higher levels of education and with this preparation are moving into positions at fairly high levels. Thus, even in northern Nigeria the relationship between education and economic success is apparent, although at present only for an elite few. In Senegal, education was the best predictor of position and salary level for all women in every region and ethnic group, even among those living in primarily rural agricultural areas. Throughout West Africa, the success in spreading education to increasing numbers of women will be closely linked with those women's ability to move into the economy and gain increasing equity with men.

Islam, of course, is still extremely important in the equation for West African women. But we need to stress most strongly that the *type* of Islam adhered to by those controlling politics and education is what will determine the influence of religious norms on women. In northern Nigeria, a conservative Muslim elite has controlled politics and society since the *jihad* of al-Hadji Usman dan Fodio. Politics thus has been deeply and closely influenced by the teachings of Islam. Islamic law has been protected by the government and frames the fabric of society in which Hausa women live. Unlike those in Nigeria, fundamentalist Islamic leaders in Senegal, including al-Hadji Umar Tal, were unable to establish political control over the region. They shared their power with the French, whose Catholic/secular influence balanced and diluted Muslim teachings. Marabouts in Senegal are conservative and promote a society in which women are more restricted than are most women currently are in Senegal. However, the marabouts are used to living in a dual world and used to interacting with and tolerating others whose ways are less strict. There is a growing group of radical reformers in Senegal who would like to purify the religion and force everyone to live by strict Islamic laws similar to those in northern Nigeria. At present they have little power or influence. Most Senegalese are Muslim, but only a minority live according to the strict Islamic teachings as the Hausa of northern Nigeria attempt to do. Thus, in Senegal, Islam is not a significant factor inhibiting women from moving into the modern economy, whereas it is the major consideration in northern Nigeria.

6

THE POLITICAL
EMPOWERMENT OF WOMEN

Nowhere in West Africa do women control the political structures or dominate the political process. In all West African countries they are permitted to vote, but their vote is usually cast for a male candidate. Political parties sometimes have women's wings and generally admit women to membership and to positions within their hierarchy, but West African women have not been national party leaders. Rarely has there been a movement or even a strike led by women based on a "women's issue," although there were a few uprisings of this nature in colonial West Africa. In Nigeria, for example, a so-called "women's war" took place in 1929 (Ifeka-Moller, 1975, pp. 127–157), and in 1973, market women rioted in Accra to protest the attempts of the Rawlings government to tax them. Across West Africa, a few women have been elected to national parliaments, and a handful have been chosen for ministerial positions or other high government office. The number and proportion are increasing, but West African women, although a majority of the population, are distinctly a minority in public office. Furthermore, although they are found in social service positions such as those associated with the ministries of health, education, or women's affairs, they are generally not named to the more sensitive or powerful ministries, such as finance, defense, or foreign affairs. Table 6.1 below gives some indication of the distribution of women in government in West Africa.

The reasons for the disparities in this distribution are not readily apparent. However, they are certainly *not* explainable on the basis of religion: Some predominantly Muslim countries have a better overall representation of women in government than do countries where Muslims are in the minority. This is not to say Islam is never a factor, for in some cases it clearly is. The presence of a military government may be part of the explanation in a few cases but not in all. Even the spread of education is not consistently linked to the amount of female representation in public office, although it clearly has a major impact on the political participation of women throughout West Africa. In this chapter, we will try to discern what has shaped the situation for women in politics in Nigeria and Senegal and then extrapolate from these instances what seems to determine the access to power for women across West Africa.

MUSLIM WOMEN IN NIGERIAN POLITICS

Muslims in northern Nigeria do not accept the proposition that it is appropriate to separate the sacred and the secular, the church and the state. Religious themes have long been a part of political culture in the Islamic sections of the country. Explicitly religious concepts of political authority and community have been important in the political rhetoric of northern Nigeria from the very beginnings of modern political activity in that region. Both the pre- and postindependence political parties there identified themselves with Islamic concepts of government, so Islamic themes have always played a powerful underlying role in the politics of developing a consensus, or *umma*. Each group maintained that not to accept the consensus claimed by it was in fact un-Islamic.

Throughout the periods of civilian politics there have been essentially two political parties in the region. (At present the military is in power, but political parties have formed in anticipation of a return to civilian rule in January 1994.) During the First Republic (1952–1966), the traditional elite was represented by the Northern People's Congress (NPC), and younger radicals were represented in the Northern Elements Progressive Union (NEPU). During the Second Republic (1979–1983), the former NPC partisans were represented by the National Party of Nigeria (NPN) and the more radical reformists of NEPU by the People's Redemption Party (PRP). Currently, two political parties are vying for control of the area (and the country)—the National Republican Convention (NRC) and the Social Democratic Party (SDP), both broad national coalitions that essentially replicate the old alignment of forces.

The more conservative NPC/NPN/NRC has been dominated by the descendants of the Fulani *jihad* and characterizes itself as appropriately representative of the community. The radical politicians in opposition have stressed the unholy nature of this leadership and their own more modern democratic underpinnings. One political personality dominated radical politics in northern Nigeria between 1952 and 1983: Mallam Aminu Kano. His impassioned rhetoric and Islamic vision are deeply ingrained in the political culture. Over the course of the past four decades Nigerian politics have reflected a consistent alignment of forces, and Aminu Kano and his followers have set the tone and substance of the radical opposition.

From the beginning of his political career, Aminu Kano was widely regarded as a religious teacher as well as a political leader, and hence

Table 6.1 Women in Public Office in West Africa

	Parliament seats (percent women)		Executive Office Economic, Political, Legal		Executive Office Social		All Ministries		Ministerial Level	
	1975	1987	Number	Percent	Number	Percent	Number	Percent	Number	Percent
Benin	—	4.1	0	0	0	0	0	0	0	0
Burkina Faso	—	—	6	4.8	19	27.5	25	13.0	3	11.5
Cameroon	5.8	14.2	1	3.1	4	30.8	5	11.1	2	6.5
Chad	—	—	0	0	1	14.3	1	2.7	1	4.2
Côte d'Ivoire	9.2	5.7	2	3.1	3	16.7	5	6.0	4	9.5
Gambia	0.0	—	2	3.9	2	25.0	4	6.8	1	5.9
Ghana	—	—	2	5.7	3	23.1	5	10.4	0	0.0
Guinea	—	—	0	0.0	0	0.0	0	0.0	0	0.0
Liberia	—	6.3	1	5.6	1	25.0	2	9.1	2	10.5
Mali	—	3.7	0	0.0	1	16.7	1	5.6	1	6.3
Mauritania	—	—	0	0.0	0	0.0	0	0.0	0	0.0
Niger	—	—	0	0.0	2	6.1	2	1.8	0	0.0
Nigeria	—	—	3	5.9	1	7.1	4	4.3	0	0.0
Senegal	4.0	11.7	1	6.7	2	22.2	3	12.0	3	12.0
Sierra Leone	1.0	—	2	3.2	1	5.3	3	3.7	0	0.0
Togo	—	5.2	0	0.0	1	20.0	1	4.3	0	0.0

Source: United Nations, 1991, pp. 39–40

throughout his adult life he was universally referred to as "Mallam." Mallam Aminu Kano, more than any other Nigerian politician, was associated with concern for the rights of women—but always as justified by Islamic teachings. His mother taught him the Quran and started his study of Arabic, and he felt strongly about the limitations placed on her life by Hausa society. To her memory he dedicated his lifelong support for women's education.

Aminu Kano was trained as an Islamic scholar, schooled in Islamic law, and educated in British schools both in Nigeria and in London. Throughout his lifetime he was well known for his deep commitment to Islamic teachings, his politically caustic poetry, and his satirical denunciation of the pompous ways of traditional emirate rulers. Unlike other Nigerian politicians of the time, he never accumulated personal wealth and lived all his life in the same humble dwelling in Kano City. He was a progressive in his practice of Islam and an early advocate of female education and the political emancipation of women. These positions, however, were always expressed with readings from the Quran and defended by quotations from the Prophet and dan Fodio (see Sklar, 1968; Whitaker, 1970; Paden, 1973). Aminu Kano and his followers stressed that the Quran is the basis of Islamic life and provides the paradigm of values and orientations toward authority and community to be followed by all Muslims. Indeed, all the early leaders of opposition politics in the Islamic sections of the country were trained and recognized as Islamic teachers (Aminu Kano, Sa'ad Zungar, and Isa Wali).

The NPC/NPN held power at the national level in both the first and second Nigerian republics. But the NEPU/PRP dominated politics in Kano City and later, when states were created by the military before the 1979 elections, in Kano and the other Islamic northern states. The leaders of the party stressed that the NPC and northern NPN leaders had betrayed the Islamic ideals set down by dan Fodio at the time of the *jihad* and attempted to place the stamp of Islamic approval on their own political program. They emphasized the political implications of Islamic concepts of government. Their ideological vision was a "radical" democracy in which principles of Islamic justice applied and in which the interests of all the people, including women, the poor, and the dispossessed, would be fairly represented.

For thirty years political dialogue was phrased in terms of Islamic reform. Campaign themes centered around notions of equality, knowledge, literacy, "modernization" (meaning reform of Islam, not development in the Western sense), and political reform according to the concepts of Islamic government. Equality was a concept that included women, but only insofar as Quranic interpretation allowed. Mallam Aminu Kano's advocacy of education and political emancipation for women did not imply support for Western feminist concepts, and both men and women clearly understood this.

Both Aminu Kano and his party repeatedly criticized and challenged the near total exclusion of women from the public world in the north during the First Republic. They asserted that Nigerian Muslim women suffered because of misinterpretations of the Quran. It was they who first made the point that four wives were sanctioned by the Prophet Muhammad only if all of them were treated equally and that because truly equal treatment is beyond human capability, the Quran does not actually endorse polygamy. They stressed that education is required for both men and women because the Prophet has said that the only way to understand Islam is through education in it. And education for women is obviously required because they are admonished to teach children. Exhortations for the education and political emancipation of women did not challenge their seclusion from public view, however. Aminu Kano argued that the seclusion of women in their homes did not mean they should be excluded from the political process. They should be permitted to go out to vote at night in the company of their husbands.

The First Republic

Largely in deference to strong Muslim lobbying, Nigeria's independence constitution of 1960 did not grant women the right to vote. The regional governments in the Eastern and Western Regions almost immediately enacted legislation extending the franchise to women, but the NPC strongly resisted such action in the North. Expanding the franchise to women was labeled incompatible with the customs of the people, and the low level of education of women was cited by the regional government as a reason not to extend the vote to them. Literacy in English for Muslim women was virtually nonexistent.

In spite of the fact that women could not vote in the north, both political parties had "women's wings" affiliated with them. Their leadership was appointed by the party heads, and they were given little or no autonomy. They relied upon the men of the party for both membership recruitment and financial underpinning. Because women could not vote, the function of the women's wings was not to involve them in politics but rather to provide entertainment at political rallies, particularly in the case of the NPC. In fact, identification with the women's wings carried a derogatory implication. Because all respectable women were in seclusion, the membership of the women's wings was recruited from women living outside of marriage and hence outside the bounds of proper society. Many of them were known to be *karuwai,* or prostitutes. Their function was to chant, sing, and dance at rallies, attracting voters and entertaining the crowds. They were provided by the parties with transportation, lodging, and food. In turn, they could solicit private business after their public performances. They did not define or present issues of interest to women. Husbands, even if they were politicians, would not allow their own wives to be involved.

NEPU/PRP did express concern about the social position of women and advocated public policies for them, especially regarding access to education. But this advocacy was couched in the language of Islamic justice, not feminist revolution. In fact, the Western feminist movement was roundly attacked. Politics, however, did provide social mobility for men, particularly men of traditionally low status. During the colonial period, the sons of slaves had been sent to schools established by the British for the sons of chiefs. Thus, a core of educated men of slave origin who were closely tied to the royal families became very important politically, especially in the First Republic. Nigeria's first prime minister, Sir Tafawa Balewa, was the son of such a family. However, the first women to receive education were upper class. They began receiving it in the 1970s, whereas men of the traditional upper classes began to receive Western education in the late 1950s.

The First Republic came to an end in 1966, when a coup d'etat resulted in thirteen years of military rule, during which time the country endured a six-year civil war. In 1975 preparation for a return to civilian rule began in earnest, and in 1976 a military decree enfranchised all women in Nigeria. The ban on politics imposed in 1966 was lifted in 1978, and parties were again allowed to organize. By then, both dominant parties agreed on the importance of education for girls and of women's right to vote. The traditional leaders of the north—particularly the highest religious leader, the Sultan of Sokoto—urged women to register and vote. Their votes were important if the northern parties were to defeat their southern rivals at the presidential level. Women in fact did register and voted in great numbers in the 1979 elections.

The Second Republic

Although defeated at the national level in 1979, Aminu Kano's party, the PRP, was voted into power in the two northern states of Kano and Kaduna. It implemented special programs for women, including appointment to public positions, as a means of demonstrating its commitment to providing greater public involvement of women in public affairs. During the Second Republic (1979–1983), Aminu Kano's program of reform for women was basically adopted. His program was one supportable within the teachings of Islam. The rhetoric and ideas of Mallam Aminu Kano kept notions of Islamic justice and equality at the center of political debate. As part of Islamic reform, his party advocated the extension of education for girls and the greater involvement of women in public affairs. During the years of the Second Republic, Universal Primary Education was already underway, and Muslim leaders exhorted parents to send their girls as well as their boys to primary school.

Shortly after the 1979 election there was a subtle but noticeable change in the language of political discussion and debate. It was echoed in the northern press in columns written by young lecturers at the two large northern universities, Bayero University in Kano and Ahmadu Bello University in Kaduna. Political parties were increasingly described as expressions of class interests, interests that were diametrically opposed to each other. The NPN and its leaders in power at the national level were cast as antagonistic to the common people, the *talakawa,* who were represented by the PRP at the state level. There were assertions about the schemes of international capitalism and U.S.-inspired imperialism designed to exploit the Nigerian working class and peasants while stripping the country of its resources with the assistance of the NPN. Aminu Kano himself increasingly invoked the specter of Western domination to account for both moral decline at the national level and the ruination of the Nigerian economy.

In this discourse there was also much concern about the place and role of women. Education for women continued to be urged, but increasingly concern was raised about "alien" notions of "women's liberation," and the superiority of the place of women in Islam was stressed. However, the main themes had become Marxist and economic in nature. The common people were characterized as exploited, forced into a relationship of dependency. In this new vocabulary, the old NEPU concern with Islamic justice and its meaning for the place of women was muted. Resentment was kindled toward the civilian government in Lagos, both on traditional grounds and on new grounds of callous indifference to the needs of "the people."

The PRP urged the adoption of a socialist economy in which these needs would be met. It embraced Universal Primary Education and urged fathers and husbands to send their daughters to school. In addition to urging increasing levels of education, the PRP advocated the nationalization of state assets in order to free the country from foreign domination. At that point, poverty would be eliminated, women as well as men would be emancipated, and all would live according to the principles of Islamic justice (see People's Redemption Party, "Plan for Redemption: Aims and Objectives of the People's Redemption Party," Kano: 1979).

Although these issues were quite removed from the immediate concerns of women, there is evidence that women voting for the first time did recognize a difference between the two parties in terms of their own interests. This awareness is illustrated by a look at the voting patterns in the two wards mentioned in Chapter 5, Kurawa and Kofar Mazugal. In Kano City in 1979, there were four administrative zones comprising 132 wards. To a certain extent, traditional social divisions were manifest, with specific wards traditionally associated with occupational categories, which in themselves carry connotations of social standing within Hausa society. Administrative and middle-rank civil servants were generally resident in the predominantly Fulani wards, such as Kurawa; traders, merchants, and craftsmen were resident in the predominantly Hausa wards, such as Kofar Mazugal.

It was in wards such as the latter that NEPU drew its votes during 1950–1965 and that the PRP won overwhelmingly in 1979. In Kofar

Mazugal, the Hausa *talakawa* formed the bedrock of PRP support, and the party won overwhelmingly. If women voted, they clearly voted as did men here. Kurawa, on the other hand, had been an NPC stronghold in a NEPU city from 1952–1965, and the NPN expected to win easily in 1979. In fact, it barely won, which lends credence to the PRP's assertion that it was women, voting for the first time, who provided the party with its overwhelming victory in Kano. (The PRP won 76 percent of the vote in Kano City in 1979.) That there was significant support for the PRP in Kurawa, where it was not expected, indicates that women were very aware that the PRP was the party with their interests at heart. Two Bayero University students surveyed 284 women in Kano in 1981 for the author, and 267 identified the PRP as "the party for women." Hence, it is reasonable to speculate that PRP drew large percentages of women's votes, suggesting some evidence of a "gender gap." Muslim women were clearly capable of making distinctions between the parties.

In the 1979 elections, in seeking to affect the women's vote, the parties again created "women's wings." But the leaders of the wings were designated by the traditional pre-Islamic women's title of "magajiya," signifying the new legitimacy for women in public roles.

The PRP continued to try to characterize women's issues as matters of religious concern. Like NEPU before it, the PRP defended its support for women's political participation on the grounds that all believers should participate as equals in the state and that Islam requires that women be educated in order to be better wives and mothers. Unlike their function in the first period of civilian rule, however, the women's wings' main task was to recruit the women's vote. The entertainment role was deemphasized. The parties also took to radio and television to try to draw out the vote. Education and participation were the only two women's issues endorsed. Although it did not encourage a discussion about the restrictions that made women inherently unequal in the structure of Islam itself, the PRP did repeatedly assert that "development cannot occur until women are educated and equal to men" (PRP, 1979).

Once the elections were over, the women's wings were largely inactive, and their leadership retreated from public view once the elections were concluded. They had no agenda of their own. The wings had been organized by male party leaders, and the party had again appointed their leaders and financed their activities. Their only agenda was to garner women's support for the party's candidates. However, the leaders of the women's wings did gain experience in the political arena and helped legitimize women's participation in politics. And the fact that women apparently voted in large numbers in their first election indicates some success for the wings' efforts. The PRP did succeed in politicizing women to some extent and brought them into the public domain, and it offered educated women an outlet for their views by putting them on the radio and television. More important, the PRP appointed two women to government positions after it came to power. By bringing them into the government, it was beginning to create new role models for Hausa Muslim women accustomed to being isolated and secluded.

To an impressive extent, during its four years in power the PRP did keep its campaign promises to women. Girls' schools were built, women's centers were established offering literacy classes, and a few women were appointed to public positions. In all of this, there was no general public outcry against government efforts, although there was enormous private pressure in individual cases.

There were also outbreaks of violence led by Muslim "fanatics." The largest of these were the Maitatsine riots in Kano in 1980. Maitatsine was a radical reformer who rallied large numbers of young and poor Quranic students to the cause of purifying Islam. He condemned all those in power as un-Islamic materialists and over a period of months took virtual control of a ward of Kano City, from which his followers launched attacks on anyone driving through it and on neighboring wards. Women were particularly targeted; several hundred who dared to venture into the Maitatsine's territory were picked up and virtually held captive in his compound. In December 1980, the Nigerian army was called in to quell the disturbances, and in the end nearly 10,000 people were killed in the confrontations between the military, the police, and the fundamentalists (Commission of Inquiry 1985). Although the Maitatsine himself was killed, periodic outbreaks of violence inspired by his followers and other Islamic militants have continued to occur in most northern cities during the past decade.

Military Rule

Ironically, it has been the military, rather than the two civilian regimes, that has advanced the cause of women's political rights in Nigeria. Women in northern Nigeria were given the vote in 1976 by military decree. Moreover, the Babangida regime, which came to power in 1986, appointed a token woman to each state cabinet, signaling that women do belong in the corridors of decisionmaking. In 1990 the military government nominated five women to serve in the 325-member Constituent Assembly charged with writing the constitution for the Third Republic. In preparing a draft for the assembly, the political bureau of the military president's office put forward the recommendation that 5 percent of the legislative seats in all three tiers of government (state, house of assembly, and senate) be reserved for women. This suggestion was turned down by the civilian assembly, however.

In one area, law, not even the military has been able to extend the protections of the Nigerian constitution to all women. Thus, women still face disadvantages vis-à-vis men because of the deference shown, both in the constitution itself and in the culture, to Islamic beliefs. Islamic law has increasingly become a symbol of Muslim identity in Nigeria. The Native Courts Proclamation of 1906 authorized British colonial officers to establish Islamic courts. From the beginning of colonial rule, in essence, the British recognized the authority of the emirs and the Islamic legal system in the northern parts of the country. This system remained substantively unchanged until the legal reforms of 1959, which assigned four categories of law (criminal, land, subversion, and taxation) to the regional governments and incorporated them into a civil law code that was legislated and secular. But the fifth category of law, civil personal law, was left outside the civil codes.

For the most part, neither the British nor the postindependence Nigerian government made any attempt to interfere with Islamic law. British common law had been incorporated into the Nigerian legal system of the country, but in the north *Sharia* law remained essentially intact. During the course of the 1978 debates in the Constituent Assembly over the content of the 1979 constitution, the question of the place of Islamic law in the Nigerian legal system nearly ended the deliberations. Several important issues were raised, including the nature of the relationship between sacred and secular law in general, the position of Islamic law in a secular state, and the separation of Islamic personal law from the general body of Islamic law. The most contentious debate, however, centered around the issue of the creation of a federal Sharia Court of Appeal, as recommended by the Constitutional Drafting Committee (CDC).

Although it was stressed in the debates that Islam is a "total way of life" and the *Sharia* sacred in its totality, the Muslims compromised in order to make a separate Islamic court system acceptable to non-Muslim members of the CDC. They argued that the *Sharia* courts should deal only with Islamic personal law, except when the parties concerned voluntarily submitted other issues to these courts. Islamic personal law was described as that dealing with marriage, divorce, legitimization and custody of children, and inheritance. Ultimately the constitution did not create a federal Sharia Court of Appeal, but it did stipulate that "the President in exercising his power to appoint the Justices of the Supreme Court and the Federal Court of Appeal, shall include in his appointees persons learned in Islamic law and these persons shall sit and determine appeals relating to Islamic law" (Section 150 [5] [ii]). Also, provisions were inserted into the constitution that exempted Islamic personal law from the human rights clauses included in the constitution.

By including the provisions insisted upon by the Muslim members of the assembly, the Nigerian constitution enshrined in law a conflict between the rights of Muslim women and the "fundamental human rights" provisions found elsewhere in the constitution. Section II(1)(a) stated that "every citizen shall have equality of rights, obligations, and opportunities before the law." Despite the fact that Islam stresses the equality of all human beings before Allah, the provisions of the *Sharia* that render a woman's testimony equal to one-half that of a man's decree that women's property rights are less than those of men, restrict women's movement, or make it easier for a man than for a woman to obtain a divorce establish that women are not equal to men. The constitution prohibited discrimination on grounds of membership in a particular community, ethnic group, place of origin, or sex. It did not prohibit discrimination based on religion.

The 1990 Constitutional Assembly entered further emotional debates concerning the place of Islamic law in a secular state, and again the assembly backed off the issue in order not to create an impasse. Muslim women as well as Muslim men supported the protections afforded Islamic law in the Nigerian constitution, and the military government did not want to reopen the issue.

Recently, the current military regime apparently joined the Organization of Islamic Associations, a move that occasioned a great political outcry on the part of Christian leaders. The Nigerian military government has remained vague about whether or not Nigeria is actually a member of this group or whether the regime has simply asked for observer status, an approach designed to reassure the Christians and appease Muslims. This is a very emotional issue, one with which the new regime will have to deal if Nigeria does in fact return to civilian rule as scheduled in 1994.

By at least making gestures to join the Organization of Islamic Associations and by agreeing to special provisions in the constitution to protect Islamic law, the military has avoided offending religious leaders. It has not been so successful in garnering the support of university students. Strikes and disturbances have periodically closed all nineteen Nigerian universities during recent years. Confrontations between the government and students reached a climax on May 24, 1986, when troops fired into a crowd at Ahmadu Bello University, the largest northern university, killing a number of students. The national union of university students was banned. Originally, the rhetoric of the students' organization was Marxist. Gradually, however, this rhetoric has been changing, and in the northern parts of the country it now invokes language of the Islamic *jihad.* The Islamic Students Organization is the strongest student organization on the northern campuses. Both the leadership and the followers speak the language of militant Islam. Muslim students have stoned Christian worshipers on their campuses, demanded strict adherence to Islamic injunctions, and insisted that female students wear black on campus. Female students have complied. The Islamic Students Organizations, supported by Iran, Iraq, Saudi Arabia, and Egypt, provide members with operating funds and travel stipends, enabling them to travel to other Islamic countries where fundamentalists are in control. In this way inter-Muslim politics play out among students in Nigeria. During the Gulf War, the Nigerian government supported the allied effort to remove Iraqi troops from Kuwait, but students at Bayero University in Kano renamed the entranceway to the campus Saddam Hussein Avenue. Pictures of Khoemeini and Ghadaffi are displayed in offices and on the walls of student hostels. Islamic consciousness presents a powerful alternative to the postindependence legacy of the colonial state.

The national trade union congresses have been disbanded by the military government, and a new national trade union organization has formed. The continuing rampant corruption under the military and the effort at structural adjustment of the economy have combined to undermine the government's ability to meet its payroll, and this problem has led to general chaos on the labor scene, as one organized sector of the work force after another calls for a general strike. Thus far, the military has succeeded in forcing teachers, shippers, dockworkers, and industrial workers back to their jobs. Although the work force has not functioned smoothly, it has not been able to organize politically, either. Workers still identify with political parties on the basis of ethnicity and religion, not ideology.

Realizing, perhaps, that its mandate is wearing thin as life becomes more difficult for ever larger numbers of Nigerians, the military government is once again directing a return to civilian rule. The process began in 1988 when the ban on political organization was lifted and continued in the 1990 decree recognizing two political parties, a left-of-center Social Democratic Party and a right-of-center National Republican Convention. A series of elections began at the local level in 1989 and will culminate in a presidential referendum scheduled for the end of 1993.

Through all the campaigning of the past five years, no national women's political interest group has formed, and no feminist agenda has been developed. A National Commission on Women has been appointed by the military government, however, and it is chaired by Bolanle Awe, perhaps Nigeria's most respected female academic. Bolanle Awe is a professor of sociology at the University of Ibadan, where she directs the Institute of African Studies. She has often spoken out on women's issues, and her work on Yoruba market women is widely respected. The commission was charged to register women to vote and to encourage them to run for office. It has been given a lot of publicity for its work, particularly by the Nigerian Association of Women Journalists, which assures its activities wide coverage in the press. Although the commission has exhorted women to run for office, mostly through the media, it has not had the means to actually assist women in their campaigns. Women seeking public office in Nigeria have the same problems as they do in the United States, and those problems are primarily financial. Nigerian men invest large sums of money in securing party nominations. Few women have access to such resources and generally do not succeed in raising the necessary funds. An accounting has not yet been made of how many women unsuccessfully sought party nominations in the elections at the local, state, and national levels.

Preparation for the Third Republic

Nigeria is scheduled to elect a civilian president in 1993. Although it is not clear which of the two parties sanctioned by the military will come to power, in regard to women some things are quite clear. Improved education and economic opportunity for women are on the agenda for both parties, but women's liberation—in the broader sense of women's freedom to make major life decisions for themselves—is not endorsed by either.

In Nigeria, the Islamic press and Islamic women associate the Western women's liberation movement with trivialization of the family, lesbianism, unwed mothers, pornography, prostitution, drugs, and alcoholism (Yusuf, 1991, p. 105). They assert that "true Islam" will liberate women in ways that Western women's liberation cannot. In Islam, in contrast to the degradation of women in Western society, women have "the right to be housed, fed, and maintained by their husbands;" to own and dispose of property; to inherit; to conduct legal transactions; to vote; to pursue education; and to pursue their rights through the *Sharia* courts (Yusuf, 1991, p. 106). Islam gives women dignity they do not have in Western countries, where, according to the accounts of Western feminists themselves, women are exploited and degraded.

Just as very few women achieved positions of political significance in the first two republics, so it is quite clear that they will not in the Third Republic either. Five political parties contested the elections in the Second Republic, and none of them nominated women for national or gubernatorial positions, nor did any have women running in more than 5 percent of the races for state assemblies (Mba, 1979). In the current series of elections, in spite of the fact that the military government has urged that the two parties include 5 percent women candidates on their slates for every office, neither party has done so. None of the more than 2,000 electoral commissioners appointed to certify the election results were women. The psychological effect has been to signify to women that their participation in the elections is indeed peripheral (Awe, 1991).

During 1990–1991, a series of elections at the local and state levels were held, and in 1992 federal representatives and senators were elected to assume office after the return to civilian rule. As mentioned above, the primary stumbling block for women seeking nominations at all stages of the electoral process has been financial. In order to stand for election to the federal legislature, both parties require a deposit of N25,000, and even local government council candidates must post N500 (Awe, 1991). Very few women can generate the backing to raise the funds for these deposits. In addition to cash deposits, candidates must provide hospitality to supporters, continuously entertaining with food and drink. Few husbands will support their wives in any such undertaking.

In the first phases of elections held in preparation for a return to civilian rule and the establishment of the Third Nigerian Republic in 1993, women candidates have been neither numerous nor successful. Of the nearly 8,000 contestants for chairmanships of local government councils, only one woman was successful. The representation of women elected to serve on the councils is less than 1 percent nationwide, and most of these are in the southern states (Awe, 1991).

In the elections to the state houses of representatives, there were 10 women candidates out of 2,005 nominated, and 3 (all southern) were elected. Of the 475 candidates fielded for the state senate elections, only 4 were women, and not one was elected. In the elections for federal House of Assembly, the two parties nominated over 5,000 candidates, of whom 42 were women; of these, 5 were elected (all non-Muslim). Twenty-three of the 994 candidates for the federal senate were women, and 3 of them were elected (Awe, 1991).

In order to seek explanations for the poor showing of women at electoral levels, particularly at the local level (where they might have been expected to do better), Professor Awe, chair of the National Commission on Women, examined party documents and interviewed party officials and female political aspirants. Answers to questionnaires randomly administered in the Ibadan market are revealing. Essentially, the market women asserted that politics had no relevance to their lives.

> I did not vote during the last elections because I saw no need for it. My success in life depends on what I do with my hands and not what anybody promises me, so I prefer to be left alone. Politics is not for women. It is for men—men who can lie and those who have the time. (Awe, 1991, p. 16)

Open distrust of politicians was the dominant theme. Awe concluded that the limitation to two political parties is disadvantaging women, because the stakes are too high and men feel they cannot make room for women.

This time around, the two parties are forbidden to establish women's wings. In the Second Republic, these wings helped women to establish confidence by giving them a chance to operate and exercise leadership within the parties. But the National Commission of Women advised that, on balance, the women's wings helped marginalize women's issues. Wrote Awe: "In virtually all cases, women in such associations have been used as cannon fodder by the political parties to gain votes. At the end of the day, when it came to power sharing and decision-making, the women were dropped" (1991, p. 9). Thus, the commission urged that women be integrated into the political parties rather than segregated within them, and the military accepted this recommendation.

The National Commission on Women maintains national and regional offices, issues critiques of national development plans, and runs seminars in order to help women organize locally. It has focused on education and women in development, particularly at the rural levels, and advocates that significant resources be channeled to women in agricultural development projects. The commission continuously urges greater participation by women in politics and stresses the necessity for complementarity in the roles of men and women so as not to antagonize or polarize the electorate along the lines of gender—hence its opposition to women's wings in the two government-recognized political parties. But with the disappearance of women's wings, women have had to try to work within the main party structure, and only in Lagos State have they managed to hold any positions of note. In the National Republican Convention, Suliat Adedeji ran for the post of publicity secretary but was defeated. In the Social Democratic Party, Iyabo Anisulowo and Sarah Jibril both vied for national posts and were defeated. One again, however, the military stepped in. In the late fall of 1992, the government dissolved the executive committees of the two parties and appointed caretaker committees to prepare for the presidential elections. Mrs. Latifa Okunnu was appointed to chair the committee for the National Republican Convention. She is, perhaps significantly, a former president of the Federation of Muslim Women's Associations of Nigeria (FOMWAN).

Both parties have planks on women in their national manifestos and constitutions to encourage women to participate fully in the economy and pledging to support their general (social) welfare. Neither party has stressed political participation for women, and their record of performance in promoting women has been negligible. According to Balanle Awe, women must have basic education and security before they can participate effectively in politics. Women are 52 percent of the overall population but 70 percent of the illiterate population (Awe, 1991, p. 18). The majority of Nigerian women live in rural areas, where their primary preoccupation is survival.

In northern Nigeria, women in seclusion can vote "but not campaign to be voted for" (p. 18). However, they do have aspirations. In 1992 women announced their candidacies for governor in Lagos and Maidugari states. In the end their parties did not support them, but their ambitions were not dismissed as illegitimate or unthinkable. There are even women who talk of running for president, and there are indications that some are beginning to build local political bases. In Anambra State in the east, two women won local elections to the 1988 Constituent Assembly. Both had long records of service at the village and local level, and both had begun to build up networks among women in their state. This support has not yet translated into state or national power, but the foundation is being laid. The Nigerian Association of Women Journalists is helping enormously to create a climate of acceptance by giving publicity to women's efforts. At present, essential data is missing, however. Bolanle Awe has not been able to collect such basic information as how many women have registered to vote and how many women each party has registered on its rolls. Therefore, comparisons about political participation of men and women are difficult to make.

In the last decade of military rule and partly in anticipation of the Third Republic, two avowedly feminist organizations have formed in Nigeria to advance the rights of women in the public arena: Women in Nigeria (WIN) and the Federation of Muslim Women's Associations of Nigeria (FOMWAN). They have taken over center stage from a third, older women's organization, the National Council of Women's Societies (NCWS). The NCWS is a confederation of more traditional women's service and social organizations such as the YWCA, the Girl Scouts, and the Red Cross. Its members are generally from the ranks of elite women, whereas the leadership of the other two organizations seeks to appeal to nonelite women.

Women in Nigeria (WIN) was founded by a coalition of university and professional women in Kaduna in 1982. It is attempting to bring women together across religious, class, and ethnic lines in order to represent their interests. Because it has attempted to be a truly national organization and has been outspoken on a number of issues, particularly in regard to child marriage and related women's health topics, WIN has been accused in Muslim areas of "Westernism" and "radicalism" and of being non- (and sometimes anti-) Muslim as well as anti–status quo. WIN, in spite of its efforts, is described in the press as too intellectual, probably because its base is in the universities.

FOMWAN, in contrast, is concerned with promoting Islam and mobilizing Muslim women in support of liberal interpretations of Islamic teachings. It has been endorsed by some learned Muslim men in its efforts to redefine the gender discourse in Islam, at least as it is practiced in Nigeria. However, there are limitations to its agenda:

> While they try to use the ulama, the ulama does the same to them—to mobilize women to vote Muslim men into power, who would then be assumed to look after "their" women. In addition, there are limits to the possible "liberality" of gender discourses within Islam. However, by keeping within already legitimated boundaries FOMWAN gains both support and material resources. (Imam, 1990, p. 22)

Because of its access to press coverage, its position as an explicitly Islamic women's organization, and the support it has received from some of the Islamic establishment, FOMWAN is particularly important. Its chief spokesperson is Bilkisu Yusuf, a former editor of the *Daily Triumph* newspaper in Kano and currently the editor of a weekly newsmagazine, *The*

Nigerian Democrat. As stated above, the organization's focus is on women's rights in Islam, particularly those rights denied to women in Hausa culture, such as inheritance rights and the right to gain custody of children upon divorce. FOMWAN also aims to gain equal access to education and equality in marriage agreements for Nigerian Muslim women. It stresses that Muslim women have an acceptable, important role to play in the development of an Islamic state in accordance with, not in juxtaposition to, Islamic teachings. FOMWAN strongly supported the effort to establish Islamic (*Sharia*) courts in each of Nigeria's thirty states, and it urges Muslim women to use these courts to protect their rights. For this reason also, the organization endorses the effort to introduce Islamic Religious Knowledge to the core of all curricula at all levels of education. FOMWAN argues that a more thorough and accurate understanding of the teachings of Islam in regard to the status of women will make young men better informed about women's rights and persuade them to join Islamic women in assuring that these rights are acknowledged and supported in the society.

FOMWAN had been especially critical of the older women's organization, the National Council of Women's Societies, particularly the efforts of that organization to introduce legislation advocating family planning and monogamy in marriage, both of which FOMWAN asserts to be un-Islamic. FOMWAN does, however, advocate family planning geared toward spacing, rather than limiting, childbirth. Its objection, like that of the Roman Catholic Church, is to such means as the use of contraceptives, intrauterine devices, injections, castration, sterilization, or abortion. In the context of Nigerian politics, FOMWAN is more liberal than the majority of both Muslim and non-Muslim men. It has taken a public position on this sensitive issue and issued a public document advocating the spacing of children. At the same time, FOMWAN successfully lobbied the government to drop its policy of urging women to use contraceptives in order to limit themselves to four children each. It stated its objection in terms very similar to those used by pro-choice advocates in the United States: "Islam teaches about every aspect of life and it is not for the government to interfere" (FOMWAN, 1988).

FOMWAN is concerned with the issue of preadolescent marriage and strongly supports efforts to bring an end to child marriage by prohibiting men from marrying girls under the age of fourteen. Although men generally now support primary-level education for girls, FOMWAN seeks to assure girls education through secondary school in order that they may be better prepared as wives and mothers. The organization has clashed with the religious establishment over Quranic interpretation. Islamic women argue in the daily press that the Quran permits women to go out of their home for valid reasons, to retain custody of their children in divorce, to discuss serious issues on an equal footing with their husbands, to claim a divorce for a host of good reasons, and not to be physically abused (Lemu, 1986). FOMWAN counters that men have distorted Islamic teachings to suit themselves. Islamic beliefs do provide a model for women's behavior and thus a model for their participation in the public domain, but it is more limited than the model aspired to by non-Muslim women. In spite of FOMWAN's clear identification with Islamic teachings, some Muslim religious leaders have condemned it, predicting that it will "suffer the same moral disintegration and degradation as their counterparts in the West" (Yusuf, 1991, p. 102). Its members, however, resist the effort to identify them with Western women's liberation by continuously stressing their adherence to the teachings of Islam concerning protections and respect for women.

As women's economic position and interests change and as they become more active in politics, their representation at the formal level will change as it has elsewhere. When that happens, we can predict that Muslim women in Nigeria will gradually expand their perception of what issues and policies are of legitimate concern to them as Islamic women. Thus, the importance of the emergence of a radical Islamic women's liberation movement in Nigeria cannot be overemphasized. The movement is articulating demands of behalf of women based on the teachings of the Quran. In so doing, it is calling for a reexamination of the judicial, educational, political, and economic systems of the secular state, both as they affect the society as a whole and as they impact upon Muslim women in particular.

Women's rights are a delicate political issue that is commanding more and more attention in the Nigerian press and media, and Muslim women are at the forefront. They recognize and accept that reform must come from within interpretations of Islamic doctrine rather than through challenges to it. But in these doctrines, they assert, are protections for women as given by Allah through his messenger, the Prophet Muhammad.

It is also important to note that research on other Islamic societies has emphasized that Muslim women are in many ways more independent of men than are Western women who have not experienced life in an all-female world (Del Vecchio Good 1978; Fallers, 1982; Papanek, 1973). Observation in Nigeria suggests that when secluded women step into public roles they retain a sense of independence from men. As teachers, midwives, or bureaucrats, they interact with a wide variety of people, and their confidence is growing. Their influence among women is considerable, all the more so because it often occurs behind the walls of seclusion, where men are absent from the discussions. At home, young professional women interact with their co-wives, relatives, women who are members of their extended families, and others from all ranks who may visit their compounds for any number of reasons. Women's public reticence is not reflected in their lively interaction with each other. In the world behind the walls of seclusion, women's views are changing. How open this changing consciousness will become is dependent, in large measure, on changing men's attitudes, and this end will be accomplished most successfully if approached from the point of view of better religious understanding. Hence, the introduction of Islamic Religious Knowledge into the school curriculum at all levels is potentially revolutionary.

Within Islam, northern Nigerian women have found ways to make their voices heard. Just as the interaction between traditional culture and Islam brought about great changes in the status of women in precolonial times, so the interplay between ideology, reality, and Islamic identity in the modern state may yet bring about a transformation in the way women are required to live. The consequences of women's efforts to transform their lives by asserting their rights within Islam may not be uniform or unidirectional, but a vision for a different future is emerging. Marriage is still the required state for Muslim women, and within marriage deference, obedience, and restrictions on movements and actions are not challenged. However, rights to protection, support, and inheritance are endorsed and asserted with renewed vigor. The call for an Islamic state offers both an alternative moral order and cause for pause. There is a need to look seriously at the consequences of pro-Islamic revolutions for women. The examples of how women fare in such states—e.g., Algeria, Iran, Pakistan, Sudan— is not encouraging.

There have been some attempts to discourage the seclusion of Muslim women in northern Nigeria, but neither the federal nor the state government has wanted to take on this issue in any overt way. Instead, the official policy has been to encourage female education, representation in the work force, and political participation. In the last decade, however, even these subtle attempts have become more tentative, retreating in the face of a rise in fundamentalism. The 1988 Kano State Commission on Women, for instance, urged greater efforts for women's education and employment but recommended single-sex workplaces (Imam, 1990). Similarly, Muslim leaders are now urging women to vote not in their own right or for their own interests but rather to support Muslim men against non-Muslim men (Imam, 1990).

With increasing numbers of women in more responsible roles, women in general will gradually change their image of themselves and their expectations, and they will make progress in West African countries as they do over time in other cultures. Such progress, however, is not likely to be evident as coherent, unidirectional change. As the messages are mixed, so the results will be. Women and their issues will become more visible, and their ability to translate these issues into public policy will become more effective, but not without reactionary attitudes in day-to-day life. How significant Mrs. Okunnu's role will prove to be in overseeing the reorganization of the National Republican Convention is yet to be evaluated.

Certainly she will be highly visible, and her appointment by the military government again reemphasizes the important role the military has played in expanding women's political voice in Nigeria.

WOMEN IN SENEGALESE POLITICS

Politics in Senegal, like those in Nigeria, are intimately related to religion—that is, to Islam. But the relationship is still a partnership between government and clergy, much as it was in the colonial period. In the preindependence period, the French clearly distinguished between themselves and the Muslim marabouts in the countryside. They used the marabouts to get the support they needed for their programs and to obtain obedience with unpopular taxes. The marabouts in turn received government assistance and even used French support to eliminate rivals within the brotherhood. Leopold Sédar Senghor, a Catholic who emerged as Senegal's leader in the late 1940s, used the same tactic as the French, skillfully supporting powerful marabouts such as Falilou M'Backé, *khalif* of the Mourides, but also preventing the brotherhoods from uniting against him as they might have, for example, within the Council of Islamic Organizations in 1957. Like the French, Senghor may have deplored the necessity of appeasing and persuading the marabouts at every turn, but it was a fact of life in Senegal. The majority of the population in rural areas had strong allegiance to one of the *turuuq*. The marabouts were the patrons to whom the peasant farmer went with his problems and to whom he paid allegiance and a tithe of his own production. They were the rural political powers, not officeholders but brokers who used elected and appointed politicians who had curried their favor (see Creevey Behrman, 1970).

Much has changed, of course, in the years since independence. In the 1960s, Senegal went through a period of more or less authoritarian control. Facing a bitter conflict with his former political rival and then prime minister, Mamadou Dia, in 1962, Senghor eliminated the position of prime minister and made opposition parties illegal. Only his government party, the Union Progressiste Senegalaise (UPS), was allowed. Mamadou Dia had pushed for social-democratic and populist policies. He strongly supported the creation of rural cooperatives and lobbied for a rural animation program to get government agents directly to rural people in an effort to create a popular base that might have eliminated the maraboutic control structure. Senghor both feared that Dia was attempting to supplant him and believed that Senegal must take a more gradual road to democratic reforms. He continued his more conservative approach and his collaboration with rural marabouts, who supported him through the major political crises (Creevey, 1977, pp. 261–277; Coulon, 1990, pp. 411–448; Fatton, 1987; Gellar, 1982).

By the end of Senghor's regime, the government had begun to liberalize. It had never been a thoroughly repressive regime; opposition leaders had remained active in the country, and criticism of the government was openly expressed (Coulon, 1990, pp. 418–419). But in the middle and late 1970s, Senghor began to allow such opposition to be legally represented. In 1974, he permitted the legalization of opposition parties, which he restricted to two: a liberal democratic party, le Parti Démocratique Sénégalais (PDS), and a Marxist party, le Parti Africain d'Indépendence (PAI). The UPS, now called the Parti Socialist (PS), retained the powerful center position as the socialist party. A fourth, "conservative" option was permitted in 1978 when the Mouvement Republicain Sénégalais (MRS) was legalized.

Abdou Diouf was named prime minister in 1971 (when this position was re-created), and from then on he was the central figure in the government administration. In 1981, after a period of vocal dissatisfaction directed against the government by radical students and labor and business leaders angry over the economic chaos of the late 1970s, Senghor retired. Abdou Diouf became president. He was labeled by many observers a "technocrat" rather than an "intellectual" and a "civil servant" rather than a "politician," in contrast to Senghor (Coulon, 1990, p. 423; Gellar, 1982, p. 25; Fatton, 1987, pp. 70–71). Diouf was faced with the need to adopt a severe austerity program to combat the continuing economic crisis and satisfy the demands of the International Monetary Fund, which had agreed to refinance Senegal's huge national debt (Fatton, 1987, p. 75; Gellar, 1982, pp. 112–114). He needed to reorganize and revitalize the government; liberalization of politics and trade unions was part of this process. Thus he immediately lifted the ban restricting the number of political parties and trade unions. The result was a proliferation of political and labor organizations: Christian Coulon pointed out in 1989 that fifteen parties were legally recognized (Coulon, 1990, p. 425). The PS, however, remained the largest and most powerful by far. Few of the opposition parties had any significant power base. The most prominent was the PDS, headed by a lawyer named Abdoulaye Wade.

Abdou Diouf, a Muslim, had participated for many years in Senghor's government. He had often appeared for Senghor at national Muslim ceremonies, such as the Magal, to speak in glowing terms of the government's obligation and devotion to the *khalif,* usually of the Mouride brotherhood. He maintained a very cordial relationship with the leaders of the Tidjaniyya *turuuq* as well, both the Niassan and the Abdul Azziz Sy groups. Indeed, he is said to have a "son-like" relationship with the *khalif* of the latter. But despite the continuing semblance of mutual devotion and support, by the end of Senghor's rule some observers felt the tie to the marabouts was relaxing. In 1980, Jean Copans argued that the government was trying to set up its own link to the people rather than going exclusively through the marabouts (Copans, 1980, p. 249). The marabouts themselves—even Abdou Lahat M'Backe, the *khalif* of the Muridiyya at this time—were distancing themselves from open political activities (Gellar, 1982, p. 35). Diouf, who desperately needed to make government more modern and effective, might well have wished to destroy the cumbersome, wasteful patronage system that existed when he became president. Indeed, he did make a number of changes almost immediately. For one thing, he replaced many of the old party faithful with better-trained technical experts in key administrative positions. Also, he attempted to eliminate corruption and inefficiency at the local level as he furthered the rural decentralization programs. More dramatically, he made some controversial gestures, such as appearing at the movie *Ceddo,* which was very critical of the marabouts. But the major marabouts had not yet withdrawn so far that they could no longer reverse themselves and act if they thought it necessary: They got out the vote for Diouf in the elections of 1983. However, Donal Cruise O'Brien, one of the foremost observers of the political role of the brotherhoods, suggests that the low turnout of voters reflected the marabouts' dissatisfaction with Diouf's policies (Cruise O'Brien, 1983). They did not abandon him nor turn to the opposition leaders, but they were warning him of the cost of opposing them.

Perhaps if the economic crisis Senegal faced had quickly been surmounted and Diouf had been able to deliver wealth and security to all other interest groups, he could have bypassed the marabouts. But such was not the situation in Senegal in the early 1980s. The country was becoming increasingly dependent on external institutions, which financed its debt and limited its political options. Diouf was forced to follow the IMF's direction to abolish the numerous parastatals and permit the flowering of free enterprise rather than promote the modified socialism he had espoused. Such developments did not help him politically. When he came to office, Diouf had called for a national coalition of support from the young intellectuals, often the source of major opposition to his predecessor. At first they did back him enthusiastically, but by 1985, disillusioned by the continuing economic crisis and the lack of decisive policies for change, they withdrew their approval (Fatton, 1987, pp. 79, 128).

Additional crises developed, some of which had been smoldering for years. One of the worst of these was the rise of separatist movement—le Mouvement des Forces Démocratiques de Casamance—in the Ziguinchor/Kolda regions. This section of the country, south of Gambia, had long felt cut off from the center of politics. More important, many felt that they had not received their due share of the economic resources available and that the ethnic groups of the region had been disfavored when political plums were handed out. The result was several paralyzing strikes and rebellions in the 1980s (Coulon, 1990, p. 426). A further problem emerged in Mauritania. Until the 1980s, Maures had been major players in the small businesses and trading networks throughout Senegal. In the 1980s, as a result of the establishment of the Senegal River dam and quarrels over claims to land ownership on both sides of the river, the relationship with Mauritania became strained to a critical point. Violent uprisings in Dakar and other parts of the country against the Maures resulted in death and property loss. Many Maures whose families had been in Senegal for generations returned to Mauritania. Diouf managed both these disturbances. By the 1990s, Ziguinchor and Kolda were largely quiet, and relations with Mauritania were much improved (although many of the Maures had not returned to Senegal). But the sources of these tensions have still not been completely resolved. The former Casamance remains on the margin of the economy and polity of the country, and conflicts remain with Senegal's neighbor to the north. In these critical circumstances, and with the high probability that other crises will develop at any time, Diouf still had to rely on the existing power structure; he had no other base to turn to.

Meanwhile, the configuration of Muslims in politics is not static. The brotherhoods themselves are adapting to the new political and economic situation. On the one hand, internal dissent is growing in the form of intellectual and scholarly Muslim beliefs, which spread among the educated and may challenge the political authority of the rural shaikhs at some point. Thus, ironically, the intelligentsia could undermine the political power the rural brotherhoods have enjoyed while actually trying to take it over for themselves (Cruise O'Brien. 1988, p. 137). Moreover, the base of the marabouts' power was the wealth they obtained from controlling the major export crop, peanuts. Now the role of peanuts and agriculture in general has declined, and many peasants are migrating to the towns and cities. Here, though, the predictable linear decline of maraboutic power stalls. In fact, most of the town dwellers are members of brotherhoods. Popular Islam—evidenced by widely publicized "miracles," heavily purchased pictures of the Senegalese marabout saints, numerous gatherings for religious songs, and the multiplication of *dahira*—flourishes in the *quartiers* of the towns, especially Dakar (Coulon, 1983, pp. 136–139). As many commentators have shown, the followers of the Muslim brotherhoods, particularly the Mouride, have become highly successful urban businessmen. Some are small traders, but others deal in real estate or own large commercial businesses, taxi fleets, even major tourist hotels. The town *talibe* is not in the same relationship to the *khalif* as he was. At the very least he is physically distanced, as the major Mouride and Tidjani leaders have remained in the countryside. But the nature of the relationship is still a strong patron-client link. The poor town dwellers contribute what they can in return for the marabout's religious grace and the political favors he can still deliver. Businessmen support the leading marabout in return for his help getting credit, easing restrictions, and facilitating business contacts, as well as for his gifts of grace, or *baraka* (Coulon, 1983, pp. 135–155; Cruise O'Brien, 1975, pp. 59–83).

The spread of education will probably lead to the spread of a more orthodox Islam. The 1991 Senegal Survey showed that educated women were significantly less likely than uneducated women to be members of brotherhoods, although many who had schooling beyond primary school still were members. However, mass education beyond a few years of primary school is still not common, even in urban areas. For the short and intermediate term, the marabouts retain their authority over their followers.

The map of Senegalese politics is changing, but the changes are taking place within a resilient political network that absorbs new groups and fits them into a pattern that has gone on for many generations, perhaps many centuries. Christian Coulon describes the political culture of the precolonial kingdoms in central Senegal as far from authoritarian; political competition between clans was "indispensable for the exercise of political power." The kings of this period were not remote, all-powerful rulers but rather chiefs with obligations to their followers, who in turn had their obligations to their chief or patron (Coulon, 1990, pp. 429–431). Writing at the time of independence, Ruth Schachter Morgenthau observed the same phenomenon in politics. She described clans in Senegal as "groups of leaders and their followers, usually living in a given region though not necessarily belonging to the same ethnic group or related by kinship" (Morgenthau, 1964, p. 126).

Alliances of these clans, she said, were the basis of the political parties contending for power as the French withdrew. Clans bound the uneducated poor, members of lower castes, free peasant farmers, and former slaves to the former nobles. In postcolonial Senegal, the leaders or patrons, who replaced the kings or traditional chiefs in this position, were the marabouts. These alliances continue; they are far-reaching and crosscut the country. Except for the recent Casamance separatist movement, politics in Senegal are not divided on regional lines. Nor are ethnic groups necessarily placed in opposition to each other by these clans. Indeed, the divisions between the major branches of the brotherhoods do not correspond to ethnic splits as such. As Donal Cruise O'Brien pointed out in 1975, most of the Mourides are Wolof, but most Wolof are Tidjani; similarly, most of the Tukulor are Tidjani, but most of the Tidjani are Wolof (Cruise O'Brien, 1975, pp. 149–182). Current data support this observation (see Chapter 3). Nor is there an exact class split either between traditional upper and lower caste/class groups or between them and the new postindustrial classes based on capital formation and the use of paid labor. The coming of Islam and of the French did permit some members of former low caste groups to rise to the position of patron, such as Ibrahima Niass, the former leader of the Kaolack Tidjani brotherhood. However, this class mobility was not typical after the first years of Islam. By the time of independence, the maraboutic group was largely composed of former chiefly or noble families. The newly developing class of technocrats, however, is still open to those of formerly lower caste families. Indeed, some Muslim leaders have opposed French education for their sons, thus—as in Nigeria—permitting families of lesser status to take advantage of the opportunity. Among present government leaders there are several whose names suggest a lower caste origin—Habib Thiam, the prime minister, comes from a family of the blacksmith caste. Nor do the Muslim leaders reject those of lower family origins in office, just as they have not rejected Catholic civil servants. It is, in fact, quite consistent with the pattern of collaboration begun with the French to have lower or noncaste men doing the job of governing.

The Western educated elite is superimposed on this fabric of clan alliances, but it does not sit apart. Beginning with the early struggles of Mamadou Dia and Leopold Senghor, educated urban Senegalese politicians found that they had to participate in the clan alliance system to win national political support. They had to get the most powerful clan leaders behind them, a feat well managed by Senghor but less well by his rival, Dia. Those political parties that have appealed primarily to the intellectuals have been doomed to failure at the polls. Yet the size of the educated class is growing, and this group controls all the tools of modern Senegalese society: the structure of laws, the policy and planning process. This group understands politics a bit differently than does the poor farmer in the countryside. It plays the political clan game, but it looks for increasing economic growth and the spread of education to make Senegalese more viable in the international system. It may even believe that democracy, in the sense of direct popular control rather than clan leader domination, is desirable. Ultimately, its ends will conflict with the patronage system of the clans, but not until the educated become more numerous than the uneducated. (See Creevey, 1993, for a more complete discussion of the Senegalese political system.)

Women in the Structure of Government

Noticeably absent from the list of the major players in politics in Senegal is a group headed by a woman or one that centers itself on defending the interests of women. All of the major political parties and the trade unions have women's branches, and women theoretically can hold any office in these organizations. All of the leaders of these organizations are men, though. There is, however, an active and vocal feminist group in Senegal headed by Marie Angelique Savane (a scholar who has acted as a consultant and a planner for various international organizations). The feminists' representative organization is called "Yewwu Yewwi," which means "raise consciousness for liberation" (*West Africa*, 1989, p. 828). It has headquarters in Dakar. The goal is clearly stated by the leaders:

> [We are] women of different religions and ethnic groups, married, divorced or single. Some are mothers, others, without children: a miniature

photo of the different statuses of women which exist in Senegalese society. Some are professional women of whom certain are not working and others are students.

We are all intellectuals with a strong consciousness of the hardly enviable and certainly unjust fate reserved for women and who commit ourselves to . . . act as a spark which will provoke a crisis of conscience and a mobilization to transform the situation of women and the relations between them and men. (*Fippu,* 1989, p. 5)

The Senegalese feminists have had an important impact on politics, which will be discussed below. Notable here, however, is the fact that this is not a mass organization but one that appeals to a relatively small group of female students and intellectuals. Although most of its membership is Muslim, it does not have the support of the maraboutic clans and certainly not of the fundamentalist (male) Muslim groups, who, like their Nigerian counterparts, see feminism as a Western perversion. To them, Yewwu Yewwi is a group of women who have been corrupted by their contacts with industrialized countries in Europe or, worse yet, with the United States (*Echo,* 1986, p. 9).

In the mainstream of Senegalese politics, women do not coalesce as one political interest group, although there are women's interest groups that do play a role. One noteworthy example is the *Dahiratou Khaury waal baraka,* made up of female disciples of a Tidjani marabout (Sheikh Tidjane Sy), which often collects money for one of its members (A. Aram Diene) who holds a seat in the National Assembly. In Senegal, however, there were no strikes or riots led by women in the preindependence period indicating any large-scale or even regional women's political effort. In the major political struggles to replace the French and thereafter to rule the independent country, women were virtually invisible. Only very recently have they had a presence in national political discussions. This presence now seems to come from the increasing strength of the growing group of educated women. There have always been a few intellectuals who wished to improve the position of women in Senegal. Now they not only are increasing in number but also are beginning to be heard.

They are supported both by foreign factors and by the continuing economic crisis in Senegal. The Senegalese government must win even further Western approval—from the IMF, from the United States, and still from France—at a time when the West has become quite self-conscious about its own discrimination against women. Senegal is thus vulnerable, because women have received so little attention. This pressure is compounded by the impact of the international women's movement, which had gained great prominence through the United Nation's Decade for women, ending with the 1985 conference in Nairobi. The economic impetus for meeting women's needs is related to the government's perception that the entire work force, including women, must be made more effective. Women have major roles in agriculture and must receive direct aid to counteract the neglect they have suffered in government agricultural programs until very recently.

In an attempt to show their good intentions, the male leaders of the PS speak now of giving more assistance to women and equalizing their situation. More women are nominated for office, and certain programs have been adopted, but the PS is cautious and afraid of offending its conservative base of support. Elite women are speaking out much more strongly and using their influence to try to improve the political situation for their gender as a whole, including the rural women still working in the fields. Their interests are not identical to those of the rural poor—the two groups would probably identify quite different things as the major problem facing women. However, the only national political voice women have currently is through the feminists and their articulate spokeswomen, who are doing their best to represent the needs of their rural sisters.

The attitude of the government toward women is shown in the changing face of those who are nominated or appointed to office. Women have been able to vote since the Loi Cadre of 1956 permitted adult suffrage, but they did not immediately appear in the government. For example, the single-house National Assembly had no women delegates until 1973, when four were elected. In 1991, there were 14 women out of 120 delegates, or 12 percent of the membership. These women take part on all the committees of the National Assembly, but they are virtually always a minority, and if they hold office it is as the secretary or vice president rather than president or director of the committee.

Major policy decisions in Senegal are made by the president (now Abdou Diouf), his prime minister, and the men heading the major ministries. The affairs of governing are managed through the ministries. There are twenty-three of these, the most important of which are interior, economy and finance, rural development, foreign service, and the armed forces. The Ministry of Education and Ministry of Health are large but less powerful. Only three women held ministerial positions in 1992. Aminata Tall (PDS), delegate minister for literacy and the promotion of national languages, is a professor of literature at the Ecole Normal (and a close friend of Adoulaye Wade's wife). Ndioro Ndiaye (PS), delegate minister for the woman, the child, and the family and a close friend of the relatives of Abdou Diouf, also has a graduate degree, but it has little to do with her present ministry: She is a professor of dental surgery. Finally, Mata S. Diallo (PS) is delegate minister for emigres. These positions are not high-ranking among the ministers in terms of status or power, and all may be seen as having responsibility for traditional "female" concerns.

The percentage of government employees that are women has increased dramatically, as indicated in Chapter 5, but it is still a small minority: Only 15 percent of civil servants are now women. The position of women in terms of their administrative/political power, their ability to make decisions or hand out favors, is shown by their percentage in the different government ranks, which naturally differs by ministry. Table 6.2 shows their percentage at all five government ranks overall and by ministry. The government ranks in Senegal are derived from the French administrative system and indicate not only relative status and authority but also level of pay. The three top ranks (from A to C) are largely determined by the amount and kind of education a candidate has received. Thus, someone with an "A" ranking will have a graduate education with a specific public administration focus; a "B" candidate will have a university degree and perhaps a year or two of graduate training but will not have a graduate degree or a degree in public administration; and a "C" candidate will have completed at least high school and probably a year or two of college. Categories D and E are difficult to distinguish and refer to unspecialized, general support and assistance. These may be lower-level secretaries, technicians, clerical workers, or general office staff. The "other" category refers to unranked workers and covers a broad range of occupations. Secretaries, chauffeurs, janitors, and handipersons all may be in this group. These are not desirable government positions because of the lack of status and benefits, as well as the lower pay.

Clearly, most of women's power is in traditional "female" fields (where they also have the most representation in the labor force) such as the education, health, and social development ministries. In the powerful ministries—economy and finance, rural development, interior, and foreign service—they have very low representation in the upper two ranks. The only ministry that is inconsistent is the armed forces, where women are 94 percent of category "B." However, this is an illusory inconsistency. These women have little role in decisionmaking. None holds the top rank: They are highly qualified and experienced secretaries needed for the administration of the very large staff of officers and soldiers. There are no women soldiers in the army (WID, 1991, p. 31). Women have their greatest strength in the weakest category—"Other." These nonranked positions indicate the mass of lower secretaries or clerks, filers, photocopiers, messengers, and maintenance people on whom the ministries depend. Relatively few Senegalese women find jobs in the unskilled labor category in the private sector (see Chapter 5), but the "other" category is not necessarily unskilled or unschooled. These may be women with some or all of a high school education but no direct training for their jobs and no admission to a civil service rank. They are relatively powerless in the Senegalese administration. If the education, health, and social development ministries are excluded (along with the armed forces and tiny commune expenditure subministry), women are on average only 8 percent of the combined "A" and "B" ranks. This is only a token representation of women in decisionmaking, yet at the same time it is a considerable increase over the first years of independence and seems strongly related to the growing pool of educated Senegalese women, the growing consciousness among both

Table 6.2   Percentage of Positions Held by Women at Each Hierarchical Level (by Ministry)

Ministry	A	B	C	D	E	Other
Residence	4	12	11	12	15	34
National Economic Council	20	0	—	12	33	22
Supreme Court	14	33	0	0	0	43
Foreign Affairs	3	8	4	4	0	24
Armed Forces	0	94	19	13	20	0
Interior	2	4	1	7	19	11
Justice	13	20	28	6	9	64
Public Works	12	10	21	6	0	62
Communications	0	13	0	6	0	31
Plan and Cooperation	12	5	24	7	0	71
Equipment	4	0	2	4	1	5
Rural Development	8	1	1	6	0	22
Economy and Finance	5	8	12	4	3	55
Industry	5	6	0	5	0	47
Hydraulic	3	2	4	1	0	55
Housing	7	5	10	7	1	53
Nature Protection	11	1	5	0	0	29
Commerce	14	10	8	4	0	87
Animal Resources	7	0	5	3	3	45
Education	18	18	39	19	26	4
Higher Education	17	12	5	12	17	24
Youth, Sport	6	8	21	6	8	72
Culture	6	28	3	0	0	30
Health	22	44	19	32	37	32
Social Development	60	48	80	31	8	64
Tourism	11	13	75	18	0	67
Commune Expenditures	17	22	38	23	0	12
Total	14	18	21	16	17	8

Source: RGPH 1988, "Repartition des Agents d'Etat par Ministère selon le sexe et la hierarchie"; Situation Economique 1988, p. 31.

women and men of a pattern of discrimination against women, and the pressure of Western powers for a modernization that includes improvement in the status of women.

Women in the civil service are appointed after obtaining the necessary educational qualifications and taking some sort of qualifying exam. Women elected to office do not have to meet specific preparation requirements. What is essential for them is that they can appeal to the electorate. Voting for the National Assembly is by national party list which means that each candidate must get votes from as broad a following as possible, receiving substantial support not only in the most populous region, Dakar, but also in the rural areas. A regional or local base is not enough to get elected. Those parties that fall below a certain minimum of votes take no seats, and those that surpass the minimum get seats according to what proportion they won (and in the order the candidates appear on the list). Decisions on who runs are made centrally by the party leadership.

Urban and rural councils are another matter. The councils have some say over the use of the limited resources that reach their area and the way government policy is administered within their jurisdiction. Here the national party leadership may have some authority over who runs for office, but local preferences and local political issues will be much more important considerations. Local leaders such as Muslim marabouts will also have great influence, and the character and political agility and personal connections of the would-be candidate are also important.

The French colonialists had permitted the creation of a limited number of towns to become what were called "communes," in which male citizens had voting privileges and could elect their own municipal councils and mayors. In the early years of Senghor's rule, after universal adult suffrage had been adopted and when Mamadou Dia was prime minister, the status of commune was conferred on every departmental capital. Each region had its own elected assembly to represent the rural population, spread across 13,000 villages throughout the country. Following Dia's arrest, in the autocratic phase of his regime, Senghor limited the powers of the communal councils and strengthened the government administration. The regional assemblies ended up as little more than sounding boards for new government programs (Gellar, 1980, pp. 39–41). In 1972, the regional assemblies were altogether abolished, and the new *arrondissements* were broken down into rural communities composed of several villages. Each community was headed by an elected rural council, which was advised by a Center for Rural Expansion (CER) made up of government agents from various services. This decentralization was intended not to lessen the power of the central government but instead to make rural development programs more effective and to increase participation of small farmers (Vengroff and Johnston, 1987, p. 275). In the 1980s, Diouf sought to expand this attempt to create a viable rural structure. The creation of the *groupements de promotion feminine* and the encouragement of the GIEs were part of the same effort.

Senegal is now divided into ten regions, each of which is subdivided into three departments. Each department is further divided into a number of urban and rural communes (depending on the number of villages and size of the population). The reform was put into effect in the first two regions in 1974, and by the communal elections of 1984 it had been implemented in all regions. Sheldon Gellar points out that in the initial years, administrative control kept many councils from making any decisions other than those suggested by the government (Gellar, 1982, pp. 41–42), but the earlier years of Diouf's rule liberalized the situation. More recent research suggests that now the rural councils, although without many resources or much authority, do "appear to provide the possibility for some popular input into the local and regional planning process" (Vengroff and Johnston, 1987, p. 287).

Women are eligible for election to the local councils. Unfortunately, data are not available to show how many women were in municipal councils prior to the 1972 reform, but it is interesting to see the position they have had in these councils in the first full elections of 1984 and the more recent ones of 1990. In 1984, there were 117 women delegates out of 1,463 elected, or 8 percent. In 1990, 16 percent (354) of the 2,213 delegates were women. In the rural areas, presumed to be more conservative in orientation, women still made considerable progress over the four-year period. In 1984, only 3 percent of the urban delegates were women (155 out of a total of 5,167), but in 1990 that percentage had more than doubled to 8 percent, or 779 of the 9,828 elected. (See full results in Creevey, 1993, pp. 207–210.)

The election results indicate some very significant points about the emergence of women into local and regional politics in Senegal. First of all, in both urban and rural councils, women have significantly increased their representation since 1984. Without any government policy enforcing affirmative action, local urban electorates returned a percentage of women delegates exceeding the percentage of government employees who are women. Conservative rural electorates did not return as many women, but the percentage of women was also going up.

Interestingly, it was neither Dakar, the modern urban center, nor Ziguinchor, urban and also home of the independent Dyola women, where the greatest strength of women was revealed. Instead, this was found in some of the more rural regions with smaller municipalities. Women succeed to office because they, like male candidates, have the support of the local clan leaders. It appears that marabouts were permitting women to be elected, although perhaps not enthusiastically. Only in M'Backe, center of the Muridiyya, is there evidence of probable maraboutic opposition, as the representation there is the lowest (although growing) of any urban council and almost the lowest as well in the combined total for the rural councils. By contrast, in Tivaouane, headquarters for the Sy family, women are well represented on the urban council, less well in the rural councils. In the conservative Tidjani Tukulor areas of St Louis, it is notable that women were elected to the municipal councils with a higher overall average than in Dakar; only in one zone, Matam, were women very poorly represented in the rural councils.

Women did not participate in the cooperatives set up in the 1960s, but they are now moving in ever larger numbers into the economic groups that are being established in response to the incentives of credit and other forms of government assistance. That percolation of rapid alterations in female economic roles is also evidenced in these regional/local electoral results. The unexpectedly high representation of women in municipal councils in the conservative river region may be an excellent indication of the profound changes in all aspects of society. Throughout Senegal, women are beginning to take a direct role in regional and local politics. They have always been active in politics, but, as they do in religious matters (see Chapter 3), they have taken an alternate path to that traveled by men. Since the arrival of Islam and the colonization of Senegal, they have not been trained or chosen for the new "modern" political posts, in keeping with the pattern seen by the French colonial rulers as normal. They have, however, continued the form of secondary political authority in clan politics, somewhat parallel to the positions they occupied in precolonial times (see Chapter 2). Thus, Sokna Muslimatou, sister of Falilou M'Backe, was a power in her own right, with her own followers and her own economic projects—such as a cous-cous factory staffed by Mouride women (Creevey Behrman, 1970, p. 110, fn. 7).

Sokna Magat Diop, the Mouride woman *khalif* discussed in Chapter 3, is certainly a current patron and clan leader. She dispenses favors, intercedes with the government, and collects economic contributions from her followers that she can use to promote those projects she thinks important. She acts through her son and less often takes an open political role than her peer marabouts do, but the authority is her own (Coulon, 1988, p. 130). In addition, women tap into the power of their male relatives for causes they favor; the wives and mothers of male marabouts intercede with their husbands or sons to get privileges for those who have appealed to them. They hold an ancillary political power that is far from insignificant.

At the village level, clearly, women have their own realm of authority, particularly over those areas of life in which women do all or most of the work. Melanie Stevens, in a village-level study in a Mouride area, observed that women at this level are powerless because they are excluded from the brotherhood organization, and they rely on their women's group to provide some sort of countervailing balance (Stevens, 1987). Although it does not control the policy decisions made in the village, the village women's group may influence them, and it does have its own economic resources (a collective field, for example) that it can use to support its projects. What is interesting in this village study is that the leadership of the group parallels the clan leadership. Thus, the first leader was the wife of the first marabout but, because she was absent from the village, his sister acted as president. When a new marabout came to the village, his wife started another women's group (Stevens, 1987, pp. 53–54). Thus, the old clan-based system continues, with women playing important, although secondary, roles. Neither Islam, the French, nor the spread of modern political positions (elected and appointed) had destroyed this system or eliminated women from it.

Growing on top of this traditional web of clan politics is a new class of women who do hold political office, either elected or appointed. Those who join the civil service probably can explain their success by their level of training and education. But at the highest levels they must also have good ties to important clan leaders (and/or to male politicians who have these clan affiliations) to obtain the jobs they strive for. Elected women seem to be more directly obligated to their clan connections, which provide them with the political support needed at the polling box. The clans, despite their conservative and traditional origin, are opening enough to allow, even support, women candidates in regional politics. The trend toward empowering women through access to political office is positive and significant.

Women and Radical Reformist Islam

However optimistically the signs are construed, though, the move forward should not disguise the fact that women in Senegal still have very little direct political decisionmaking power. What is more worrisome is that the present trend could be slowed or even stopped if the current balance of power shifts dramatically. Throughout this study, the positive impact of Western education on the situation for women has been cited. Ironically though, the continuation of the spread of education may bring with it the conditions that will destroy the gains women have made.

At issue here is the clan basis of politics controlled by marabouts. These men as a whole are conservative. They place a great deal of importance on a traditional interpretation of the Quran and the *suras,* which definitely prescribe a subordinate position for women. In Senegal, however, the brotherhoods and their leaders have allowed many preexisting social and political customs to continue. Even the ordering of the brotherhoods may be influenced by pre-Islamic matrilineal inheritance patterns—among the Mourides, for example, the brother of the *khalif,* rather than the son, inherits his position. After the conversion to Islam, the traditional political position of women reemerged in the maraboutic clan structure, despite their exclusion from the public face of the religion. Their open roles in the economy and in society have continued. Indeed, only a very few Senegalese women have been veiled (a minority of those related to one of the Mouride *khalifs*), and even these women have had considerable direct political power, as discussed above. But this laissez-faire attitude, which has typified the marabouts, is in conflict with the point of view of the radical reformist Muslims.

By definition, an orthodox Muslim is one who accepts the teachings of the Prophet and believes they should be observed as they were written in the Quran and embodied in the schools of law developed immediately after Muhammad died. The state itself, according to these beliefs, should be governed by the precepts of Islam. Democracy and popular rule are in conflict with the notion of a government obeying the written word of Allah. In a state such as Senegal, based on a secular constitution, strictly orthodox Muslims are constantly faced with an unacceptable compromise where no compromise is allowed (Hiskett, 1992).

Orthodox beliefs are most important to people who have studied the religion. It was the *sufi* brotherhoods that brought about conversion in Senegal, and when they originally spread to West Africa their ranks contained both highly sophisticated intellectual religious scholars and untrained or educated worshipful followers. The strictly orthodox Muslim is not patient with the superstition of popular Islam permitted by the brotherhoods, and he does not participate in the cult of the marabouts as saints. To him, the marabout should be a teacher and/or a recluse whose abstemious devotion to his religion is a model for his followers. Nor should lackadaisical observance of Islamic laws and rituals be tolerated by the marabouts, according to the orthodox; the faithful should observe all the teachings of Islam. Further, they should learn Arabic so that they can understand the Quran and its teaching properly, rather than relying on the *baraka* of the marabout and his wisdom to intercede for them. Although Islam does not distinguish between the sacred and the secular and thus does not differentiate between the affairs of the "church" and those of the "state," it also does not recognize the role of chief-surrogate or patron that the Senegalese marabouts have taken on. The strictly orthodox look askance on the political maneuvering of the major Muslim leaders.

Of course, there are many different versions of what is acceptable in Islam by different Muslim groups; some are more liberal in their attitudes toward women than others. The problem for women in Senegal currently is that the more extreme version of Islamic orthodoxy, echoing the strong nationalist and anti-Western attitudes from radicals in Iran, Egypt, Sudan, Algeria, India, and Morocco, has been gaining in popularity among intellectuals. These intellectuals, who may be called fundamentalists by most common definitions of the term (see Caplan, 1987; Kaplan, 1992), have very restrictive notions about women. So far, the continuing political power of the marabouts has acted as a buffer protecting Senegalese women against the extremes of seclusion, veiling, and withdrawal from many facets of public life, all of which the fundamentalists demand. Should the clan system be eroded and the marabouts lose their bases of power, though, the more liberal orthodox leaders and the fundamentalists would be in open conflict. Quite probably, the present group of politicians, allied to the West and having primarily Western education themselves, would seek to soften the demands of the fundamentalists. But if this fundamentalist rhetoric were strong and constantly before the public eye, both the more liberal Muslims and the politicians who side with them would inevitably be pushed to the right.

The question in Senegal today concerns what kind of foothold the fundamentalists have and how rapidly they are gaining power. There has been an orthodox, nonbrotherhood Islamic presence in Senegal for many generations. Christian Coulon points out that the reformers began to get their message to Senegal as early as the late 1920s. But the first Senegalese reform group was the Muslim Fraternity, founded in St Louis in 1935 and headed by Abdel Kader Diagne. The Muslim Fraternity and, later, post–World War II organizations such as the Union Culturelle Musulmane (UCM) criticized the French for interfering in Islam and castigated the marabouts for their corruption of the religion. But they had little following even among university students, and their voices became somewhat muted when Senegalese leaders took control of the state in 1960 (See Creevey, 1993, pp. 215–218).

In the years of political liberalization at the end of the Senghor regime, followed by the accession to power of Diouf, numerous other Muslim orthodox reformist groups emerged alongside the UCM, the fraternity, and the other reformist student groups of the 1950s and 1960s. Some of these were radical fundamentalist groups, such as the one currently publishing *The Muslim Student*; others, including numerous unions of teachers of Arabic, had more specific and limited reform agendas. Most groups are loosely affiliated in a national organization called La Fédération des Associations Islamiques du Sénégal (FAIS), which has had a decidedly progovernment tone despite the more critical attitude of some of its members. The splits among the membership remain—some groups work with the marabouts, others are completely distant and critical. Some marabouts appeal to the reformists for assistance for matters of common interest—for example, because they wish to open and expand an Arabic and religious training school. (Serigne Mourtada M'Backe, a Mouride leader, opened such a school near Touba and staffed it with teachers of Arabic having a reformist orthodox background.) Some previously hostile groups have found elements in the brotherhood-dominated popular Islam that they can support—the UCM, for example, sponsored seminars on Ahmadu Bamba, founder of the Muridiyya (Coulon, 1983, pp. 127–141).

The government has an interest in allying itself with the reformists as much as it can without threatening either its base of support with the marabouts or its access to assistance from the West. Thus, it not only allowed the UCM to reopen its schools, which had been closed by the French, but also supported a variety of other extensions of the teaching of Arabic, both privately and in the public school system. Muslim holidays replaced the Christian holidays formerly observed. An Institute of Islamic Studies was established at the University of Dakar, and more recently an Islamic Institute was established near the Great Mosque of Dakar. Among other things, the institute has occupied itself with translating the Quran and the *suras* into Wolof (Coulon, 1983, pp. 128–133). Senegal has accepted assistance from North Africa and the Middle East, which has taken the form primarily of the construction of several huge mosques—in Dakar, in Touba, in Kaolack—and numerous smaller ones as well. Senegal also has received scholarships to send Senegalese students to complete their higher education in Muslim universities.

Although Muslim reformers are not unified among themselves and do not have, in any case, a mass base of support, they have become a force in politics with which the government must deal. Following the precedent established by the French during colonial days, the government plays the various reform groups off against each other and against the marabouts. When one side opposes something, the government will turn to the other for support. One of the more interesting issues that shows this balancing act was the debate over the Family Code of 1972 (revised in 1989). Here, too, the relative power of the feminists versus the moderate reformist and fundamentalist Muslim groups in the post-Senghor era is illustrated.

Before 1972, Senegal had several different legal bases in uneasy coexistence with each other. Basic civil rights were guaranteed to everyone under a single code—all men and women had the right to vote, hold office, and receive the minimum wage and were treated equally under criminal law. Issues relating to the family were another matter. These could be tried under French law, in traditional courts, or in Muslim law courts, depending on the nature of the issue and the interested party's own claim of affiliation. Moreover, regional and local variations in interpretation were common, particularly in the latter two systems. Like most rulers of independent West African states, Senghor was forced to find a consistent system of law to be adopted nationally. The Family Code was his effort at providing a coherent national body of civil law. However, it was based not on one system but on all three, with heaviest emphasis on French and Islamic laws.

The Family Code spelled out the specific rules and obligations of marriage, divorce, and inheritance. A slightly different variation applied to those who declared themselves Muslim, but many features were common to all citizens and based on French law. For example, after 1972, all marriages had to be witnessed by the civil service, either through a separate ceremony or through the presence of a civil official at the religious ceremony. Brides had to be at least sixteen and had to agree to the marriage. Self-declared Muslims were faced with a number of decisions. Both man and woman had to agree whether the marriage would be monogamous or polygamous. No longer could men divorce women by simply declaring three times that they did so; divorce had to be heard by a civil court and was granted only for specific reasons, such as infidelity or unalterable incompatibility. Women could equally bring suit for divorce in family court.

Divorced husbands were now forced to pay alimony and child support, although they retained the right to determine where the children would be raised (*Journal Officiel de la Republique du Senegal,* May 1979).

The adoption of the Family Code caused an explosion of angry reactions throughout the countryside. The strongest opponents were the marabouts, who declared the code completely contrary to the principles of the Quran (Magassouba, 1985, p. 113). The major marabouts had maintained an organization called the Superior Islamic Council (descended from the ineffective Council of Islamic Organizations of the 1950s). Through this body, they made pronouncements on subjects about which they mutually agreed, usually on general religious matters. The council was totally unified against the Family Code. In a resolution signed by El Hadj Seydou Nourou Tall, El Hadj Abdul Aziz Sy, and Cheikh Amadou M'Backe, leading marabouts of the council declared their unalterable opposition.

> By virtue of . . . our position in the Religion, we must eliminate all equivocation in reaffirming solemnly our unalterable wish to categorically reject any measure, even official, which does not respect the sacred principles of our religion. Certainly Islam includes recommendations which can be modified in different circumstances depending on the place but there are also imperative and unchangeable prescriptions, which never, for any reason whatever, can be modified. (*L'Etudiant Musulman* 5 [April–June 1991], p. 14)

The Quran and the traditional schools of Islamic law most clearly do spell out the requirements of marriage and divorce and inheritance. The code included many elements from these prescriptions but also many that were modified specifically to improve the position of women. Thus, its opponents called it the "Women's Code" (Code de la Femme) as opposed to the "Family Code" (Code de la Famille) (Sow, 1989, p. 9), and they accused Senghor of being too French and too Christian and seeking to subvert Islam as the French would have wished him to do (Dieng, 1991, p. 13). Senghor, however, was in the position of trying to establish a code that would be accepted both by Muslims and by his Western allies, who demanded more just and equitable treatment for women. His code, moreover, was not inconsistent with codes adopted in other modernizing countries that were incontrovertibly Muslim, such as those implemented by the governments of Jemal Attaturk in Turkey and Habib Bourguiba in Tunisia. These modernizing leaders were also widely criticized by conservative Muslims, but Senghor, as a non-Muslim, was more vulnerable than they.

The post–Family Code period has witnessed the nadir of relations between the powerful marabouts and the government. The marabouts were furious—even Abdou Lahat M'Backe, *khalif* of the Mourides at the time —and Senghor was intransigent. The strategy of Senghor was again to try to divide the opposition, to convince some respected Muslims that the code was acceptable so they could balance the anger of others. In this case, he appealed to more liberal orthodox Muslims groups to help explain and justify the changes introduced in the code. He had to appeal to the most moderate of these, such as the government union of Arabic teachers; the fundamentalists were just as opposed as the marabouts (Coulon, 1983, p. 134). He also turned a blind eye to the actual implementation of the new law, especially in the rural, marabout-controlled zones. Thus, the marabouts ordered their disciples not to have anything to do with the civil registration of marriage, and they did not. In the urban centers, though, the law was more carefully monitored and enforced (Magassouba, 1985, p. 114).

The accession of Diouf symbolized to many marabouts a new, more resolutely Muslim regime, one less tainted by Christianity and former ties with the French. Consequently, despite Diouf's having been prime minister in 1972 and therefore complicit in the establishment of the code, the effort to abrogate it was begun afresh. But there was no widespread public outcry as there had been when the code was first published, only a certain sense of inertia. The outrage of the marabouts faded; it was easier to ignore the code than to continue to fight over it. They simply continued to advocate disobeying it whenever possible. The fundamentalists, however, were just as vocal as before in their dislike of the code and the results they perceived in Senegalese society. Diouf received many appeals and demands for a revision of the code and for a move to the adoption of a true Islamic code consistent with one of the major Muslim schools of law. In response, Diouf made strong efforts to emphasize his own ties with Islam, but he did not repeal the Family Code.

During this time, the feminists, who had viewed the code as some sort of victory for women, had also seen many ways in which the code in fact legalized their inferior or second-class status. They, too, brought all possible pressure to bear for reform of the code, but in their case a liberalization of it was sought. The issues the feminists underlined in the code were several. In the first place, the man was clearly seen as the holder of family power: "The husband is head of the family. He exercises this authority in the common interest of the menage and of the children" (Article 152). He would determine where the married couple would live (Article 153), a setback for Senegalese women, among whom polygamy had been customary and thus separate residence possible (Sow, 1989, p. 10). Men retained the paternal power and decisionmaking authority over children (Article 283); a wife only obtained that authority by a special dispensation of the court in extreme instances, such as when the father had deserted the family (Article 277).

It was also a symbol of a husband's power that the *livret,* the legal document recording all transactions of the married couple, was given to the husband to keep, although he was supposed to give a copy to the wife if divorce should take place. But the provision that created the highest level of indignation among most feminists was Article 154, which stated that a woman may take a job only with her husband's consent: "The wife may exercise a profession, even separate from that of the husband, as long as he does not oppose it and make his opposition known to the third party who is trying to hire the wife." In fact, according to most traditional laws, Senegalese women had worked and, as long as they satisfied the traditional obligations to the family, did what they chose to earn their revenue. Article 154 thus diminished their independence (Sow, 1989, p. 10), although many educated Senegalese men tried to say that this was the ordinary situation—husbands needed to be able to, and usually did, decide on the disposition of time of the family members.

The laws in regard to marriage embodied in the code were not fully satisfactory to feminists either, despite some improvements. In the first place, polygamy remained legal and even seemed to be considered the normal, as opposed to an unusual, situation. Although women were supposed to explicitly agree to polygamy, marriages could take place without a contract (either for or against polygamy) being signed. Where the couple made no definite contract, polygamy was presumed in force. Furthermore, should the husband take a second wife even though there had been a contract for monogamy, there was no provision for punishment. The worst he had to fear was divorce from his first wife (Sow, 1989, p. 10). And although couples could chose one of three types of contracts at marriage, the right of the husband to the major family property was generally assumed in all three unless the wife had a special claim, such as a separate residence maintained apart from the husband.

Feminists also argued that the family maintenance provision was undermining women. The code now required women to help pay the family costs. Under traditional and Muslim law, men were responsible for all such costs; women could contribute from their income as they chose. Although taking responsibility seemed reasonable to educated Senegalese women, the fact is that they already contributed substantially through their domestic and child-care responsibilities, contributions that were totally ignored. Finally, there had been little improvement in the highly discriminatory inheritance laws that existed before the code. Muslim women received half of what their brothers received, and wives scarcely inherited anything at the death of their husbands. The inequalities in inheritance were extended through every degree of kinship, male cousins always being preferred over female, and so forth.

The fundamentalists remained adamant that the code was a direct attack on Islam, basing their disapproval on the incontrovertible fact that the law included secular elements and was not purely drawn from the *Sharia*. The response of the government was that the code permitted all citizens to choose various options according to their religion. Muslims could choose the options largely drawn from Islamic law. Non-Muslims could make other choices. But this explanation did not satisfy the fundamentalists (Diop and Sow, 1989, pp. 8–9). As they insisted repeatedly:

> The fundamental problem which the personal statute poses to Muslims comes from the indivisibility of law and faith in Islam. Implicitly [the Code] invites them, these Muslims, to reduce Islam to some moral precepts and ritual acrobatics, that is to say to amputate from the *Sharia* of God one of the essential branches, the family regime. (Dieng, 1991, p. 14)

Men, these critics pointed out, should not have to *choose* what is guaranteed them by their own faith (polygamy). Nor should Islamic privileges and obligations be limited, as the code did with polygamy and in many other ways. The law has been laid down, the fundamentalists insisted, and cannot be changed just to suit the needs of modernizers who wish to please the wealthy West.

Whether or not the law has been inscribed and can only be interpreted in one fashion is an issue that has divided Muslim scholars for centuries. Some highly respected Muslim scholars claim that reinterpretation is not only necessary but normal in Islam; others, of course, claim that there can be no reinterpretation, that what is written is immutable (Esposito, 1982, pp. 10–134). In the Family Code controversy, the fundamentalists took the strictest line and were supported by the marabouts, despite the various examples of the latter's own deviations from Islamic law within the brotherhoods. Less religious, educated Muslims, who otherwise would not have taken sides in the matter of reinterpretation, allied themselves with the coalition of Muslim leaders and fundamentalists claiming that the code was destroying family life, encouraging women to seek divorce, and breaking down traditional morals. One of the major criticisms of these more moderate conservatives was that the code in fact discriminated against men, who not only had had the major financial responsibility for the family during the marriage but now, upon divorce, had to support their ex-wives and children (under certain conditions) for such lengthy periods that they were being impoverished (interview, Momar N'Diaye, June 1992). As one Senegalese observer sarcastically commented:

> The Senegal of the Code still lives this paradox which consists of seeing a law applied—sometimes with extreme rigor—in urban centers where women use at will, often in an immoderate fashion, this new weapon given them by the legislator, while [the Code] is virtually ignored in the countryside where the greatest majority of women are not even sure of its existence. (Magassouba, 1985, p. 114)

Feminists responded that men were not being disadvantaged, merely having to deal with the responsibilities they had been able to ignore in the past. Women, they pointed out firmly, were still deeply subordinate even under the new laws. But their perception was not shared by many men.

Diouf's government waited for several years before calling a major conference on possible reforms to the code in January 1987. It was attended by many lawyers and spokesmen for the fundamentalists and feminists. The issues surrounding the code were debated for several weeks, and much of the angry rhetoric of Muslim critics resurfaced in the newspapers. Finally, in January 1989, several revisions to the code were passed (*Journel Officiel*, February 18, 1989). The principal changes included a repeal of the provision that husbands had the right to refuse to allow their wives to work: "The wife, just as the husband, has full control of her civil status, her rights and powers are limited only by the present act" (Article 371).

Other favorable revisions from the point of view of feminists included provision of a copy of the all-important *livret* to the wife at the time of marriage (Article 28); this document had often been withheld by the angry ex-husband after divorce. Also, underage girls received permission to annul a marriage, even if a child had been conceived (Article 142); a wife no longer had to make her legal residence in her husband's house (Article 13); and a divorced woman was given the right to use her husband's name as her last name unless the husband took specific action to prevent her (Article 62). One alteration, however, was directed at the moderate conservatives' complaint: Women were no longer able to claim support payments for themselves and their children (past a few specified months) unless they could prove an inability to support themselves *and* the former husband had the resources to pay (Article 261).

On balance, the revisions alleviated some of the inequalities for women embodied in the original Family Code. The authority of the husband was diminished; the freedom of the woman enhanced. From the point of view of the fundamentalists, nothing had been improved; if anything, the specifics outlined in traditional Muslim law had been further whittled down by the changes. The government certainly had made no move to adopt a Muslim law system (as Sudan had done in 1989). But women were not entirely satisfied, either. Despite the positive steps, they still did not have an equal place in society, even legally. Power within the family (and over the children) was still first of all in the hands of the husband. Polygamy still was accepted as normal. And inheritance was still totally inequitable.

However, women in Senegal have a reasonable chance of gaining more equal access to and control of the economic and political resources of society. Many factors are coming together to provide support for the feminists' cause. First is the continuing spread of Western formal education throughout Senegal. The more people—both men and women—who do receive schooling, particularly secondary education or higher, the more they are likely to be sympathetic to treating women as equal individuals. There are now Senegalese women on the faculty of the university and the staff of the prestigious l'Institut Fondemental d'Afrique Noire (IFAN). Women head government agencies and are responsible for large projects in rural and urban areas. They are role models for both men and women, showing that women are competent and need to be treated as such. Second, Senegalese are increasingly exposed to foreigners from Western industrialized countries, which favor a policy promoting women. The economic dependence of Senegal on these countries means that this policy cannot be ignored, despite government obligations to conservatives inside the country. Also, Western nations finance Senegalese feminist activities—their conferences, seminars, and publications, the education of young scholars, and research trips abroad for more established figures. The voices from these groups are heard on radio shows, and their leaders are interviewed in the national paper, *Le Soleil.* Even the negative press they often receive keeps their ideas before the public. Thus, although the Western support of feminists is only a trifle in the scheme of what is needed to help women, it is of significance in keeping the feminist voice before the public and training other women for future work.

More fundamental change is taking place in the countryside, where economic and social stimulation is breaking down traditional role patterns. Society is opening enough to allow women to take new economic and political opportunities. Many women still live traditional lives in the rural villages, their routines made up of farming and domestic work much as they were a hundred years ago. But few of these women are untouched by what is happening. New ideas and new customs are reaching them, and they will react, just as other women in nearby areas in the country are doing. There seems to be no possibility that this tide of reform will be reversed.

But feminists are not completely sanguine about the developments in Senegal. They still face a current in society that directly opposes their efforts and has strong roots in the dissatisfaction many Senegalese have with the interference of the West and the continuing poverty in their country. The fundamentalists appeal to these Senegalese by casting religious issues in a nationalistic framework. The insistence of women on greater political and social equality is cited as merely another instance of the corruption of society by the West. *Echo* quotes the following accusation of fundamentalists against Senegalese feminists:

> Listening to certain talk, sometimes disrespectful [to religious leaders] and breaking the bounds of social norms subscribed to by the overwhelming majority of the population, observers cannot fail to wonder whether Senegalese feminists have not stayed in the era of 100 flowers— the famous period of gaudy exhibitionist, bra-burning, mass hysteria, women's lib. (*Echo* 1986, I (2–3), p. 9)

Marie Angelique Savane, president of both Yewwu Yewwi and AAWORD (an international group of African women supporting research), boldly counters that fundamentalists are only a minority of Muslims and are out of date, having forgotten that change is an integral aspect of life. "As for fundamentalist ideas," she said in an interview, "their time has come and gone long ago" (*Le Soleil,* 1989, p. 92).

She is right that fundamentalists are only a minority in Senegal, but their influence stretches beyond their actual numbers. They can and have collaborated with the marabouts in the past in battles for Islam; should they incite a maraboutic campaign against the feminists, the prospects for immediate improvements for women would be dimmer. However, the marabouts have had little direct interest in the urban-based feminist organizations. Of course, they still oppose the code and all the changes it implies, but their opposition is muted; disobedience is more typical than efforts to overturn it by force. The marabouts are simply less concerned about the role of women than are the fundamentalists. The marabouts are, and have been, quite comfortable with the open public economic and political activities of women, even those close to them in their family hierarchies. They are more tolerant, and that is the main reason Islam has not been effectively used as a weapon to stop the advance of women. The fundamentalists on their own have no power to influence government policy except to slow it down. But in another political climate—for example, if the West were to withdraw or the clan structure to crumble—it is not certain that the positive balance would remain as it is. No one interested in promoting women in Senegal can afford to ignore the right-wing danger represented by the Islamic fundamentalists.

CONCLUSION

Although the involvement of Muslim women in politics follows two very different paths in northern Nigeria and Senegal, some important similarities emerge that show how Islam has been a factor in the process of political development for women in West Africa. The first similarity is that although equal rights are provided for in the constitutions of both nations, Muslim women have less than equal rights; they have fewer protections than not only their male peers but also their Christian sisters. In Nigeria, Muslim women are exempted from the equal rights provisions of the constitution, and in Senegal Muslims are under the jurisdiction of Islamic law for family matters. Muslim women do not enjoy equal inheritance rights, and they are forced to tolerate polygamy. Furthermore, there is no avowed equality in the family because of the recognized authority of husbands as family heads. This is not to say that Muslim women have no rights, for of course they do, even in the family domain, and these rights are more extensive than those guaranteed to women in many other countries. But the fact remains that Muslim law, based on the *Sharia,* does discriminate against women more than do current Western codes.

A second similarity is the role of the Muslim leaders in blocking and even attempting to reduce the freedom and privileges of women in both northern Nigeria and Senegal. In both cases there is a growing group of young Muslims, particularly in the universities, who are strongly influenced by Islamic militants in the Middle East and North Africa and identify the women's movement as a Western perversion. Enthusiastically espousing nationalist anti-Western rhetoric, these radical Muslim students would be happy to see removed all revisions or modifications of *Sharial* law. The northern Nigerian Islamic militants go further than their Senegalese brothers, calling for Muslim women students to wear black and more openly discussing the need for women's submission and obedience. The political culture of Senegal does not encourage this degree of anti-feminism, but even the Senegalese fundamentalists go quite far in their warm support of the traditional rights of men to unilaterally divorce, to have full rights over the family (including whether and where the wife works), and so on. All these things, they claim, are prescribed by the *Sharia* and cannot be altered. Fundamentalists are immovably opposed to granting women equal political rights. The fundamentalists are fairly powerful in northern Nigeria, where radical Islamic militants find their echo in the conservative elders of the community, who still control regional and local politics. In Senegal, fundamentalists remain a tiny minority whose relationship with the Islamic leaders in the countryside is quite inconsistent. The fundamentalists have strongly criticized the marabouts for corruption and distortion of Islam. The marabouts, in turn, feel little in common with the urban-based radical fundamentalists, who are uprooted from common society in the countryside. So far there have been instances of cooperation, as in the united front against the Family Code, but the marabouts have not identified themselves with the radical reformist tone of the young militants and have followed their own path. The government has cleverly tried to keep a wedge between them, playing off both sides in its eternal balancing act. Where the fundamentalists are a minority cut off from the mainstream of politics, they will have little influence on the role of West African women in the political system.

A third similarity is the pressure to include women in politics imposed by the need to modernize and compete in the world market. In northern Nigeria, even conservative leaders have begun to urge women to get involved in politics, at least to the extent of voting. Their motivation is to assure votes for northern (male) politicians and the northern political agenda. The national government, despite its military nature, urges even more strongly that women be involved in politics and the economy as part of its effort to bring about more balanced and rapid development in Nigeria. Our study has shown that Nigerian Muslim women have responded (and men have permitted them to do so). Slowly, carefully protected by justifications drawn from the dictates of Islam, women are beginning to move into the economy and into politics. So far they hold few political offices, and their economic activities, except for those of the few upper class educated Muslim women, are carried on from behind the wall of seclusion, but there are clear beginnings.

The same types of incentives have been exerted in Senegal, but much more openly and directly and with less careful appeal to Islamic traditions or laws. Here, women have begun to respond quite dramatically, both in the economy and in politics. The interaction effect has produced a much more open environment; the activities of women are now public, with much less effort to veil them behind some kind of token male leadership. The same factors operate throughout West Africa, drawing women out of their traditional roles. Where economic change is rapid and widespread, the advance of women is generally also rapid. Where economic change is slow or nonexistent, the advance of women is equally slow. In all cases, education interacts with economic and political incentives, and its impact is compounded. The more women who have access to education beyond the primary school level, the more economic and political change there will be.

A final similarity is the role of feminists in the two countries in getting women's needs on the political agenda, in helping women to define their own rights, and in defining the obligations of the state to defend those rights. In both Nigeria and Senegal, the membership of feminist organizations is drawn from small minorities of elite educated women. On the face of it, their background and interests have little in common with most women in their countries. Yet they play a role much larger than their numerical representation in the population. They have formed the only organizations that persistently articulate the issues facing women and denounce the current lack of attention by government and society to these matters. Despite being openly criticized in both societies (the press in each characterizes them as "bra burners"), they get heard, even if only through the negative coverage often given them by the press. The governments, with an eye to Western criticism of the position of women, cannot altogether ignore the demands they make. There is, of course, a big difference between Yewwu Yewwi, with its explicit baiting of the fundamentalists, and FOMWAN, with its careful redefinition of the meaning of Islamic law and its strong effort to define all women's issues as Islamic ones. But the role of these groups is similar in their respective societies. They have little political power as such, but their influence on the educated and on policymakers grows daily.

In 1993 West African women were far from achieving a position in politics equal to men in their societies. But the initial steps toward achieving greater equality in access to political decisionmaking power were being taken. Precolonial political patterns, the colonial experience, the degree of economic change, the spread of education, exposure to the West, and rule by the military (or, conversely, the reemergence of democratic politics) all act together to create the political fabric and determine the rate at which women move into the modern political system. Religion generally is one additional factor that under the right circumstances can be crucial. Women in a Muslim society with a secular state where fundamentalists are weak do not seem to face barriers to their progress because of their religion. However, where orthodox Islam is strong and Muslims are a powerful minority, the government must be careful not to challenge *Sharia* law in any way. Here Islam can be the major factor defining women's legitimate political role. What is important is not simply whether or not a West African woman is Muslim but how the political system of her society is structured and what influence or power is accorded her religion.

7

CONCLUSION: ISLAM AND THE
CHANGING STATUS OF WOMEN

Across West Africa, women are struggling to make their lives, and those of their families, better. In all too many cases, their sole preoccupation is with the basic elements of survival. Obtaining food and water, warding off the dangers of disease and civil war—these are their primary concerns. But gradually, an ever-larger number of women are becoming aware that they have less status, less involvement in the development process, and less access to choices opened by economic and political change than men do. Without necessarily focusing on this inequality, women are beginning to demand more. Their needs are many and diverse. They want more education. In the urban areas, they are seeking access to salaried employment and promotions, and they are demanding salaries commensurate with their work. In the agricultural sector, they seek credit and access to the inputs necessary for crop improvement and the training needed to improve their skills. Increasingly, they recognize that these are only a few of the changes essential to improving their lives.

The structure of West African women's demands depends on many factors. Their situations differ across ethnic groups, across regions in the same country, and across countries. A comparison of some of these myriad and complex problems can provide useful information that may help to empower the women most directly concerned. In particular, it is worth trying to analyze major factors common to the entire West African region that inhibit the advance of women. The foundations of many of these barriers were laid long ago in precolonial and colonial days. Throughout the region, the status of women was defined as secondary to that of men. Colonial influences exacerbated the problem by undermining whatever status women held in precolonial societies as important agricultural producers and relegating them to a dependent position they had not occupied formerly.

Our concern has been with one specific factor: the role religion, particularly Islam, plays in shaping the lives and status of women. We have found in this study an extraordinarily complex relationship between Islam and the lives of West African women. In the first place, the timing of the spread of Islam into a particular region and the political situation into which it came were very significant in determining the role it would later play in women's lives. Conversion itself occurred over time, coming in waves and spurts at different historical points throughout the region. It was brought both by peaceful traders and by fanatically devoted Muslim conquerors. Whole societies generally did not convert at one time or on their first contact. Generally, sections of the nobility, commoners among specific ethnic groups, or some combination of social castes would decide the religion would reinforce their standing in the society and thus become the early converts. Military conquests inevitably followed, often under the banner of purifying the "corrupt" Islam of partially converted societies, and the entire society would be drawn into the Islamic fold.

The date and circumstances of the introduction of Islam to a society is highly significant in predicting its impact on women's lives. Throughout West Africa, Islam has had the greatest impact on women's lives among those who were converted earliest and who were relatively isolated for centuries thereafter from contact with other cultures. In coastal regions where the colonialists arrived before the Muslims, Islam came later, and the whole society was less likely to convert to it. Consequently, its influence on the ordering of social norms and traditions was less total.

We stress, however, that early and more complete conversion to Islam does not necessarily imply a linear process of dwindling status for women. Islam did provide certain individual rights to women that they had generally not enjoyed under traditional societal norms, including respect, specific inheritance privileges, and the right to whatever income they earned. It required their husbands to support them and set up certain rules for divorce. But Islam, through its teachings and the cultural norms imported from North Africa and the Middle East, reinforced the patriarchal elements already present in society. The Muslim brotherhoods featured male hierarchies, and technically no women could be members. The public political roles of noble women—as political brokers, king makers, and patrons in their own rights—were eliminated; and the roles women played as religious leaders of pre-Islamic cults were no longer publicly acknowledged.

In the older Islamic societies, women's traditional political and religious roles were deeply submerged, but they did not vanish altogether. In societies that converted later and were located where contact with the West was greater, certain aspects of these earlier roles persisted openly and were more likely to be tolerated even within the brotherhood framework. Our two case studies present two ends of this continuum. In northern Nigeria, the Hausa developed and deepened a patriarchal society that stripped women of all their public roles, firmly subordinated them to men, and even locked them in seclusion. In Senegal, the degree of domination and distortion of preexisting traditions is less than it is in Hausaland.

It is also relevant that the British protected the traditional Hausa rulers under the policy of Indirect Rule and with certain exceptions left Islamic law intact. The Hausa state structure also was left in place, further protecting Hausa culture in general from British influence. Eventually there was a strong nationalist incentive to emphasize (and thus exacerbate) the differences between Islamic northern Nigerian and British-dominated southern Nigerian cultures. In contrast, the French stripped the local rulers in West Africa of their traditional authority and firmly retained all political power in their centralized colonial capitals. Because they were few in number and because they were, after the end of the nineteenth century, not seriously threatened by Muslim uprisings, the French were actually able to use the brotherhoods to help rule their territories. Brotherhood leaders, militarily defeated early on, tacitly accepted the authority of the French and collaborated with them. Both sides gained and both sides lost from the interaction. We conclude that this pattern of collaboration limited the influence of both Islam and colonialism on the cultures of the indigenous societies.

Certain aspects of women's lives are generally overlooked by outside scholars. For one thing, Islam encourages the education of women within the religion, and Islamic women, especially those of more elite families, often receive an elaborate training in the rituals and philosophy of their religion. In turn, these women can and do teach others, primarily women. Furthermore, in their roles as wives, daughters, mothers, and sisters of powerful Islamic leaders, women have considerable influence in their societies. In northern Nigeria, this role is played out from within the network of women; in Senegal, women's authority in certain cases applies equally to men. Because women are not secluded, they speak openly to men, and men do not hesitate to request the help of powerful, well-connected women. Indeed, the greatest difference between Muslim women in Senegal and Nigeria is the opening of public roles for women in the former, to the point where Senegalese women now head religious support organizations comprising both men and women members. This transition accompanies the economic and political liberalization of Senegalese society. In northern Nigeria, this transition is only beginning: Islamic women there still work in and through women-only organizations and networks. Women are secluded in society, although men are excluded from the women's world thus created.

One of the most significant challenges to the conservative impact of Islam in West Africa is the spread of Western education. Women are most likely to assert their rights to equality when they are educated, especially beyond the primary level. Educated men, too, are more likely to accept the necessity of improving the situation for women if their societies are to progress. We found that the spread of education is first and foremost limited by the availability of resources. The poorest West African countries have the lowest rates of education and the worst ratio of girls to boys in school. Within most nations, the inequity of resources and investments means that children, both girls and boys, are much more likely to be educated in large towns and cities than they are in villages or rural areas. Islam plays a role in generating suspicion or even resistance to Western education, but this depends again on the extent to which Islam is a defining feature of people's lives. In countries (such as Senegal) where Muslim leaders have accommodated outside influences over many generations, Islam is not a major factor inhibiting girls' education. Conversely, in countries or regions such as northern Nigeria, where the Islamic influence is nearly total and suspicion of Western education holds sway, Islam has been a major factor inhibiting the education of girls.

Political, social, and economic changes continue, some of which seem to move society forward and some of which appear to be retrogressive. For instance, northern Nigerian Muslim leaders, for a variety of reasons (including the need to keep their region competitive with the rest of Nigeria), have endorsed the education of women. Also, many northern Nigerians have sought higher education abroad, including in the West, and have inevitably brought back ideas favorable to the liberation of women. Because education is so key to the advancement of the whole society, many Muslim leaders now encourage—indeed, require—young girls to go to school. More and more Hausa girls are going to school at all levels. This positive trend is somewhat vitiated, however, by the efforts to alter the curricula of schools, especially at the secondary and postsecondary levels, to make them compatible with the teachings of Islam. Reaffirmation of faith and disavowal of critical analysis is at the heart of this type of revision and certainly dilutes the extent to which education leads to independent thinking and rationality about daily life.

In other regions of West Africa, conservative Muslim leaders have tried to prevent the spread of Western education, especially to the children of the highest-ranking disciples and leaders. But the importance of education for acquiring good positions in a salaried economy is clear to all, Muslim and non-Muslim alike, and remains an overriding concern of most people. Thus, it is only in special circumstances that the concerns of conservative Muslim leaders about the negative impact of Western education have observable consequences in regard to the availability of educational opportunities. Overall this opposition has not been effective where resources adequate to establish schools exist and where the economy demands a more skilled work force. Hence, Muslim leaders in northern Nigeria have modified their opposition, and the government has acquiesced to their concerns by introducing Islamic Religious Knowledge into an otherwise Western curriculum.

Historically, West African women have played an essential role in the production process. Although the teachings of Islam dictate that men must support the family, the religion does not require that women not work.

Only in those societies in West Africa that adhere to the Islamic rule mandating seclusion of women has Islam been a major factor inhibiting the movement of women into the modern wage sector. Certainly the seclusion of women in Hausa society has seriously circumscribed the economic roles they filled. Where once they worked in the fields like other women in surrounding areas, after the *jihads* of the early nineteenth century Hausa women disappeared into their compounds. Whether or not this withdrawal was a sign of *better* status for women (this was an area where slavery had been common), the impact of seclusion was to block women's integration into the processes of modern economic development. Even here, though, women developed important economic networks of their own in the informal sector, especially in urban areas. Through their domestic enterprises and, with the help of their children, in public marketplaces, they have garnered incomes that have helped sustain their families in hard economic times. Only recently, have a few upper class women have begun acquiring higher education and taking positions in professional and government service.

This pattern is in striking contrast to that found in the southern regions of Nigeria, where women play a much larger role in the economy and control the large urban marketplaces. In fact, it is in contrast to that found in all the coastal countries of West Africa, including Muslim Senegal. In the latter, there has been a dramatic change in the percentage of women in the wage labor force since independence and in the move of Senegalese women in rural areas to join new economic groups to market their produce. Here, Islam has not been a major factor preventing women from economic involvement: Muslim women are as likely as Catholic women in Senegal to work. Differences in patterns of adaptation to the labor market seem to be dictated primarily by the availability of resources and secondarily by certain ethnic differences.

As West African women move into the labor force, they are simultaneously becoming more involved in national politics. Political parties and government office had been defined by both Western colonialists and Muslim leaders as the concern of men, not women. Few women played important roles in the West African independence struggles, nor did they occupy positions in the newly independent governments established across the region after 1960. But the situation is now changing, both because of pressure from the outside and because West African women themselves are beginning to demand a role in the political process. The women who are articulating these demands are almost always drawn from the educated elite, which is growing in all West African nations. They have established women's organizations (some government-sponsored, some independent) through which many of the their needs are beginning to be acknowledged. It is still true that women play only peripheral roles in the parties and government structures, but they are beginning to appear in leadership positions in ministries and departments traditionally associated with the needs of women. The willingness of most West African governments to support this change has been a response both to the insistence of Western donor countries and to a growing perception that part of the slowness of the development process is caused by a failure to reach women with the plans and programs adopted.

In many countries, the movement of women into the political arena does not seem to be significantly affected by the proportion of Muslims in society. In these nations, the importance of religion is accepted as a given, but religious leaders are assumed to defer to secular politicians on routine matters. It is the latter who make policy and run the business of national government. This is particularly true in countries such as Senegal, where the dominance of Islam is not challenged, or in regions such as southern Nigeria, where Christianity is dominant and separation of church and state is insisted upon.

The situation in northern Nigeria is different because Muslims are much more Islamically conscious and feel threatened by the more Christian south. They insist that "Islam is a total way of life" and do not believe in separation of church and state. This is not to say that Muslim groups in Senegal do not ever influence politics. The brotherhoods are extremely powerful politically, but they do not dominate the national political decisionmaking process. The government is careful not to offend the most powerful leaders, but it has not hesitated to make decisions that are unpopular with them when necessary. Because the Muslim leaders are not organized into a unified whole, the secular government has been able to play the interests of different Muslim groups off against each other and institute reforms, such as the Family Code, that are seen as violating some of the basic tenets of Islam.

In cases where the national government is controlled by strictly orthodox Muslim men and where the main challenges to that government come from non-Muslims, the impact of Islam on the move of women into politics would be expected to be considerable and largely inhibitory. In Nigeria, where the large northern states are Islamic and control the federal government, this impact is pivotal at both the local and national levels. Everywhere, the ability of women to participate in political parties is limited by male beliefs concerning appropriate roles for women. In northern Nigeria, women historically were expected to play only those roles assigned to them by the male leadership of the national political parties. Until the present, they have been expected to work or speak out on only those women's issues accepted by Muslim men as legitimate. Today, as Nigeria attempts its third transition from military to civilian rule, women are encouraged to bring out the female vote and to speak out on such issues as women's role in economic development and education. Issues such as equality in marriage or changes in the marriage laws or divorce rights are not addressed.

In traditional Islamic teachings, the male/female dichotomy is definitive, and public discussions that threaten this separation are not encouraged. Only those reforms considered that can be justified by appeal to Islamic teachings are considered legitimate, but these can result in real change for the lives of women in Islamic societies. In northern Nigeria, Islamic women in organizations such as FOMWAN seek significant changes under the protection of Islamic knowledge. FOMWAN has close ties with the Supreme Council for Islamic Affairs in Nigeria and works to stress the relevance of the ideals of early Islam to contemporary situations. Thus, reform that affirms rather than challenges Islam can be endorsed by both men and women. Here, where women live in seclusion, separated from the life of men in nearly every way, they may have a psychological foundation for seizing separate opportunities for their own advancement. But in public they must have the support of men to function at all. Men who are supportive of providing more education and related opportunities for women can gain their political support. Hence, there is a gender gap to be exploited, as long as such exploitation does not challenge Islam directly.

Muslim women in northern Nigeria continue to face significant disadvantages vis-à-vis men because of the protections given by the culture, and by the Nigerian constitution itself, to Islamic law. It is not likely that in the near future the ideal of sexual equality in such matters as inheritance, employment, divorce, free choice in marriage, or freedom of association and movement will be accepted—or even for that matter, granted legitimacy as matters to be publicly addressed. At present, such issues are defined as matters of religious law, not public policy.

Partly because matters such as these are defined as religious rather than political issues, changes are not likely to come through the legal system. The reactions of Muslims in Nigeria to the attempt to encode human rights provisions into the Nigerian constitutions of 1979 and 1992 are instructive. In both cases, Muslim delegates to the constitutional conventions were able to "protect" the *Sharia* by exempting Muslims from the guarantees of the federal constitution. Hence, any attempt to directly confront the subordination of women as decreed in *Sharia* law will be vigorously attacked and is likely to continue to be doomed to failure. Rather, legislation in other areas that can actually be endorsed by Muslim leaders will probably be the avenue of significant change for women. This is especially true in the area of education. Islamic leaders in both Nigeria and Senegal agree that learning is endorsed for women as well as for men. Yet education is the real threat to continued female subordination. Educated women inevitably find expression for their knowledge, and this expression inevitably begins to affect the way they view themselves and the way society views them. Thus, it is education—which is *endorsed* by Islamic teaching—rather than a direct challenge to Islam itself that is likely to lead to increased participation of women in politics in northern Nigeria. And women are bound to change the political agenda.

In other West African countries with Muslim majorities, women also face certain political disadvantages owing to Islamic teachings. Senegal, despite its secular government, allows Muslims to follow the prescripts of Islamic law in matters dealing with marriage, child maintenance, divorce, and inheritance. Thus, Muslim women have fewer rights in these areas than do other Senegalese women and are relatively less equal to men. But there is a significant difference between Senegal and Nigeria. Northern Nigerian women discuss their political goals in terms of a reinterpretation of Muslim law. If they can legitimately show that the law and the scriptures could be construed to mean something different from current custom, then they can advocate this change. Thus, the leaders of FOMWAN point out that Muhammad could not have meant to endorse polygamy, as he insisted that all wives be treated equally, a feat that is not humanly possible. In Senegal, feminists do not feel obliged to make such reinterpretations and indeed sometimes show quite an open disregard for Muslim law. Thus, Marie Angelique Savane, head of the Senegalese feminist movement Yewwu Yewwi, is quoted in the national newspaper, *Le Soleil*, as saying "the Shari'a is no longer adequate for managing the world" (*Echo*, 1986, p. 9). Such public rejection of the *Sharia* would be unthinkable for Muslim feminists in northern Nigeria, but in Senegal statements of this type cause little reaction except among the small groups of fundamentalists who cite them as further proof of the corruption and degradation of feminists in Senegal.

In Nigeria, then, the path to liberation and advancement for Muslim women will be somewhat different than the path followed by non-Islamic women. It will not be fought simply in the battle for political representation but rather will be grounded in the belief that within the Islamic tradition it is possible to give public recognition to women with interests separate from men's, and the logic of separate solutions that flows from that. The end picture envisioned is one of complementarity, not antagonism, in Islam between the interests of men and women. Any antagonism between men and women is blamed on the destructive influence of colonialism and the West. Islam offers an alternative moral order. Hence, Islamic associations demand that the state continue to endorse the authority of Islam over women. Both the state and Nigerian Islamic women's organizations stress the necessity of improving women's status, but neither advocates restructuring gender relations. The public agenda for women is cautious and ambiguous. The importance of educating women to make them better able to contribute to national development is recognized, but their actual roles are always seen as being supportive of or peripheral to those of men. Islamic leaders condemn the secular lifestyles of Western women and insist that Muslim women live in seclusion and adopt the most conservative Islamic dress, going out only under cover of darkness or with the permission of husbands. Women's rights are placed squarely within the confines of the family and the rights of men.

In Senegal and other West African countries where the tenor of politics remains largely secular and cosmopolitan in spite of the presence of an overwhelmingly Islamic population, the discourse of politics is only slightly different than it might be in non-Islamic societies. Women openly point to the need to end discrimination in the workplace and in political organizations. They discuss birth control and women's health issues, including abortion (although this is not endorsed by the national feminist movements). They object to polygamy without feeling compelled to justify this concern through reinterpretation of Muslim law, and they decry the inequities in inheritance built into the Muslim family code. They do not attack the importance of the role of the family in society, but they reinterpret the structure of the family on a more egalitarian (and less patriarchal) basis. Disadvantaged as they are by the application of Islamic law, they nonetheless feel free to openly object to their limitations and to put pressure on the government to reduce such inequities. They have even had some success, as our discussion of Senegal shows, although even there Muslim women are still disadvantaged legally. Women are less outspoken in their feminism in West African countries such as Mali, Chad, and Niger, which have had fewer contacts and interactions with the West and whose rulers are more conservative. But even in these societies, the constraints on women are not primarily justified through Islamic law as they are in northern Nigeria.

There is a question as to whether or not Islamic fundamentalism, now a strong force throughout the Muslim world, will become a major force in Senegal and other West African societies. The merging of militant Islamic fundamentalist teachings with anti-Western nationalism is in many ways threatening the advancement of women. In Nigeria, as in many other Islamic countries, the flight into militant Islam can be explained as an attempt to retain power and/or dignity in the face of a dysfunctional economic system and mounting public unrest. There are some indications that this could happen elsewhere, even in Senegal. As the militants come to dominate public discourse, the tolerance for new ideas and alternate social orders will likely disappear, and women will be deprived of the ideological foundation necessary as a basis for their claims to gender equality. One need only look at Tunisia, Algeria, or Sudan, neighboring on West Africa, to see how drastically and quickly the advantages gained by women in their liberation struggles may be undermined or destroyed. So far, in most of West Africa, the militant fundamentalists remain a small minority in society and are often associated with university students. But continuing economic problems, disagreements with the treatment of African nations by Western countries, and public dissatisfaction and despair can radically alter politics in societies that now appear secular and even relatively liberal.

The position of West African women in Islamic countries may depend in large part on the outcome of the effort of Islamically committed women to fashion reforms that do not challenge the fundamentals of their religion. Their effort to forge an Islamic alternative to Western feminism should alert our interest and study. We stress again the necessity of seeing the diversity behind the unity of Islam. Although Islam prescribes a "total way of life" and adherence to the fundamentals of the religion as laid down in the seventh century, in fact differing contexts have produced many different types of Islamic societies. Some of these differences are found in the emergence of varying interpretations of Islamic law, theology, and mysticism. But even if the more observant Muslim women in Nigeria appear on first encounter to live more limited lives than their secular Senegalese Muslim sisters, they may in fact be at the forefront of a reinterpretation of Islam having revolutionary consequences in their own society. They are challenging it to live up to the tenets of the religion and, in so doing, are leading the way toward reinterpretations of Islamic doctrine that may usher in a new Islamic tradition in Nigeria and influence Islam throughout West Africa as well.

BIBLIOGRAPHY

Adas, Michael (1979). *Prophets of Rebellion: Millenarian Protest Movements Against the European Colonial Order.* Chapel Hill: University of North Carolina Press.

Afshar, Haleh (ed.) (1985). *Women, Work and Ideology in the Third World.* London: Tavistock Publications.

Al-Hibri, Azizah (ed.) (1982). *Women and Islam.* Oxford: Pergamon Press.

Almond, Gabriel and Sidney Verba (1962). *The Civic Culture.* Boston: Little, Brown and Co.

Anderson, J.N.D. (1970). *Islamic Law in Africa.* London: Frank Cass. Orig. pub. London: Her Majesty's Stationery Office, 1954.

Andre, P. J. (1992). *L'Islam et les races. Vol II: Les Rameaux (mouvements régionaux et sectes).* Paris: Paul Guethner.

Ardener, Shirley (1975). "Introduction." In Shirley Ardener (ed.), *Perceiving Women.* New York: John Wiley and Sons.

———— (1978). *Defining Females: The Nature of Women in Society.* New York: John Wiley and Sons.

Awe, Bolanle (1991). "Women and Politics in the Transition and Beyond." Paper presented at the International Conference on Democratic Transition and Structural Adjustment in Nigeria, January 9–12, 1991, Lagos, Nigeria.

Awosika, Keziah (1981). "Women's Education and Participation in the Labour Force: The Case of Nigeria." In Margherita Rendel (ed.), *Women, Power, and Political Systems.* New York: St. Martin's Press, pp. 81–93.

Balandier, G., and P. Mercier (1952). *Les Pecheurs Lebou: Particularisme et Evolution.* St Louis: Centre IFAN.

Bana, Fames et al. (1984). "The Impact of Territorial Administrative Reform on the Situation of Women in Senegal." In Bana, Fames et al., *Rural Development and Women in Africa.* Geneva: International Labor Organisation, p. 108.

Barkow, Jerome (1972). "Hausa Women and Islam: The Underestimation of Women's Economic Activities." In Nici Nelson, (ed.), *African Women in the Development Process.* London: Frank Cass, pp. 10–28.

———— (1973). "Muslims and Maguzawa in North-Central State, Nigeria: An Ethnographic Comparison." *Canadian Journal of African Studies* 7 (l), pp. 59–76.

Barkow, Jerome, and Keziah Awosika (1981). "Women's Education and Participation in the Labour Force: The Case of Nigeria." In Margherita Rendel (ed.), *Women, Power, and Political Systems.* New York: St. Martin's Press, pp. 81–93.

Barry, Boubacar (1985). *Le Royaume de Walo: Le Senegal avant la Conquete.* Paris: Karthala.

Bashir, M. K. (1972). "The Economic Activities of Secluded Married Women in Kurawa and Lallokin Lemu, Kano City." Zaria: Ahmadu Bello University, Department of Sociology, B.Sc. Thesis.

Bay, Edna G. (1982). *Women and Work in Africa.* Boulder: Westview Press.

Beck, Lois, and Nikki Keddie (eds.), (1978). *Women in the Muslim World.* Cambridge: Harvard University Press.

Behrman, Lucy C.—See Creevey, Lucy.

Beik, Janet (1991). "Women's Roles in the Contemporary Hausa Theater of Niger." In Catherine Coles and Beverly Mack (eds.), *Women in Twentieth-Century Hausa Society.* Madison: University of Wisconsin Press, pp. 232–244.

Bello, Aishatu Salibu (1983). "The Problems and Prospects of Mass Education with Special reference to Women." Kano: Bayero University, Faculty of Education, M.Ed. Thesis.

Beneria, Lourdes (1982). "Accounting for Women's Work." In Lourdes Beneria (ed.), *The Sexual Division of Labor in Rural Societies.* New York: Praeger, pp. 119–147.

Bivar, A. D. H., and Hiskett, Mervyn (1962). "The Arabic Literature of Nigeria to 1804: A Provisional Account." *Bulletin: School of Oriental and African Studies.* 25 (1), pp. 142–158.

Boserup, Ester (1970). *Women's Role in Economic Development.* New York: St. Martin's Press.

Boyd, Jean (1989). *The Caliph's Sister, Nana Asma'u, 1793–1865: Teacher, Poet and Islamic Leader.* London: Frank Cass.

Boyd, Jean, and Murray Last. (1985). "The Role of Women as 'Agents Religieux' in Sokoto." *Canadian Journal of African Studies.* 19 (2), pp. 283–300.

Bray, Mark (1981). *Universal Primary Education in Nigeria: A Study of Kano State.* London: Routledge and Kegan Paul.

Brigaud, Felix. (1962). *Histoire Traditionnelle du Sénégal: Etudes Sénégalaises.* No. 9, Connaissance du Sénégal. St. Louis: C.R.D.S.

Bromley, Ray, and Chris Gerry (eds.) (1979). *Casual Work and Poverty in Third World Cities.* New York: John Wiley and Sons.

Brosselard, M. Charles (1859). *Les Khouans: de la constitution des ordres religieux musulmans en Algérie.* Algiers: A. Bourget.

Brown, Godfrey N. and Mervyn Hiskett (ed.) (1975). *Conflict and Harmony in Education in Tropical Africa.* London: George Allen & Unicorn.

Bruce, J. (1989). "Homes Divided." *World Development* 27 (7) (July), p. 980.

Bujiria, Janet M. (1986). "Urging Women to Redouble their Efforts . . . Class, Gender, and Capitalist Transformation in Africa." In Claire Robertson and Iris Berger (eds.), *Women and Class in Africa.* New York: Africana Publishing Company, pp. 117–140.

Bunster, Ximena, et al. (eds.) (1977). *Women and National Development: The Complexities of Change.* Chicago: University of Chicago Press.

Callaway, Barbara (1984). "Ambiguous Consequences of the Socialization and Seclusion of Hausa Muslim Women in Nigeria." *Journal of Modern African Studies* 22 (3), pp. 429–450.

——— (1987). *Muslim Hausa Women in Nigeria.* Syracuse: Syracuse University Press.

——— (1991). "The Role of Women in Kano City Politics." In Catherine Coles and Beverly Mack (eds.), *Women in Twentieth-Century Hausa Society.* Madison: University of Wisconsin Press, pp. 145–163.

Callaway, Barbara, and Enid Schildkrout (1985). "Law, Education, and Social Change: Implications for Hausa Muslim Women in Nigeria." In Lynn Iglitzen and Ruth Ross (eds.), *The Women's Decade, 1975–1985*. Santa Barbara: ABC-Clio Press, pp. 181–205.

Callaway, Barbara, and Lucy Creevey (1989). "Women and the State in Islamic West Africa." In Sue Ellen Charlton, Jana Everett, and Kathleen Staudt (eds.), *Women, the State and Development*. Albany: State University of New York Press, pp. 88–93.

Cammack, Paul, David Pool, and Wm. Tordoff (1990). *Third World Politics: A Comparative Introduction*. Baltimore: John Hopkins University Press.

Caplan, Lionel (1987) "Introduction." In Lionel Caplan (ed.), *Studies in Religious Fundamentalism*. Albany: State University of New York Press, pp. 1–22.

Cardaire, Marcel (1954). *L'Islam et le terroir africain*. Kouluba: Imprimèrie du Gouvernement.

—— (1962). "Quelques aspects de l'Islamisation sénégalais." *Academie des Sciences d'Outre-Mer* 17 (June 15), p. 259.

Carney, Judith, and Michael Watts (1991). "Disciplining Women? Rice, Mechanization, and the Evolution of Mandinka Gender Relations in Senegambia." *Signs* 16 (4) (Summer), pp. 651–681.

Chailley, M., et al. (eds.) (1963). *Notes et Etudes sur l'Islam en Afrique Noire*. Paris: J. Peyronnet.

Charlton, Sue Ellen (1984). *Women in Third World Development*. Boulder: Westview Press.

Charlton, Sue Ellen, Jana Everett, and Kathleen Staudt (eds.) (1989). *Women, The State and Development*. Albany: State University of New York Press.

Christelow, Allen (1991). "Women and the Law in Early-Twentieth-Century Kano." In Catherine Coles and Beverly Mack (eds.), *Women in Twentieth-Century Hausa Society*. Madison: University of Wisconsin Press, pp. 130–145.

Cloud, Kathleen (1970). "Sex Roles in Food Production and Distribution Processes in the Sahel." In Lucy Creevey (ed.), *Women Farmers in Africa: Rural Development in Mali and the Sahel*. Syracuse: Syracuse University Press, pp. 19–49.

Coleman, James S. (1960). *Nigeria: Background to Nationalism*. Cambridge: Harvard University Press.

Coles, Catherine (1983). *Muslim Women in Town: Social Change Among the Hausa of Northern Nigeria*. Madison: University of Wisconsin, Ph.D. Dissertation.

—— (1988). "Urban Muslim Women and Social Change in Northern Nigeria." *Working Papers on Women in International Development* 19. East Lansing: Michigan State University.

—— (1991). "Hausa Women's Work in a Declining Urban Economy: Kaduna, Nigeria, 1980–1985." In Catherine Coles and Beverly Mack (eds.), *Women in Twentieth-Century Hausa Society*. Madison: University of Wisconsin Press, pp. 163–192.

Coles, Catherine and Beverley Mack (eds.) (1991). *Women in Twentieth-Century Hausa Society*. Madison: University of Wisconsin Press.

Code de la Famille—see Government of Senegal.

Comaroff, John L. (1987). "Sui Genderis; Feminism, Kinship Theory and Structural 'Domains.'" In Jan Fishburne Collier and Sylvia Junko Yanagisako (eds.), *Gender and Kinship: Essays Toward a Unified Analysis*. Stanford: Stanford University Press, pp. 53–85.

Copans, Jean (1980). *Les Marabouts de l'Arachide*. Paris: Le Sycomore.

Coulon, Christian (1983). *Les Musulmans et le Pouvoir en Afrique Noire*. Paris: Karthala.

―――― (1989). "Women, Islam and Baraka." In Donal Cruise O'Brien and Christian Coulon (eds.), *Charisma and Brotherhood in African Islam.* Oxford: Clarendon Press, pp. 113–133.

―――― (1990). "Senegal: The Development and Fragility of Semidemocracy." In Larry Diamond, Juan Linz, and Seymour Martin Lipset, *Politics in Developing Countries: Comparing Experiences with Democracy.* Boulder: Lynne Rienner Publishers, pp. 411–448.

Coulson, Noel, and Doreen Hinchcliffe (1978). "Women and Law Reform in Contemporary Islam." In Lois Beck and Nikki Keddie (eds.), *Women in the Muslim World.* Cambridge: Harvard University Press, pp. 37–51.

Creevey (Behrman), Lucy (1970). *Muslim Brotherhoods and Politics in Senegal.* Cambridge: Harvard University Press.

―――― (1971). "French Muslim Policy and the Senegalese Brotherhoods." In Daniel F. McCall and Norman R. Bennett (eds.), *Boston University Papers on Africa.* Vol. V: *Aspects of West African Islam.* Boston: Boston University Press, pp. 185–208.

Creevey, Lucy (1977). "Muslim Politics and Development in Senegal." *Journal of Modern African Studies* 15 (2), pp. 261–277.

―――― (1979). "Ahmad Bamba 1850–1927." In John Ralph Willis (ed.), *Studies in West African Islamic History.* Vol. 1: *The Cultivators of Islam.* London: Frank Cass, pp. 278–307.

―――― (ed.) (1986). *Women Farmers in Africa: Rural Development in Mali and the Sahel.* Syracuse: Syracuse University Press.

―――― (1991). "The Impact of Islam on Women in Senegal." *Journal of Developing Areas* 25 (3) (April), pp. 347–368.

―――― (1993). *The Sword and the Veil: Islam and Women in Senegal.* Storrs, CT: Unpub. mss.

Cruise O'Brien, Donal (1971). *The Mourides of Senegal: The Political and Economic Organization of an Islamic Brotherhood.* Oxford: Clarendon Press.

―――― (1975). "Clans, Clienteles and Communities: A Structure of Political Loyalties." In Donal Cruise O'Brien, *Saints and Politicians: Essays in the Organization of a Senegalese Peasant Society.* Cambridge: Cambridge University Press.

―――― (1975b). "Land, Cash and Charisma: An Economic Sociology of the Mouride Brotherhood." In Donal Cruise O'Brien. *Saints and Politicians,* pp. 59–64.

―――― (1988). "Charisma Comes to Town: Mouride Urbanization 1945–1986." In Donal Cruise O'Brien and Christian Coulon (eds.), *Charisma and Brotherhood in African Islam.* Oxford: Clarendon Press, pp. 135–155.

Cultru, P. (1913). *Premier Voyage du Sieur de la Courbe fait à la coste d'Afrique en 1685.* Paris: Emile Larose and Edouard Champion.

Dan Shehu, Malam Isa (1971). "Wak'ar Shehu Karamonin." *African Language Studies* 12, p. 17.

Davison, Jean (ed.) (1988). *Agriculture, Women and Land: The African Experience.* Boulder: Westview Press.

"Debates on Feminism in Senegal; Visions vs. Nostalgia." (1986). *Echo* 1 (2–3), p. 9.

Del Vecchio Good, Mary Jo (1978). "A Comparative Perspective on Women in Iran and Turkey." In Lois Beck and Nikkie Keddie (eds.), *Women in the Muslim World.* Cambridge: Harvard University Press, pp. 482–500.

Depont, Octave, and Xavier Coppolani (1897). *Les Confrèries religieuses musulmanes.* Algiers: Adolphe Jourdan.

Diamond, Larry, Jaun J. Linz, and Seymour Martin Lipset (1990). *Politics in Developing Countries: Comparing Experiences with Democracy.* Boulder: Lynne Rienner Publishers.

Dieng, M. (1991). "Code de la Famille du Sénégal; Les dessous anti-islamiques." *Le Militant Musulman* 5 (April–May), pp. 13–14.

Dieng, Oumar (1954). "Chez Serigne Dame." *Le Reveil Islamique* 3 (February).

Dikko, Saude (1982). "The Role of Women Title Holders in the Zaria Political Setup." Kano: Bayero University, B.A. Thesis.

Diop, Abdoulaye-Bara. (1981). *La Société Wolof: Tradition et Changement: les Systèmes d'Inégalité et de Domination.* Paris: Karthala.

——— (1985). *La Famille Wolof.* Paris: Karthala.

Diop, Cheikh Anta (1960). *L'Afrique noire précoloniale.* Paris: Présence Africaine.

Diop, Fatimatou Zahra, and Fatoumata Sow (1989). "Le Code de la Famille; une arme pour la Libération des Femmes." *Fippu* 2 (April), pp. 8–9.

Dodd, B. (ed.) (1973). *Out of School Education for Women in African Countries.* Geneva: UNESCO. 82 (4), pp. 52–57.

Dube, Leela (1986). "Introduction." In Leela Dube, Eleanor Leacock, and Shirley Ardener (eds.), *Visibility and Power: Essays on Women in Society and Development.* Delhi: Oxford University Press, pp. xi–xliv.

Dunbar, Roberta Ann (1970). *Damagarum (Zinder, Niger), The History of a Central Sudanic Kingdom.* Ph.D. Dissertation. Los Angeles: University of California.

——— (1991). "Islamic Values, the State, and the Development of Women: The Case of Niger." In Catherine Coles and Beverly Mack (eds.), *Women in Twentieth-Century Hausa Society.* Madison: University of Wisconsin Press, pp. 69–90.

Dywer, D., and Bruce, J. (eds.) (1988). *A Home Divided: Women and Income in the Third World.* Stanford: Stanford University Press.

Echard, Nicole (1991). "Gender Relationships and Religion: Women in the Hausa Bori of Ader, Niger." In Catherine Coles and Beverly Mack (eds.), *Women in Twentieth-Century Hausa Society.* Madison: University of Wisconsin Press, pp. 207–221.

Echo. Publication of the Senegalese feminist organization. Yewwu Yewwi.

Edholm, F., O. Harris, and K. Young (1977). "Conceptualizing Women." *Critique of Anthropology* 3, pp. 101–130.

Entwisle, Barbara, and Catherine M. Coles (1990). "Demographic Surveys and Nigerian Women." *Signs* 15 (January), pp. 259–284.

Esposito, John L. (1980). *Islam and Development: Religion and Sociopolitical Change.* Syracuse: Syracuse University Press.

——— (1982). *Women in Muslim Family Law.* Syracuse: Syracuse University Press.

——— (1992). *The Islamic Threat: Myth or Reality?* London: Oxford University Press.

l'Etudiant Musulman. Journal of a Muslim student's association in Senegal.

Fage, J. D., (1978). *A History of Africa.* New York: Alfred Knopf.

Fall, Aminata Sow (1979). *La Grève des Battus ou les Dechets Humains.* Dakar: Les Nouvelles Editions Africains.

Fallers, Lloyd, and Margaret Fallers (1982). "Sex Roles in Edremit." In J. Peristiany (ed.), *Mediterranean Family Structure.* Cambridge: Cambridge University Press, pp. 88–145.

Fapohunda, Eleanor (1983). "Female and Male Work Profiles." In Christine Oppong (ed.), *Female and Male in West Africa.* London: George Allen Unwin, pp. 32–53.

Fatoumata-Diarra, Andree Michel Agnes, and Helene Agbessi-Dos Santos (eds.) (1981). *Femmes et Multinationales*. Paris: Karthala.

Fatton, Robert (1987). *The Making of a Liberal Democracy: Senegal's Passive Revolution, 1875–1985*. Boulder: Lynne Rienner Publishers.

Feinstein, Alan (1987). *African Revolutionary: The Life and Times of Nigeria's Aminu Kano*, revised edition. Boulder: Lynne Rienner.

Folbre, N. (1988). "The Black Four of Hearts: Toward a New Paradigm of Household Economics." In D. Dwyer, and J. Bruce (eds.). *A Home Divided: Women and Income in the Third World*. Stanford: Stanford University Press.

Frishman, Alan (1991). "Hausa Women in the Urban Economy of Kano." In Catherine Coles and Beverly Mack (eds.), *Women in Twentieth-Century Hausa Society*. Madison: University of Wisconsin Press, pp. 192–207.

Froelich, J. C. (1961). "Le Reformisme le l'Islam en Afrique noire de l'Ouest." *Revue de Défense Nationale* 17, (January), pp. 83–89.

Gaden, Henri (1912). "Legendes et coutumes sénégalaises; Cahiers de Yoro Dyao." *Revue d'éthnographie et de sociologie* 3, p. 123.

Gamble, David P. (1957). *The Wolof of Senegambia Together with Notes on the Lebu and Serer*. Western Africa, Part XIV. London: International African Institute.

Garnsey, Elizabeth (1982). "Women's Work and Theories of Class and Stratification." In Anthony Giddens and David Held (eds.), *Classes, Power and Conflict: Classical and Contemporary Debates*. Berkeley: University of California Press, pp. 425–469.

Gastellu, Jean-Marc (1981). *l'Egalitarianisme économique des Serers du Sénégal, Travaux et Documents d'O.R.S.T.O.M.* 128. Paris: ORSTOM.

Geismar, L. (1933). *Recueil des coutumes civiles des races du Sénégal établi par L. Geismar, administrateur en chef des colonies*. St. Louis: Imprimèrie du Gouvernement.

Gellar, Sheldon (1982). *Senegal: An African Nation Between Islam and the West*. Boulder: Westview Press.

———— (1987). "Circulaire 32 Revisited: Prospects for Revitalizing the Senegalese Cooperative Movement." In John Waterbury and Mark Gersovitz (eds.), *The Political Economy of Risk and Choice in Senegal*. London: Frank Cass, pp. 123–159.

Gibb, H.A.R. (1955). *Mohammedanism: An Historical Survey*. New York: Mentor Books.

Gibb, H.A.R. and Bowen, H. (1957). *Islam, Society and the West*. London: Oxford University Press.

Giddens, Anthony, and David Held (eds.) (1982). *Classes, Power and Conflict: Classical and Contemporary Debates*. Berkeley: University of California Press.

Giele, J. Z. and Audrey Smock (1977). *Women's Roles and Status in Eight Countries*. New York: John Wiley and Sons.

Ginat, Joseph (1982). *Women in Muslim Rural Society: Status and Role in Family and Community*. New Brunswick: Transaction Books.

Glele, Maurice Ahanhanzo (1981). *Religion, culture et politique en Afrique Noire*. Paris: Presence Africaine.

Gouilly, Alphonse (1952). *L'Islam dans l'Afrique Occidentale Francaise*. Paris: Editions Larose.

Government of Mali (1988). *Annuaire Statistique du Mali 1985*. Bamako: Direction Nationale de la Statistique.

Government of Senegal: Dakar Archives (DA) (1936). Abdel Kader Diagne to Governor General (November 18), 19G 38 (108)FM.

————: DA (1912). Governor General to Lieutenant Governor (November 8), No. 2099, Dossier.

————: DA (1904). "Rapport sur la situation politique en l'AOF" (1st trimester) 2G 4.5.

————: DA (1926). Rapport Politique du Senegal, 2G 26:10.

————: DA (1936a). Abdel Kader Diagne to Governor General (November 18), 19G 38 (108) FM.

————: DA (1936b). Speech by Thierno Boubakar Ben Omar Hadji on the occasion of the arrival in St. Louis of the Minister of Colonies and the Governor General, 19G, 38 (108) FM.

————: DA (1936c). Daigne to Governor General (December 4) and attached clippings, 19G 38 (108) FM.

————: DA (1936d). Governor General to President of the Muslim Fraternity (November 26) 16G (108) FM.

————: DA (1937). Gaigne to Governor General (May 24) and Governor General to Diagne (June 3), 19G 38 (108) FM.

———— (1975). *Situation Economique du Senegal 1974*. Dakar: Ministère des Finances et des Affaires Economiques.

———— (1979) *Code de la Famille*. Dakar: published in *La Journel Officielle* (revision published in April 1989).

———— (1988). *Recensement Général de la Population et de l'Habitat* (RGPH). Dakar: Ministère de l'Economie et des Finances, Direction de la Statistique, Bureau Informatique.

———— (1988a). *Situation Economique 1987*. Dakar: Ministère de l'Economie et des Finances, Direction de la Statistique.

———— (1989). *Les Principaux Resultats Provisoires du Recensement de la Population de l'Habitat du Senegal*. Dakar: Direction de la Prevision et de la Statistique.

———— (1989a). "Repartition des Agents d'Etat par Sexe selon la Situation Matrimoniale." DTAI/MEF (May).

———— (1989b). *Journal Officiel de la Republique du Senegal* (Mai).

———— (1989c). *Situation Economique 1988*. Dakar: Ministère de l'Economie et des Finances, Direction de la Statistique.

Gravrand, Henry (1985). *La Civilisation Sereer: Cosaan: Les Origines*. Abbeville: Les Nouvelles Editions Africaines.

Greenberg, Joseph (1946). *The Influence of Islam on a Sudanese Religion*. New York: J. J. Augustin.

———— (1947). "Islam and Clan Organization Among the Hausa." *Southwest Journal of Anthropology* 3, pp. 196–211.

Grown, Caren A., and Jennifer Sebstad (1989). "Introduction: Toward a Wider Perspective of Women's Employment." *World Development* 17 (7) (July), p. 940.

Guyer, Jane I. (1986). "Intra-Household Processes and Farming Systems Research: Perspectives from Anthropology." In Joyce L. Moock (ed.), *Understanding Africa's Rural Households and Farming Systems*. Boulder: Westview Press, pp. 92–104.

Haddad, Yvonne Yazbeck, and Ellison Banks Findly (eds.) (1985). *Women, Religion and Social Change*. Albany: State University of New York Press.

Hailey, Lord (1944). *Native Administration and Political Development in Tropical Africa, 1940–1942*. London: Her Majesty's Stationery Office.

Hargreaves, John D. (1967). *West Africa: The Former French States*. Englewood Cliffs: Prentice Hall.

Harris, Barbara J. and JoAnn K. McNamera (eds.) (1984). *Women and the Structure of Society: Selected Research from the Fifth Berkshire Conference on the History of Women*. Durham, NC: Duke University Press.

Hartmann, Heidi (1982). "Capitalism, Patriarchy and Job Segregation by Sex." In Anthony Giddens and David Held, *Classes, Power and Conflict: Classical and Contemporary Debates*. Berkeley: University of California Press, pp. 425–469.

Hassan, Yusuf Fadl (1975). "Interaction Between Traditional and Western Education in the Sudan: An Attempt Towards a Synthesis." In G. N. Brown and M.

Hiskett (eds.), *Conflict and Harmony in Education in Tropical Africa,* London: George Allen and Unwin, pp. 118–183.

Hijab, Nadia (1988). *Womenpower: The Arab Debate on Women at Work.* Cambridge: Cambridge University Press.

Hill, Polly (1969). "Hidden Trade in Hausa Land." *Man* 4 (3), pp. 392–409.

―――― (1971). "Two Types of West African House Trade." In Claude Meillassoux (ed.), *The Development of Indigenous Trade and Markets in West Africa,* London: Oxford University Press, pp. 303–318.

―――― (1972). *Rural Hausa: A Village and a Setting.* London: Cambridge University Press.

―――― (1974). "Big Houses in Kano Emirate." *Africa* 54 (April), pp. 117–135.

―――― (1977). *Population, Prosperity and Poverty: Rural Kano 1900 and 1970.* London: Cambridge University Press.

―――― (1986). *Development Economics on Trial: The Anthropological Case for a Prosecution.* Cambridge: Cambridge University Press.

Hilliard, F. H. (1957). *A Short History of Education in British West Africa.* London: Thomas Nelson and Sons, Ltd.

Hinchcliffe, Doreen (1975). "The Status of Women in Islamic Law." In Godfrey N. Brown and Mervyn Hiskett (ed.), *Conflict and Harmony in Education in Tropical Africa.* London: George Allen and Unwin, pp. 455–466.

Hiskett, Mervyn (1960). "Kitab al-Farq: A Work on the Habe Kingdoms Attributed to Uthman dan Fodio." *Bulletin: School of Oriental and African Studies* 23 (3), pp. 553–579.

―――― (1973). *The Sword of Truth: The Life and Times of Usman dan Fodio.* New York: Oxford University Press.

―――― (1975). "Islamic Education in the Tradition and State Systems in Northern Nigeria." In Godfrey N. Brown and Mervyn Hiskett (ed.), *Conflict and Harmony in Education in Tropical Africa.* London: George Allen and Unwin, pp. 134–152.

―――― (1984). *The Development of Islam in West Africa.* London: Longmans.

―――― (1985). "Enslavement, Slavery and Attitudes Towards the Legally Enslavable in Hausa Islamic Literature." In John Ralph Willis (ed.), *Slaves and Slavery in Muslim Africa.* London: Oxford University Press, pp. 106–124.

―――― (1992). "Islamic Theocracy vs. Democratic Pluralism: A Dilemma of Present Day Africa." Presented at the Conference on Islam and Nationhood at Yale University (November 12).

Hitti, Philip K. (1956). *History of the Arabs from the Earliest Times to the Present.* London: Macmillan.

Hogben, S. J., and A.H.M. Kirk-Greene (1966). *The Emirates of Northern Nigeria: A Preliminary Survey of Their Historical Traditions.* London: Oxford University Press.

Houtsma, M., et al. (eds.) (1892). *Encyclopedia of Islam.* London: Luzac.

Humphrey, John (1985). "Gender, Pay and Skill: Manual Workers in Brazilian Industry." In Haleh Afshar (ed.), *Women, Work and Ideology in the Third World.* London: Tavistock Publications, pp. 214–231.

Ifeka-Moller, Caroline (1975). "Female Militancy and Colonial Revolt: The Women's War of 1929, Eastern Nigeria." In Shirley Ardener (ed.), *Perceiving Women.* New York: John Wiley and Sons, pp. 127–157.

Iglitzin, Lynne B., and Ruth Ross (eds.) (1986). *Women in the World: 1975–1985, The Women's Decade.* Santa Barbara: ABC-CLIO Press.

Imam, Ayesha M. and Renee I. Pittin (1984). *The Identification of Successful Women's Projects: Kaduna State Nigeria.* International Labour Organization Report, Geneva.

Imam, Ayesha M. (1985). "Ideology, Hegemony and Mass Media." Sociology Department Seminar Paper. Zaria, Nigeria: Ahmadu Bello University.

——— (1990). "Politics, Islam and Women in Kano, Northern Nigeria." Presented at the Roundtable on Identity Politics and Women (October 8–10). Helsinki: United Nations University.

——— (1991). "Ideology, the Mass Media, and Women: A Study from Radio Kaduna, Nigeria." In Catherine Coles and Beverly Mack (eds.), *Women in Twentieth-Century Hausa Society*, Madison: University of Wisconsin Press, pp. 244–255.

Imperato, Pascal James (1989). *Mali: A Search for Direction*. Boulder: Westview Press.

Jackson, Cecile (Sam) (1978). "Hausa Women on Strike." *Review of African Political Economy* 13 (May–August), pp. 21–36.

——— (1985). *The Kano River Irrigation Project*. Kumarian Press Case Studies on Women's Roles and Gender Differences in Development. New York: Kumarian Press.

Jaggar, P. J. (1976). "Kano City Blacksmiths: Precolonial Distribution Structure and Organization." *Savanna* 2 (1), pp. 11–26.

James, Wendy (1978). "Matrifocus on African Women." In Shirley Ardener (ed.), *Defining Females: The Nature of Women in Society*. New York: John Wiley and Sons, pp. 140–162.

Joekes, Susan (1985). "Working for Lipstick? Male and Female Labour in the Clothing Industry in Morocco." In Haleh Afshar (ed.), *Women, Work and Ideology in the Third World*. London: Tavistock Publications, pp. 183–213.

Journet, Odele (1981). "Les Femmes Diola au Developpement des Cultures Commerciales." In Fatoumata-Diarra, Agnes Andree Michel, and Helene Agbessi-Dos Santos (eds.), *Femmes et Multinationales*. Paris: Karthala, pp. 117–138.

Kabir, Zainab (1985). "On the Women's Liberation Movement: Myth and Realities." Paper presented at the Conference of Muslim Sisters' Organisation, Kano, Nigeria.

Knipp, Margaret Mary (1987). *Women, Western Education and Change: A Case Study of the Hausa-Fulani of Northern Nigeria*. Evanston: Northwestern University, Ph.D. Dissertation.

Khurshid, Ahmad (1974). *Family Life in Islam*. Leicester: The Islamic Foundation.

Last, Murray (1967). *The Sokoto Caliphate*. London: Longmans, Green and Co.

——— (1983). "From Sultanate to Caliphate: Kano ca. 1450–1800." In Bawuro M. Barkindo (ed.), *Studies in the History of Kano*. Ibadan: Heinemann Educational Books, pp. 67–92.

Lazreig, Marnia (1990). "Gender and Politics in Algeria: Unraveling the Religious Paradigm." *Signs* 15 (4) (Summer), pp. 755–780.

Leacock, Eleanor (1986). "Women, Power and Authority," In Leela Dube, Eleanor Leacock, and Shirley Ardener (eds.), *Visibility and Power: Essays on Women in Society and Development*. Delhi: Oxford University Press.

Leacock, Eleanor, and Helen Safa (eds.) (1986). *Women's Work: Development and the Division of Labor by Gender*. Massachusetts: Bergin and Garvey.

Le Chatelier, A. (1899). *L'Islam dans l'Afrique Occidentale*. Paris: G. Steinheil.

Lemu, Aisha (1986). "The Ideal Muslim Husband," Part 2. *New Nigerian,* Friday, May 16, p. 20.

——— (n.d.). *A Degree Above Them: Observations on the Condition of the Northern Nigerian Muslim Women*. Islamic Education Trust, Minna; Zaria, Nigeria; Gaskiya Corporation.

Levy, Reuben (1977). *The Social Structure of Islam*. London: Cambridge University Press.

Lovejoy, Paul E. (1988). "Concubinage and the Status of Women Slaves in Early Colonial Northern Nigeria." *Journal of African History* 29, pp. 245–246.

Lubeck, Paul. (1986). *Islam and Urban Labor in Northern Nigeria: The Making of a Muslim Working Class.* Cambridge: Cambridge University Press.

Lugard, Frederick (1970). *Political Memoranda: Revision of Instructions to Political Officers on Subjects Chiefly Political and Administrative, 1913–1918.* 3d ed. A.H.M. Kirk-Greene. London: Frank Cass.

MacGaffney, Janet (1986). "Women and Class Formation in a Dependent Economy, Kisangani Entrepreneurs." In Claire Robertson and Iris Berger (eds.), *Women and Class in Africa.* New York: Africana Publishing Company, p. 161.

Mack, Beverly (1988). "Haj'iya Madaki: A Royal Hausa Woman." In Patricia Romero (ed.), *Life Histories of African Women.* Atlantic Highlands, NJ: Ashfield Press, pp. 47–77.

———— (1990). "Service and Status: Slaves and Concubines in Kano, Nigeria." In Roger Sanjek and Shellee Colen (eds.), *At Work in Homes: Household Workers in Perspective.* American Ethnological Society Monograph 3. Washington, D.C.: American Anthropological Association, pp. 14–34.

———— (1991). "Royal Wives in Kano." In Catherine Coles and Beverly Mack (eds.), *Women in Twentieth-Century Hausa Society.* Madison: University of Wisconsin Press, pp. 109–130.

Magassouba, Moriba (1985). *l'Islam au Sénégal: Demain las Mollahs?* Paris: Karthala.

Martin, Carol (1983). "Skill-Building or Unskilled Labour for Female Youth: A Bauchi Case." In Christine Oppong (ed.), *Female and Male in West Africa.* London: George Allen and Unwin, pp. 223–235.

Marty, E. (1917). "Les Mourides d'Ahmadou Bamba (rapport à m. le Gouverneur Générale de l'Afrique Occidentale)." *Revue du Monde Musulman* 25 (December).

Marty, Martin (1992). "The Fundamentals of Fundamentalism." In Lawrence Kaplan (ed.), *Fundamentalism in Comparative Perspective.* Amherst: University of Massachusetts Press, pp. 15–23.

Marty, Paul (1917). *Etudes sur l'Islam au Sénégal.* Vol. 1: *Les Personnages.* Paris: Ernest Leroux.

Massignon, Louis (1929). "Tarika" and "Tassawuf." In M. Houtsma, et al. (eds.), *Encyclopedia of Islam.* London: Luzac, pp. 667–672, 681–685.

Mba, Nina (1979). *Nigerian Women Mobilised.* London: Zed Press.

M'Bow, Penda (1989). "Religions et statuts de la femme." *Fippu* (April), p. 45.

McCall, Daniel F., and Norman R. Bennett (eds.), (1971). *Boston University Papers on Africa.* Vol. V: *Aspects of West African Islam.* Boston: Boston University.

McGee, T. G. (1979). "The Poverty Syndrome: Making Out in the Southeast Asian City." In Ray Bromley and Chris Gerry (eds.), *Casual Work and Poverty in Third World Cities.* New York: John Wiley and Sons.

Mernissi, Fatima (1987). "Professional Women in the Arab World: The Example of Morocco." *Feminist Issues* 7 (Spring), pp. 47–65.

Mitchell, Richard C., David G. Morrison, and John N. Paden (1989). *Black Africa: A Comparative Handbook.* 2d ed. New York: Paragon House.

Moghadam, Valentine (1992). "Development and Patriarchy: The Middle East and North Africa in Economic and Demographic Transition." *Working Papers.* Helsinki: World Institute for Development Economic Research of the United Nations University (WIDER).

Monteil, Vincent (1964). "Lat Dyor, Damel du Kayor (1842–1886) et l'Islamisation des Wolofs." *Archives de Sociologie des Religions* 9 (17), pp. 103–104.

Moock, Joyce L. (ed.) (1986). *Understanding Africa's Rural Households and Farming Systems.* Boulder: Westview Press.

Moreau, Rene Luc (1982). *Africains Musulmans; des communautés en mouvement.* Paris: Présence Africaine.

Morgen, Sandra, and Ann Bookman (1988). "Rethinking Women and Politics: An Introductory Essay." In Bookman and Morgen (eds.), *Women and the Politics of Empowerment.* Philadelphia: Temple University Press, pp. 3–29.

Mukhopadhyay, Carol C., and Patricia J. Higgins (1988). "Anthropological Studies of Women's Status Revisited, 1977–1987. *Annual Review of Anthropology* 17, pp. 461–495.

Nelson, C. (1974). "Public and Private Politics: Women in the Middle Eastern World." *American Anthropologist* 1 (3), pp. 551–563.

Nicholson, Linda (1986). *Gender and History: The Limits of Social in the Age of the Family.* New York: Columbia University Press.

Nicolas, Guy (1965). *Circulation des richesses et participation sociale dans une société Hausa du Niger.* Bordeaux: Editions du Centre Universitaire de Polycopiage de l'A.G.E.B.

Paden, John (1973). *Religion and Political Culture in Kano.* Berkeley: University of California Press.

———— (1986). *Ahmadu Bello: Sardauna of Sokoto.* London: Hodder and Stoughton.

Palmer, H. R. (1914). "Bori Among the Hausas." *Man* 14 (52), pp. 113–117.

———— (1928). *Sudanese Memoirs.* 3 vols. Lagos: Government Printer.

Papanek, Hanna (1973). "Purdah: Separate Worlds and Symbolic Shelter." *Comparative Studies and History* 15 (3), pp. 289–325.

Parpart, Jane L. (ed.). (1989). *Women and Development in Africa: Comparative Perspectives.* Lanham: University Press of America.

Pellow, Deborah (1985). "Muslim Segmentation: Cohesion and Divisiveness in Accra." *Journal of Modern African Studies* 23 (3), pp. 419–444.

———— (1991). "From Accra to Kano: One Woman's Experience." In Catherine Coles and Beverly Mack, *Women in Twentieth-Century Hausa Society*, Madison: University of Wisconsin Press, pp. 50–69.

People's Redemption Party (PRP) (1978). "The Platform of the People: The General Programme and Election Manifesto of the People's Redemption Party." Kano. Mimeograph.

Pittin, Renée I. (1976). "Social Status and Economic Opportunity in Urban Hausa Society." *Proceedings: Conference on Nigerian Women and Development in Relation to Changing Family Structure.* Ibadan: Unversity of Ibadan.

———— (1978). "Sex Role Stereotypes and the Behavior of Women: The Ideal/Real Dichotomy." In Fred Omu, et al., *Proceedings of the National Conference on Integrated Rural Development and on Women in Development.* Benin: University of Benin Press, pp. 886–900.

———— (1979). *Marriage and Alternative Strategies: Career Patterns of Hausa Women in Katsina City.* London: School of Oriental and African Studies, Ph. D. Dissertation.

———— (1984). "The Migration of Women in Nigeria: The Hausa Case." *International Migration Review* 18 (Winter), pp. 1293–1314.

———— (1987). "Documentation of Women's Work in Nigeria." In Christine Oppong (ed.), *Sex Roles, Population and Development in West Africa.* Portsmouth, N.H.: Heinemann, London: James Currey, pp. 25–44.

Prindle, Deborah Zubow (1991). *Role of Secondary Cities in African Rural Development: Case Studies of Kikwit, Zaire and Kayes, Mali.* Philadelphia: University of Pennsylvania, Ph. D. Dissertation in City and Regional Planning.

Quesnot, F. (1963). "Les cadres maraboutiques de l'Islam sénégalais." In M. Chailley, et al. (eds.), *Notes et Etudes sur l'Islam en Afrique Noire.* Paris: J. Peyronnet.

"Qui Sommes Nous." (1989). *Fippu, Journal of Yewwu Yewwi, Pour La Libération des Femmes* 2 (April), p. 5.

Quinn, Charlotte Alison (1979). "Maba Diakhou and the Gambian Jihad, 1850–1890." In John Ralph Willis (ed.), *Studies in West African Islamic History.* Vol. 1: *The Cultivators of Islam.* London: Frank Cass, pp. 233–258.

Ragab, Ibrahim A. (1980). "Islam and Development." *World Development* 8 (7–8) (July/August), pp. 513–522.

"Raising Consciousness." (1989). *West Africa* (May 22–28), pp. 828–829.

Remy, Dorothy (1975). "Underdevelopment and the Experience of Women: A Nigerian Case Study." In Rayna R. Reiter (ed.), *Toward an Anthropology of Women.* New York: Monthly Review Press, pp. 356–371.

RGPH—See Government of Senegal.

Rinn, Louis (1884). *Marabouts et Khouan: Etude sur l'Islam en Algérie.* Algiers: Adolphe Jourdan.

Robertson, Claire C. (1984). *Sharing the Same Bowl: A Socioeconomic History of Women and Class in Accra, Ghana.* Bloomington: Indiana University Press.

Robertson, Claire C., and Iris Berger (eds.) (1986). *Women and Class in Africa.* New York: Africana Publishing Company.

Robinson, C. H. (1896). *Hausaland, or Fifteen Hundred Miles Through the Central Soudan.* London: Sampson Low, Marston & Co.

Robinson, David (1975). *Chiefs and Clerics: Abdul Bokar Kan and Futa Toro, 1853–1891.* Oxford: Oxford University Press.

——— (1985). *The Holy War of Umar Tal: The Western Sudan in the Mid-Nineteenth Century.* Oxford: Clarendon Press.

Rosaldo, Michelle Zimbalist (1974). "Woman, Culture and Society: A Theoretical Overview." In Michelle Zimbalist Rosaldo and Louise Lamphere (ed.), *Woman, Culture, and Society.* Stanford: Stanford University Press, pp. 17–42.

——— (1980). "The Use and Abuse of Anthropology: Reflections on Feminism and Cross Cultural Understanding." *Signs* 5 (3), pp. 389–417.

Rosaldo, Michelle Zimbalist, and Louis Lamphere (eds.) (1974). *Women, Culture, and Society.* Stanford: Stanford University.

Saadawi, Nawal E. (1980). *The Hidden Face of Eve: Women in the Arab World.* London: Zed Press.

Sabbah, Fatima (1984). *Women in the Muslim Unconscious.* New York: Pergamon Press.

Sacks, Karen (1974). "Engels Revisited: Women, the Organization of Production and Private Property." In Michelle Zimbalist Rosaldo and Louise Lamphere (eds.), *Women, Culture, and Society.* Stanford: Stanford University Press, pp. 219–222.

Sadji, Abdoulaye (1958). *Maimona.* Paris: Presence Africaine.

Sa'id, Halil Ibrahim (1978). *Revolution and Reaction: The Fulani Jihad in Kano and Its Aftermath, 1807–1919.* Ann Arbor: University of Michigan, Ph.D. Dissertation.

Sanasarian, Elizabeth (1986). "Political Activism and Islamic Identity in Iran." In Lynne B. Iglitzin and Ruth Ross (eds.), *Women in the World: 1975–1985, the Women's Decade.* Santa Barbara: ABC-CLIO Press, pp. 207–224.

Sanday, Peggy Reeves (1981). *Female Power and Male Dominance: On the Origins of Sexual Inequality.* Cambridge: Cambridge University Press.

Saunders, Margaret O. (1978). *Marriage and Divorce in a Muslim Hausa Town (Mirria, Niger Republic).* Bloomington: Indiana University, Ph.D. Dissertation.

Savane, Angelique (1986). "The Effects of Social and Economic Changes on the Role and Status of Women in Sub-Saharan Africa." In Joyce L. Moock (ed.), *Understanding Africa's Rural Households*. Boulder: Westview Press, pp. 104–124.

Schildkrout, Enid (1978). "Age and Gender in Hausa Society: Socio-Economic Roles of Children in Urban Kano." In J. S. LaFontaine (ed.), *Age and Sex as Principles of Social Differentiation*. ASA Monograph 17. New York: Academic Press, pp. 109–137.

———— (1978b). "Changing Economic Roles of Children in Comparative Perspective." In C. Oppong, G. Adaba, M. Bekombo-Priso, and J. Mogey (eds.), *Marriage, Fertility and Parenthood in West Africa: Changing African Family*. No. 4, Pt. 1. Canberra: Australian National University.

———— (1979). "Women's Work and Children's Work: Variations Among Moslems in Kano." In Sandra Wallman (ed.), *Social Anthropology of Work*. ASA Monograph 19. London: Academic Press, pp. 69–85.

———— (1981). "The Employment of Children in Kano, Northern Nigeria." In Gerry Rodgers and Guy Standing (eds.), *Economic Role of Children in Low-Income Countries*. Geneva: International Labour Office, pp. 81–112.

———— (1982). "Dependence and Autonomy: The Economic Activities of Secluded Hausa Women in Kano, Nigeria." In Edna Bay (ed.), *Women and Work in Africa*. Boulder: Westview Press, pp. 55–81.

———— (1983). "Dependence and Automony: The Economic Activities of Secluded Hausa Women in Kano." In Christine Oppong, ed., *Female and Male in West Africa*. London: George Allen and Unwin, pp. 107–126.

———— (1986). "Widows in Hausa Society: Ritual Phase of Social Status?" In Betty Potash (ed.), *Widows in African Societies: Choices and Constraints*. Stanford: Stanford University Press, pp. 131–152.

———— (1988). "Haliya Husaina: Notes on the Life History of a House Woman." In Patricia Romero (ed.), *Life Histories of African Women*. Atlantic Highlands, NJ: Ashfield Press, pp. 78–98.

Sen, Gita, and Caren Grown (1987). *Development Crises and Alternative Visions: Third World Women's Perspectives*. New York: Monthly Review Press.

Simmons, Emmy B. (1975). "The Small-Scale Rural Food Processing Industry in Northern Nigeria." *Food Research Institute Studies* (Stanford) 14 (2), pp. 147–161.

———— (1976). "Economic Research on Women in Rural Development in Northern Nigeria." In *Overseas Liaison Committee America Council on Education* series, paper no. 10.

Simms, R. (1981). "The African Woman As Entrepreneur: Problems and Perspectives on Their Roles." In F. Steady (ed.), *The Black Woman Cross-Culturally*. Cambridge, MA: Shenkman, pp. 141–168.

Situation Economique du Sénégal 1988—see Government of Senegal.

Sivaud, Ruth Leger (1985). *Women . . . a world survey*. Washington, DC: World Priorities.

Sklar, Richard L. (1983). *Nigerian Political Parties: Power in an Emergent African Nation*. New York: Nok Publishers International.

Smith, Donald E. (1970). *Religion and Political Development*. Boston: Little, Brown and Co.

———— (1974). *Religion and Political Modernization*. New Haven: Yale University Press.

Smith, Jane I. (ed.) (1980). *Women in Contemporary Muslim Societies*. Cranbury, NJ: Associated University Presses.

———— (1985). "Women, Religion and Social Change in Early Islam." In Yvonne Yazbeck Haddad, and Ellison Banks Findley (eds.), *Women, Religion and Social Change*. Albany: State University of New York Press, pp. 19–35.

Smith, Jane I. (1987). "Islam." In Arvind Sharma (ed.), *Women in World Religions.* Albany: State University of New York Press, pp. 235–250.

Smith, Mary F. (1981). *Baba of Karo: A Woman of the Muslim Hausa.* 2d Edition. New Haven: Yale University Press. Orig. pub. London: Faber and Faber, 1954.

Smith, Michael G. (1955). *The Economy of the Hausa Communities of Zaria.* London: Her Majesty's Stationery Office, Colonial Research Studies 16.

——— (1959). "The Hausa System of Social Status." *Africa* 29 (3), pp. 239–252.

——— (1960). *Government in Zazzau.* London: Oxford University Press.

——— (1962). "Exchange and Marketing Among the Hausa." In P. Bohannan and G. Dalton (eds.), *Markets in Africa.* Evanston: Northwestern University Press, pp. 229–334.

——— (1978). *The Affairs of Daura: History and Change in a Hausa State, 1800–1958.* Berkeley: University of California Press.

——— (1981). "Introduction." In Mary F. Smith, *Baba of Karo: A Woman of the Muslim Hausa,* New Haven: Yale University Press.

——— (1983). "The *Kano Chronicle* as History." In Bawuro M. Barkindo, ed., *Studies in the History of Kano,* Ibadan, Nigeria: Heinemann Educational Books, pp. 31–56.

——— (n.d.). "Government in Kano." Manuscript.

Smith, Wilfred Cantwell (1959). *Islam in Modern History.* New York: New American Library.

Sow, Fatou (1973). "Dependance et Developpement; Le Statut de la Femme en Afrique Moderne." *Notes Africaines* 139 (July), 65.

——— (1985). "Muslim Families in Contemporary Black Africa." *Current Anthropology* 26 (5) (December), p. 566.

——— (1989). "La Décennie des Nations Unies pour la Femme (1975–1985) au Sénégal; Bilan et Perspectives." University Cheikh Anta Diop de Dakar, Institut Fondamental d'Afrique Noire/Cheikh Anta Diop, 9.

——— (1990). "Les Groupements Féminins autour de Nabadji-Civol (Departement de Matam-Sénégal)." *Rapport de la Mission de l'Association Francaise des Femmes Diplomées.* Dakar: Institut Foundemental d'Afrique Noir (IFAN), Janvier.

——— (1991). "Le Pouvoir économique des femmes dans le Department de Podor." Dakar: IFAN, Janvier.

Stamp, Patricia (1990). *Technology, Gender and Power in Africa.* Ottawa: International Development Research Center.

Staudt, Kathleen (1982). "Sex, Ethnicity and Class Consciousness in Western Kenya." *Comparative Politics* 14 (1), pp. 149–158.

——— (1986). "Stratification: Implications for Women's Politics." In Claire Robertson and Iris Berger (eds.), *Women and Class in Africa.* New York: Africana Publishing Company, pp. 197–215.

Stephens, Connie (1991). "Marriage in the Hausa Tatsuniya Tradition: A Cultural and Cosmic Balance." In Catherine Coles and Beverly Mack (eds.), *Women in Twentieth-Century Hausa Society.* Madison: University of Wisconsin Press, pp. 221–232.

Stevens, Melanie (1987). "Gender and Solidarity: A Village in Rural Senegal." Radcliffe College: Unpublished manuscript.

Stichter, Sharon B. (1984). "Appendix: Some Selected Statistics on African Women." In Margaret Jean Hay and Sharon Stichter (eds.), *African Women South of the Sahara.* London: Longman, pp. 188–194.

Stichter, Sharon B., and Parpart, Jane L. (eds.) (1988). *Patriarchy and Class: African Women in the Home and the Workforce.* Boulder: Westview Press.

Sudarkasa, Niarra (1986). "The Status of Women's Indigenous African Societies." *Feminist Studies* 12 (Spring), pp. 91–103.

Sule, Balaraba B. M. and Priscilla E. Starratt (1991). "Islamic Leadership Positions for Women in Contemporary Kano Society." In Catherine Coles and Beverly Mack (eds.), *Women in Twentieth-Century Hausa Society*. Madison: University of Wisconsin Press, pp. 29–50.

Suret-Canale, Jean (1964). *Afrique Noire Occidentale et Centrale: géographie, civilisations, histoire*. Paris: Editions Sociales.

Sy, Cheikh Tidjane (1969). *La Confrèrie Sénégalaise des Mourides*. Paris: Présence Africaine.

Tabari, Azar, and Nahid Yageneh (eds.) (1982). *In the Shadow of Islam: The Women's Movement in Iran*. London: Zed Press.

Tahir, Ibrahim (1976). *Scholars, Sufis, Saints, and Capitalists in Kano, 1904–1974*. Cambridge University, Ph.D. Dissertation.

Thomas, Louis-Vincent (1958). *Les Diola: Essai d'Analyse Fonctionnelle sur une Population de Basse-Casamance*. Dakar: IFAN.

Tibenderana, Peter Kazenga (1985). "The Beginnings of Girls' Education in the Native Administration Schools in Northern Nigeria, 1930–1945." *Journal of African History* 26, pp. 93–109.

Tokman, Victor E. (1989). "Policies for a Heterogeneous Informal Sector in Latin America." *World Development* 17 (7) (July), p. 1067.

Trevor, Jean (1975a). "Western Education and Muslim Fulani/Hausa Women in Sokoto, Northern Nigeria." In Godfrey Brown and Mervyn Hiskett (eds.), *Conflict and Harmony in Education in Tropical Africa*. London: George Allen and Unwin, pp. 247–270.

——— (1975b). "Family Change in Sokoto, A Traditional Moslem Fulani/Hausa City." In John Caldwell (ed.), *Population Growth and Socioeconomic Change in West Africa*. New York: Columbia University Press, pp. 236–253.

Trimingham, J. Spencer (1959). *Islam in West Africa*. Oxford: Clarendon Press.

Trincaz, Jacqueline, and Pierre Trincaz (1983). "L'Elatement de la Famille Africaine, Religions et Migrations, Dot et Polygamie." *Cahiers d'ORSTOM, ser. Sci. Hum.* Vol. XIX, No. 2, pp. 195–202.

Trincaz, Pierre (1979). "Transformation Sociales dans les Zones Neuves du Sénégal Oriental." *Cahiers d'ORSTOM ser. Sci. Hum* 16 (1–2): 2, pp. 19–36.

——— (1987). "L'Importance de la Famille dans les Processus d'Insertion Urbaine des Serer du Bassin Arachidier." *Colloques et Séminaires; l'Insertion Urbaine des Migrants en Afrique, Actes du Seminaire CRDI-ORSTOM-URD*. Lome (February), pp. 33–39.

United Nations (1991). *The World's Women: Trends and Statistics*. New York.

United States Agency for International Development (USAID) (1991). "Facts on Women in Senegal." Draft Research Report prepared for the Women in Development Office, Dakar.

Venema, Bernard (1978). "The Wolof of Saloum: Social Structure and Rural Development in Senegal." Wageningen PUD, PUDOC.

——— (1970). "The Changing Role of Women in Sahelian Agriculture." In Lucy Creevey (ed.), *Women Farmers in Africa*. Syracuse: Syracuse University Press, pp. 84–88.

Vengroff, Richard, and Alan Johnston (1987). "Decentralization and the Implementation of Rural Development in Senegal: The Role of Rural Councils." *Public Administration and Development* 7, pp. 275–287.

Vengroff, Richard (Principal Investigator) (1990). "Etude sur les G.I.E.s au Sénégal." Ecole Nationale d'Economie Appliquée, supported by USAID-Dakar, pp. 5–9.

Vengroff, Richard, and Momar N'Diaye (1991). "Senegal Maps Informal Sector Survey." Unpublished Manuscript.

Verrière, Louis (1965). "La Population du Sénégal (Aspects Quantitatifs)." Dakar: University of Dakar.

Wallace, Anthony F. (1966). *Religion: An Anthropological View.* New York: Random House.

Waterbury, John, and Mark Gersovitz (eds.) (1987). *The Political Economy of Risk and Choice in Senegal.* London: Frank Cass.

Watts, Michael (1983). *Silent Violence: Food, Famine and Peasantry in Northern Nigeria.* Berkeley: University of California Press.

————— (1987). *State, Oil, and Agriculture in Nigeria.* Berkeley: Institute of International Studies, University of California.

Weekes, Richard V. (ed.) (1984). *Muslim Peoples: A World Ethnographic Survey.* Westport: Greenwood Press.

Wehr, Hans (1961). *Dictionary of Modern Arabic.* Edited by J. Milton Cowan. Ithaca: Cornell University Press.

Whitaker, C. S. (1970). *The Politics of Tradition: Continuity and Change in Northern Nigeria 1946–1966.* Princeton: Princeton University Press.

Whyte, Martin King (1978). "Cross Cultural Codes Dealing with the Relative Status of Women." *Ethnology* 17 (April), pp. 211–237.

Willis, John Ralph (ed.) (1979). *Studies in West African Islamic History.* Vol 1: *The Cultivators of Islam.* London: Frank Cass.

Williams, John Alden (1980). "Veiling in Egypt as a Political and Social Phenomenon." In John L. Esposito (ed.), *Islam and Development; Religion and Sociopolitical Change.* Syracuse: Syracuse University Press, pp. 71–85.

Wilson, Boydena R. (1984). "Glimpses of Muslim Urban Women in Classical Islam." In Barbara J. Garris and JoAnn K. McNamera (eds.), *Women and the Structure of Society: Selected Research from the Fifth Berkshire Conference on the History of Women.* Durham: Duke University Press, pp. 5–11.

World Bank (1986). *World Development Report 1986.* New York: Oxford University Press.

————— (1988). *World Development Report 1988.* New York: Oxford University Press.

————— (1990). *World Development Report 1990.* New York: Oxford University Press.

Yazbeck Haddad, Yvonne, and Ellison Banks Findley (eds.) (1985). *Women, Religion and Social Change.* Albany: State University of New York Press.

Yeld, Rachel (1960). "Islam and Social Stratification in Northern Nigeria." *British Journal of Sociology* II (11), pp. 2–28.

Youssef, Nadia. (1974). *Women and Work in Developing Societies.* Berkeley: Institute of International Studies, University of California.

Yusuf, Bilkisu (1985a). "The Rights of Women under the Shariah." Paper presented at the Muslim Students Society, Training Programme December, Kano, Nigeria.

————— (1985b). "Nigerian Women in Politics." In Renée Pitten and Aisha Imam (eds.), *Women in Nigeria Today.* London: Zed Press.

————— (1991). "Hausa-Fulani Women: The State of the Struggle." In Catherine Coles and Beverly Mack (eds.), *Women in Twentieth-Century Hausa Society.* Madison: University of Wisconsin Press, pp. 90–109.

INDEX

213

ABOUT THE BOOK
AND THE AUTHORS

Callaway and Creevey explore the impact of Islam on the lives of West African women, particularly (but not exclusively) in Nigeria and Senegal.

Focusing on whether Islam acts as a barrier to women in the process of social change and development, they address a series of important questions: Is the pattern of training and education different for Muslim and non-Muslim girls? Comparatively, what is the domestic life of a Muslim woman like? How do Muslim women fare in the economy, in both the wage-labor force and in the informal sector? Do Muslim women act as a political group, and are they involved in politics in any way that differs from the political participation of other West African women? In short, how is a Muslim woman's life different from that of her animist or Christian sister?

These questions are placed in the context of the ongoing controversy over the role of Islam in the secular realm; the particular history of West Africa; and the position of women in pre-Islamic West African society, which has an important bearing on their present situation.

The authors also examine the impact of modernization and industrialization, as well as nationalist reactions to colonialism and neocolonialism, on Islamic women in West Africa.

BARBARA CALLAWAY, a political scientist, is associate provost for academic affairs at Rutgers-The State University of New Jersey—New Brunswick. She is author of *Muslim Hausa Women in Nigeria: Tradition and Change.*

LUCY CREEVEY is professor of political science and director of the Women's Studies Program at the University of Connecticut. She is author of *Muslim Brotherhoods and Politics in Senegal* and editor of *Working with Women Farmers in Africa.*